OF ENGLAND
55 B.C. to 1399

D. C. HEATH AND COMPANY   LEXINGTON, MASSACHUSETTS/TORONTO/LONDON

ORIGINAL WOODCUTS BY HUGH PRICE
MAPS BY NORMAN CLARK ADAMS

Published simultaneously in Canada.

Printed in the United States of America.

International Standard Book Number: 0–669–97931–7

Library of Congress Catalog Card Number: 75–2636

Foreword

Carl Becker once complained that everybody knows the job of the historian is "to discover and set forth the 'facts' of history." The facts, it is often said, speak for themselves. The businessman talks about hard facts, the statistician refers to cold facts, the lawyer is eloquent about the facts of the case, and the historian, who deals with the incontrovertible facts of life and death, is called a very lucky fellow. Those who speak so confidently about the historian's craft are generally not historians themselves; they are readers of textbooks that more often than not are mere recordings of vital information and listings of dull generalizations. It is not surprising then that historians' reputations have suffered; they have become known as peddlers of facts and chroniclers who say "this is what happened." The shorter the historical survey, the more textbook writers are likely to assume godlike detachment, spurning the minor tragedies and daily comedies of humanity and immortalizing the rise and fall of civilizations, the clash of economic and social forces, and the deeds of titans. Anglo-Saxon warriors were sick with fear when Viking "swift sea-kings" swept down on England to plunder, rape, and kill, but historians dispassionately note that the Norse invasions were a good thing; they allowed the kingdom of Wessex to unite and "liberate" the island in the name of Saxon and Christian defense against heathen marauders. Nimbly the chronicler moves from the indisputable fact that Henry VIII annulled his marriage with Catherine of Aragon and wedded Anne Boleyn to the confident assertion that this helped produce the Reformation in England. The result is sublime but emasculated history. Her subjects wept when Good Queen Bess died, but historians merely comment that she had lived her allotted three score years and ten. British soldiers rotted by the thousands in the trenches of the First World War, but the terror and agony of that holocaust are lost in the dehumanized statistic that 750,000 British troops died in the four years of war.

In a brief history of even one "tight little island," the chronology of events must of necessity predominate; but if these four volumes are in any way fresh and new, it is because their authors have tried by artistry to step beyond the usual confines of a textbook and to conjure up something of the drama of politics, of the wealth of personalities, and even of the pettiness, as well as the greatness, of human motivation. The price paid will be obvious to anyone seeking total coverage. There is relatively little in these pages on literature, the fine arts, or philosophy, except as they throw light upon the uniqueness of English history. On the other hand, the complexities, the uncertainties, the endless variations, and above all the accidents that bedevil the design of human events—these are the very stuff of which history is made, and these are the "truths" that this series seeks to elucidate and preserve. Moreover, the flavor of each volume varies according to the tastes of its author. Sometimes the emphasis is political, sometimes economic or social; but always the presentation is impressionistic—shading, underscoring, or highlighting to achieve an image that will be more than a bare outline and will recapture something of the smell and temper of the past.

Even though each book was conceived and executed as an entity capable of standing by itself, the four volumes were designed as a unit. They tell the story of how a small and insignificant outpost of the Roman Empire hesitantly, and not always heroically, evolved into the nation that has probably produced and disseminated more ideas and institutions, both good and bad, than any state since Athens. The hope is that these books will appeal both, as individual volumes, to those interested in balanced portraits of particular segments of English history and, collectively, to those who seek the majestic sweep of history in the story of a people whose activities have been wonderfully rich, exciting, and varied. Erasmus once wrote: "The important thing for you is not how much you know, but the quality of what you know." In this spirit these volumes were originally written and have now been revised for a second time, not only to keep pace with new scholarship, but equally important to keep them fresh and thought-provoking in a world that is becoming both more nostalgic and more impatient of its past.

Lacey Baldwin Smith
Northwestern University

Contents

ILLUSTRATIONS

MAPS

GENEALOGICAL TABLES

MUIREADOCH'S CROSS, COUNTY LOUTH (ca. 500). *Courtesy Irish Tourist Board.*

I
THE BEGINNINGS
55 B.C. to A.D. 1066

Roman Britain and the
Anglo-Saxon Settlements

History, as the recorded annals of civilized man, began in England in the year 55 B.C., when Julius Caesar's troops waded ashore on the beaches north of Dover.[1] Caesar was a man of remarkable military ability and boundless confidence. He was an astute opportunist who rose to power amidst the violent political turmoil of the late Roman Republic and a great creative statesman who laid the groundwork for Rome's transformation from republic to empire. It was this man, this military adventurer and political genius, who first brought England into the orbit of civilization.

Caesar's invasion of Britain was almost an afterthought to his campaigns against the Gauls. Between 58 and 50 B.C., prior to his rise to supreme power in Rome, he undertook the conquest of an extensive territory known as Gaul, which corresponds very roughly to modern France and was then inhabited by semicivilized Celts. Although Caesar could not realize it, the conquest of Gaul was to have an incalculable influence on the development of Western civilization in later centuries. For Gaul extended far to the north of the Mediterranean Basin, and Caesar's victories brought Roman government and culture into the Western European heartland. The Romanization of Gaul proved to be a crucial factor in providing medieval and modern Europe with its enduring classical heritage.

---

[1] Several good general accounts of Roman Britain are available: R. G. Collingwood and J. N. L. Myres, *Roman Britain and the English Settlements* (2nd ed., Oxford, 1937), J. A. Richmond, *Roman Britain* (Baltimore, 1955), Peter Hunter Blair, *Roman Britain and Early England*, 55 B.C.–A.D. 871 (New York, 1963), and Sheppard Frere, *Brittania: A History of Roman Britain* (London, 1967).

The First Invasions

In the course of his campaigns, Caesar discovered that the Celts in Gaul were receiving support from their fellow Celts on the remote island of Britain. Desiring to teach them to respect the might of Rome, he undertook two military forays into Britain, the first in 55 B.C., the second a year later. Caesar's first raid was inconclusive, but in 54 B.C. he marched across Kent, forded the Thames River, and won a notable victory over a Celtic coalition. He demanded hostages from the defeated Britons, secured a promise of regular tribute payments, and then withdrew across the Channel. But the Britons never paid the promised tribute, and Caesar was too preoccupied with the consolidation of his Gallic conquest and the advancement of his political fortunes in Rome to return to Britain in force. The first encounter between classical Mediterranean civilization and the distant Celtic island was not followed up for nearly a century.

Nonetheless, Caesar's raids had succeeded in bringing Britain to Rome's attention, and, with the organization of Celtic Gaul into Roman provinces, the Britons began to feel the impact of Roman civilization. The close relations between Gaul and Britain continued much as before; the two lands remained tightly linked by bonds of commerce and kinship. A group of Celtic inhabitants of Yorkshire called the *Parisi*, for example, was related to a group in Gaul that gave its name to the future capital of France. The Romans, having subdued the Celts of Gaul, were almost bound to undertake the conquest of the Celts of Britain.

In A.D. 43 the conquest began in earnest: the emperor Claudius sent four Roman legions across the Channel into Kent with the intention of bringing Britain under the authority of Rome. The Claudian invasion marks the real beginning of Roman Britain. Thenceforth the primitive culture of the British Celts was penetrated and transformed by the conquering legions of a huge cosmopolitan state and by the administrators and entrepreneurs who followed them.

Rome, by the time of Claudius' invasion, had achieved a high degree of imperial stability. It had weathered the stormy decades of the late republic and had submitted to the rule of an emperor. In doing so the Romans abandoned a tradition of self-determination for a new, authoritarian regime that promised order and political coherence. With the coming of imperial government, the interior districts of the empire entered a prolonged, unprecedented epoch of security and peace. The empire that Claudius ruled was a prosperous, intelligently governed state embracing the ancient lands along the Mediterranean and extending northward across Gaul to the English Channel. Within its vast frontiers, guarded by well-trained legions, the cultures of Greece, Italy, and the ancient Near East were drawn together into one immense political and economic unit, unencumbered by national boundaries or tariff barriers, and spanned by a superb road system and by the protected seaways of the Mediterranean. Imperial unity brought to the upper classes of the ancient world a degree of prosperity hitherto unknown, though great masses of peasants and urban dwellers remained, as they always had, in a state of hopeless impoverishment.

The Roman economy, like almost all economies prior to the industrial revolution, was fundamentally agrarian, but the city was the nexus of Roman politics and civilization. The city, with an extensive agrarian district surrounding it, was the essential unit of local government, and it was on the cities that the Romans lavished most of their considerable architectural and engineering talents. Administrators, poets, scholars, even great landowners, made their homes in the cities. As half-civilized districts such as Gaul fell under Roman control, old tribal centers were transformed into cities, and new cities were built where none had existed before. And each city sought to adorn itself with impressive temples, baths, and public buildings on the model of Rome itself. Hence the paradox that the Roman Empire was economically rural yet culturally urban.

These cities, scattered across the empire, were centers of cultural synthesis, where the various traditions of the Mediterranean world spread and intermingled. But it was above all the Latin culture of Rome itself that inspired the architecture and literature of the European cities and dominated the curricula of their schools. Great Latin authors and poets such as Lucretius and Cicero, Virgil and Horace, set the canons of style for a Latin literary tradition that spread across the West. United politically by the Roman legions, the Roman Empire was united culturally—at least in its western provinces—by the power and magnetism of Roman literature and art.

The empire was united legally by Roman jurisprudence. It may well be that Rome made its most creative and enduring contribution in the field of law. As Rome won its empire, the narrow law code of the early republic evolved gradually into a broad, humane system of legal precedents and principles—a product of centuries of practical experience—designed to deal justly with conflicts among men of diverse cultures. Although essentially pragmatic in its development, Roman law was influenced by the Greek concept of natural law—the belief in universal and discoverable norms of human conduct, applicable not merely to certain civilized peoples but to all men. A concept of this sort was naturally attractive to Roman jurists, faced as they were with the task of bringing all the peoples of the empire under a single canopy of jurisprudence.

Such, in brief, was the civilization that Rome brought to Britain. The student of English history must never allow his preoccupation with the British Isles to obscure the fact that Claudius' invasion of A.D. 43 constituted an encroachment by a highly civilized empire on a small, remote, and backward land. In Roman times, Britain could never be anything but an outwork—a distant frontier district of an age-old Mediterranean civilization.

Britain's history before the Roman contact is utterly undocumented, but the investigations of archaeologists provide us with at least a general picture of its economic and cultural development. It is a picture of repeated incursions and invasions from across the Channel, of incessant tribal rivalries, and of gradual technological and economic progress as Britain's inhabitants evolved from the Stone Age to the Bronze Age and finally, beginning in the fifth century B.C., to the Iron Age. The majestic stone trilithons at Stonehenge—a religious center of the early Bronze Age—testify to the engineering skills the island's inhabitants possessed nearly two millennia before the Roman invasion.

The pattern of pre-Roman invasions and settlements was governed by the island's geography. Clearly visible from the continent, England's Kentish shore is separated from France by a channel only twenty-one miles wide at its narrowest point. Accordingly, repeated waves of invaders and traders crossed from the continent to southern Britain in prehistoric times. England itself is divided geographically into two major districts: a lowland area—with rich, heavy soil broken by occasional ranges of hills—which covers approximately the southeastern half of England; and a highland zone dominating the northwestern half of the land—a district of mountainous terrain rich in mineral resources but with generally infertile soil. Cornwall and Devon at the southwestern tip of England, Wales in the west, and most of northern England and Scotland are hilly or mountainous, and England's chief mountain range, the Pennine Chain, points southward like a great finger from the northern hill country into the heart of the midland plain.

The earlier prehistoric invaders tended to concentrate in the southeast lowlands zone, but they settled chiefly in the hilly portions of that zone rather than in the lowlands themselves. For the lowlands were thickly wooded, and their heavy soil defied the primitive plows of the early settlers. On the eve of the Roman invasion, however, Britain's Celtic inhabitants had developed plows that were adequate to the task of tilling this rich soil and were beginning the age-long process of clearing the land of woods and brush. By the standards of the time, the Celtic settlement of lowland Britain was quite dense, and grain was being produced in such quantities that it became an important export commodity. A Roman author of the early first century A.D. mentions several other British exports that found regular markets in the empire: cattle, hides, dogs, iron, and slaves. And for centuries, traders of the Mediterranean world had been aware of the rich tin deposits in Cornwall. The considerable prosperity of pre-Roman Britain is illustrated by the fact that a few of the island's chieftains, following the example of neighboring Roman provinces, were beginning to coin money.

As the first century progressed, everything pointed to a Roman invasion of Britain. The independence of the British Celts posed difficulties for the Roman administration of Celtic Gaul. British resources and prosperity suggested to the Romans that from the financial standpoint a conquest of the island would be well worth the effort. Finally, intertribal warfare among the Britons—and appeals by defeated British chieftains for Roman support—indicated that a conquest would not be unduly difficult. The invasion of A.D. 43 was a calculated act of imperial policy undertaken with every expectation of success.

Roman Britain

The British Celts, divided among themselves and distinctly inferior to the Romans in military organization, could offer only temporary resistance to the Claudian invasion. In the years following A.D. 43 the Roman legions repeatedly breached the Celtic defenses, storming hilltop fortresses and occupying first the southeastern lowland zone and finally, after some difficulty, the highland districts of the north and west. The administration of the able Roman governor Agricola (A.D. 78–84) marks the essential completion of the conquest. By then, Roman authority extended over virtually all of modern England, Wales, and southern Scotland.

The Roman conquest of the lowland zone was relatively easy, although it was threatened briefly by a rebellion of several British tribes in A.D. 60 under the leadership of a Celtic queen named Boudicca. Historians of earlier generations romanticized this uprising and pictured Boudicca, quite wrongly, as the first British patriot—a primitive Joan of Arc. The rebels won some initial victories, burned London and other newly established towns, and then fell before an army of well-trained legionaries. Boudicca died, perhaps from poison at her own hand, and the lowlands were tamed. The consolidation of Roman authority in the highland zone was far more difficult, for the savage hill peoples of Wales, the north, and the northeast could be controlled only by the continued presence of large Roman garrisons at strategic points.

Hence, Roman Britain was divided administratively into two districts, corresponding to the island's two great geographic zones: a civil district in the southeast, where Roman civilization flourished in an atmosphere of peace, and a military district in the highland areas where Roman legions remained on guard against uprisings and invasions and where Roman civilization made comparatively little impact. Three legions guarded the military district, each of them consisting of some thirty to forty thousand men. One legion was stationed at Chester, where it was in a position to dominate Wales. Another was stationed at Carlisle to overawe southern Scotland and guard the northern frontier. A third made its base at York and served as a strategic reserve. These three legions were generally successful in upholding Roman authority, but they were never able to rid their districts of rebellion.

Under the emperor Hadrian (117–138) construction began on a great wall, more than seventy miles long, spanning the narrow neck of Britain between Solway Firth and the mouth of the Tyne River. This ambitious fortified line was intended to secure Roman Britain's northern frontier from incursions by savage tribes to the north. Later in the second century the Antonine Wall was erected still farther northward, across the narrows between the Firth of Clyde and the Firth of Forth. The Antonine Wall was an advance position that the Romans were unable to hold for long, and during the third and fourth centuries they were usually content to draw their northern line at the Wall of Hadrian. At times Roman punitive ex-

ROMAN BRITAIN

Military Occupation
Not permanently occupied
Extent of Conquest, 40 A.D.
Roman Roads

SCOTLAND

ANTONINE WALL

NORTH

SEA

HADRIAN'S WALL, 123 A.D.
R. Tyne

Carlisle

Isle
of Man

York

IRISH SEA

IRELAND

R. Humber

Anglesea

Lincoln

The Wash

Chester

Wrexeter

Severn R.

High Cross

Avon R.

Gloucester

Verulamium (St.
Albans)

Colchester

Cirencester

London

Caerwent

R. Thames

Bath

Silchester

Canterbury
Dover

Salisbury

Winchester

Lymme

Exeter

Dorchester

Chichester

Pevensey

Axminster

Isle of Wight

English Channel

FRANCE

HADRIAN'S WALL
Built by the Roman emperor to keep out marauding northern tribes, the
still-impressive wall stretches across the Northumberland countryside.
British Travel.

peditions probed far north of Hadrian's Wall, and at other times northern
tribesmen broke through the fortifications and carried their devastation far
to the south. But during most of the later age of Roman occupation, Hadrian's Wall marked the northern frontier.

The lowlands zone, after Boudicca's revolt, enjoyed unbroken peace
and considerable prosperity. Here Roman institutions were gradually imposed upon a Celtic and pre-Celtic substructure, and the Britons came to
know not only the high taxes but also the settled life, the thriving economy,
and the amenities of upper-class urban living that were customary in the
Roman provinces. The military camps and commercial centers of Britain
were bound together by a network of Roman roads; Roman law courts
brought with them a rational system of justice quite unknown to Britain
prior to the Roman conquest. And with the coming of Roman civilization,
towns and cities grew and flourished as never before.

In Britain, as elsewhere in the empire, the cities were of three basic *li: ? Roman*

2. celtic

3.

types: (1) the *colonia,* usually a newly established urban center occupied by a colony of retired legionaries and their families, (2) the *municipium,* normally a previously existing town whose inhabitants received from the imperial government a charter conveying certain important privileges, and (3) the *civitas,* an older tribal center that developed urban institutions in imitation of the colonia and municipium. The inhabitants of coloniae and municipia were Roman citizens; those of the civitates were not. All three, however, enjoyed a degree of local self-government and exerted political control over fairly extensive surrounding lands. All three were governed by local senates comprised of wealthy townsmen, and by annually elected magistrates who supervised finances, public buildings and the courts. And all three sought to adorn themselves with public buildings, temples, and baths built of stone in the Roman style. Still, the civitates remained fundamentally Celtic tribal centers and were never so thoroughly Romanized as were the municipia and the coloniae.

Only four British cities are known to have possessed colonia status: Colchester, Gloucester, Lincoln, and York, and there is evidence to suggest only one municipium: Verulamium (the later St. Albans). Extant contemporary documents do not state specifically that London was a colonia or a municipium, but there can be no question that it was the foremost city of Roman Britain. Indeed, it was the Romans who made London a significant center of trade. Whereas most of the chief British cities of the Roman era were between 100 and 200 acres in extent, London occupied some 325 acres. Situated on the Thames at the crucial point where the river was broad enough to accommodate ocean-going ships and yet narrow enough to be bridged,[2] London assumed in Roman times the dominant commercial position that it was destined to occupy in medieval and modern times. Then, as now, it was the commercial nexus of Britain.

It was only natural, therefore, that London should be the focal point of the Roman road system. Stretching from London far and wide across the land, the Roman roads formed a vast five-thousand-mile system of paved thoroughfares running in nearly straight lines over the countryside, enabling men and supplies to move across the island at speeds unmatched until the nineteenth century.

In Roman Britain, as elsewhere in the empire, farming was the basic economic activity. Historians of former generations used to distinguish between two radically different agricultural communities: the village—pre-Roman in origin and little affected by the Roman occupation—and the villa—a typically Roman institution that consisted of a luxurious home surrounded by extensive fields. Recent research, based on more sophisticated archaeological techniques and on aerial photography, has modified this traditional view. We now realize that the buildings unearthed at a particular site often represent successive levels of development rather than one agrarian com-

---

[2] This was precisely analogous to Rome's position on the Tiber.

plex existing at a single moment in time. Consequently, scholars today doubt that the agricultural village played a particularly significant role in either Roman or pre-Roman Britain. Instead, the rudimentary agrarian unit was the small family farm, a few acres in extent, consisting typically of a couple of houses, a number of pits for storing grain, and farmlands laid out in small, squarish fields. Farms of this type abounded in both Celtic and Roman times, and their inhabitants were little influenced by the coming of the Romans.

The older conception of the villa, with its gracious Roman provincial architecture, its mosaics and rich furnishings, glass windows and under-floor heating, also requires modification. Such villas did indeed exist, but they were exceptional. The great majority of the Roman villas were far more modest establishments, and some were actually squalid. Altogether, between 600 and 700 villas have been identified in Britain, most of them concentrated in small areas of the southeastern lowlands. Life in the villas, whether luxurious or impoverished, was distinctly Roman in style and organization, and it is through the villas that Rome made its impact on the British countryside. The typical villa owner was a Roman or a Romanized Briton, who used hired laborers or slaves, sometimes in large numbers, to work his lands. In the later years of the Roman settlement, much villa land, as elsewhere in the empire, was leased to tenant farmers, with the consequence that many of the advantages of large-scale farming were lost.

A sharp distinction still must be made between the Celtic farm and the Roman villa, but it must also be remembered that the laborers on the villa's fields profited no more from Roman civilization than Celtic farmers did. In Britain, as elsewhere in the empire, Rome's impact on the agrarian masses was remarkably slight. Rome had always lagged in agrarian technology, and she contributed little to Celtic farming practices because she had little to offer. Some progress was made during the Roman occupation toward the clearing of forests and draining of swamps, but the bulk of that task was left to the later Anglo-Saxons. And it was the achievements of the pre-Roman Celts that enabled Roman Britain to export agricultural products to the continent.

The Romans did, however, contribute significantly to the development of the British economy in areas other than agriculture. Britain had been exploiting its mines long before the Claudian invasion, but Rome introduced a far more efficient—and more ruthless—mining technology than before. In particular, the Romans developed lead mines in Britain and made lead a major export commodity, along with copper, bronze, and iron.

Perhaps, after all, Rome's greatest gift to Britain was peace. For more than three centuries, the Roman legions shielded lowland Britain from invaders and prevented intertribal warfare. As a frontier province of the Roman Empire, Britain fell under the direct authority of the emperor. But apart from the rare occasions when the emperor actually visited the island, imperial control was exercised by an imperial agent entitled *legatus* who was, in effect, a provincial governor. His responsibilities included both administration of justice in the civil zone and command of the armies in the military zone. Responsibility for the collection of imperial taxes and the supervision of imperial estates was entrusted to another official, the *procurator*, who was administratively independent of the governor and subject to the emperor alone. It was up to the procurator to see that Britain paid its way and that the occupation was financially worthwhile to Rome.

Such was the administrative structure of Britain in the era following the Claudian invasion. In subsequent centuries, as the empire evolved steadily toward military despotism, Roman administrative organization underwent several major revisions, and the administration of Britain changed accordingly. Early in the third century the island was divided into two separate provinces, which probably approximated its two zones: military and civil. Toward the end of the same century Emperor Diocletian designated Britain as one of the twelve dioceses into which he divided the empire. Britain was now ruled by a *vicarius*, whose headquarters seems to have been at London. The island was further subdivided by Diocletian into four provinces.

Throughout the epoch of the Roman occupation, the key units of local government were the towns—the coloniae, municipia, and civitates—which managed their own local affairs through their senates and magistrates and supervised considerable areas of the surrounding countryside. In the final catastrophic years of Roman Britain it was the towns that took the lead in striving to defend their civilized heritage against the incursions of the barbarians.

Decline and Fall

The Roman age of British history began and ended as a result of forces that transcended Britain itself. The fall of the Roman Empire in the West is a venerable problem for which numerous scholars have proposed numerous solutions, none of them satisfactory.[3]

Many different factors contributed to the transformation from Roman to medieval Europe. For one thing, the educated classes of the empire underwent a profound change in outlook during the third and fourth centuries, turning from the humanism and rationalism of Greek antiquity and the practical, worldly values of early Rome to the mysticism and quest for eternal salvation that characterized the earlier Middle Ages. This change in mood marked the end of the viewpoint and value system of traditional Greco-Roman civilization. But did the new transcendental spirit destroy the

---

[3] Gibbon's classic, *The Decline and Fall of the Roman Empire* (many editions), is majestic in style and fearlessly opinionated. Compare Lynn White, Jr., ed., *The Transformation of the Roman World: Gibbon's Problem after Two Centuries* (Berkeley, 1966), and Bryce Lyon, *The Origins of the Middle Ages: Pirenne's Challenge to Gibbon* (New York, 1972).

old humanistic values, or did the failure of these values give rise to the new mysticism?

Much has been written on the political and economic problems that afflicted the Roman Empire. It has been said that the Roman political system never solved the problem of imperial succession, that the Roman economy was inefficient and parasitical, that the Roman bureaucracy was bloated and corrupt. One should be cautious about condemning an empire that endured for five hundred years in the West and another thousand years in the East. Nevertheless, some of these criticisms stand. The economy of the early empire depended too heavily on slave labor and on booty from conquered peoples. When, in the course of the second century, imperial expansion ceased, the economic system in the West began to falter and finally broke down almost completely. Rome experienced no industrial revolution; her cities, particularly those in the West, tended to be military and administrative centers rather than centers of industrial production. Many of them harbored large masses of unemployed paupers and street people; and all of them teemed with soldiers and bureaucrats, who consumed the wealth of the empire. In the end, the largely agrarian imperial economy proved incapable of supporting the bureaucracy, the army, and the unproductive cities.

The economic breakdown was marked by widespread demoralization. So many artisans, tenant farmers, and civic officials dropped out of their jobs and out of society that the emperors were forced to make laws freezing men in their vocations and making them hereditary. By the early fourth century, a caste system had come into being in the Roman Empire. The economy continued to function after a fashion, but demoralization was growing. The lightly taxed landed aristocracy remained prosperous, but the more productive classes of the empire—the workers in field and town, and the urban middle classes—were becoming dangerously alienated.

Economic breakdown was accompanied by political disintegration. The emperors of the second century tended to be long-lived and dedicated but, as the third century dawned, the army came to exert increasing power in Roman politics. The middle decades of the third century were marked by frequent assassinations, disputed successions, and struggles between army units for control of the throne. In these years, barbarians breached the frontiers repeatedly, and large sections of the empire repudiated the authority of the emperor in Rome. At length, in the later decades of the century, a series of determined emperors succeeded in restoring the frontiers and re-establishing imperial control over the Roman state. The most celebrated of these rulers, the warrior-emperor Diocletian (284–305), pulled the empire together by resorting to a military despotism of the most thoroughgoing sort and enforcing strict controls over economic activity.

Diocletian's policy of law and order through despotism was carried on by Constantine (306–337) and his successors. Constantine's reign is marked by two epoch-making events: (1) the construction of Constantinople on the Bosphorous—the great city that served as the capital of the Eastern or Byzantine Empire for more than 1,100 years thereafter, and (2) the conversion of Constantine to the Christian religion.

Both these events were responses to age-old trends. The center of gravity of the Roman Empire had been shifting eastward for many decades; the older eastern cities were more productive and more prosperous than those of the west, and the eastward movement symbolized the new political order that abandoned the constitutional traditions of the city of Rome for the absolutism of the east. The great autocrat Diocletian had spent nearly all his reign in the eastern half of the empire, and now Constantine erected his new capital there.

Constantine's conversion may be regarded as a response not only to the growing strength of Christianity within the empire but also to the gradual drawing together of the classical and Christian traditions. The growth of a transcendental spirit in Roman culture made the inhabitants of the empire ever more receptive to the mystical doctrines of the Christian religion; the increasing emptiness and hopelessness of daily life in the empire created a growing need for the doctrines of human dignity before God and personal salvation which Christianity offered. The Christians, for their part, had incorporated into their theology many elements from classical philosophy—particularly the philosophy of Plato—and had adopted numerous administrative ideas from Rome itself. The steadily closing chasm between Church and Empire was bridged by the conversion of Constantine.

By the fourth century, Christianity had spread from its Near Eastern homeland across the entire empire. In Constantine's time it was still a minority religion, but its adherents were among the most vigorous and dedicated inhabitants of the Roman state. Previous emperors had persecuted Christians intermittently for their refusal to worship the official deities, but persecution seemed to encourage the Church to greater efforts. With Constantine's conversion, the persecutions gave way to a policy of toleration and encouragement, and before the fourth century had ended, Christian emperors were persecuting pagan and heterodox sects. Converts now flooded into the Church, and Roman intellectuals such as St. Ambrose, St. Jerome, and St. Augustine of Hippo devoted their lives to its service. The new religion harmonized perfectly with the otherworldly mood of the late empire, and long before the end of imperial rule in the West, Christianity had won the allegiance of the Mediterranean world. By the fifth century, Greco-Roman civilization had virtually fused with the Judeo-Christian religious tradition.

The progress of Christianity in Roman Britain is difficult to trace. Christian archaeological remains from this period are scarce, and written references to the Roman-British Church occur only occasionally. Christian evangelism doubtless came late to remote Britain, but by the third century the process of conversion had begun. Early in the century St. Alban and two fellow Christians were martyred at Verulamium, and three British bishops, a priest, and a deacon are recorded as being present at an ecclesiastical council in Gaul during Constantine's reign.[4] Thus, fourth-century Britain possessed an ecclesiastical hierarchy and was active in the affairs of the imperial Church. Toward the end of the fourth century, Britain went so far as to produce a heresy all its own. The British priest Pelagius, who emphasized the importance of free will over divine grace, had the distinction of being attacked by the noted theologian St. Augustine of Hippo. Pelagius left Britain as a young man and seems to have spent most of his life in Rome, but his teachings became popular among the British upper classes. Orthodox continental churchmen are recorded as preaching against Pelagianism in Britain in the fifth century. At about the same time, British evangelists such as St. Patrick (*c.* 389–461) were spreading the Gospel beyond the Roman frontiers into Ireland and southwestern Scotland.

As it turned out, Christianity was Rome's most enduring legacy in Britain. At a time when Roman civilization was losing its hold on the inhabitants of the empire, Christianity was reaching masses of people and affecting their lives in a way that Greco-Roman culture had failed to do even at its height. In later years, when Roman government was all but forgotten, when Germanic barbarians had occupied the fertile lowland zone and driven its former British inhabitants into the western hills, the British held fast to their Christian faith and built an impressive new culture upon it.

The ebbing of Roman authority in Britain was an inevitable consequence of Roman political and economic disintegration in the West. But because of its isolated location on the periphery of the empire, Britain was spared much of the agony and chaos of the third century, and its cities remained relatively prosperous throughout the fourth.

The history of Roman Britain is punctuated by occasional irruptions of semicivilized peoples from across its frontiers, most frequently the Scots and the Picts. The term "Scot" was used by men of this period to refer to members of the various tribes of Ireland (not Scotland). These Scots undertook periodic attacks against Britain's western shore but met with no permanent success. "Pict" was the common term for the tribes across the northern frontier in what we would now call Scotland. With a few disastrous exceptions, Hadrian's Wall held firm against their incursions.

As the Roman period of British history drew toward its end, signs of increasing insecurity began to appear. An intensification of sea raids by Germanic barbarians is suggested by the appearance of elaborate fortifications along the southeastern coast. In the fourth century these coastal fortresses were placed under the authority of a single military commander known, significantly, as the count of the Saxon Shore. In 367 the British defenses were shattered by a combined attack of Picts from the north, Scots

---

[4] At Arles in A.D. 314. The British delegates to the council represented the metropolitan churches of the four provinces into which Britain had been divided since Diocletian's time.

from the west, and Saxons from the south and east. Hadrian's Wall was breached, the count of the Saxon Shore was killed, and London itself was placed under siege. The situation was saved, however, by the timely appearance of a large Roman army from the continent led by Theodosius, a talented general and future emperor. By 370 Britain was secure once again, and its earlier prosperity returned.

As the fourth century closed, Roman Britain remained vigorous and its cities still flourished. But the Roman Empire as a whole was in desperate circumstances. An entire Germanic tribe, the Visigoths, had crossed the empire's Danube frontier in 376, and by the first decade of the fifth century was threatening Rome itself. As Roman troops were ordered southward from Britain and the Rhine frontier to strengthen the defenses of Italy, Gaul and Britain were left exposed. In the winter of 406 a mixed multitude of Germanic tribesmen poured across the frozen Rhine into defenseless Gaul, virtually cutting Britain loose from the empire. In the chaos that followed, an ambitious Roman-Briton general, Constantine III, led what was left of the Roman garrison in Britain southward across the Channel in an abortive attempt to save Gaul for the empire and win an imperial title for himself.

The year 410 marks the essential termination of Roman authority in Britain. In that year the Visigoths entered Rome and pillaged the city for three days. At about the same time Britain, stripped of its legions, was struck hard by barbarian raids. At this point our sources thin out and the sequence of events is clouded. One contemporary writer speaks of a native British uprising against the Roman administration—perhaps against the officials left behind by the usurper Constantine III rather than against Rome herself. A letter of A.D. 410 from Emperor Honorius to the civitates of Britain, evidently in response to their appeal for military help, commands them to see to their own defense. With Visigoths rampaging through Italy, there were no troops to be spared for a remote island outpost. The Roman legions and administrators were gone from Britain for good.

The Germanic Invaders

As the fifth century progressed Britain became, from the standpoint of the civilized districts of the Mediterranean Basin, the "land of legend"— the Isle of the Dead. To the modern historian the post-Roman epoch is almost equally obscure. Aside from a few oblique, secondhand references from continental writers, the historian must depend on a handful of unreliable Celtic sources and a few accounts written long afterwards by descendants of the Germanic invaders. None of these sources is at all satisfactory, but none can be ignored. The most important of them is a history of the conquest of Britain written by a Briton named Gildas sometime in the 540s. Riddled with factual errors, Gildas' account was a bitter, emotional outcry against the shortcomings of contemporary British Christians rather than an objective history. Yet it is the only contemporary narrative of the invasion epoch to which historians can turn. On the Germanic or "English" side, there is a certain amount of suggestive but ambiguous material in early epics such as *Beowulf*. The opening sections of the *Anglo-Saxon Chronicle,* which were first written in their present form in the late ninth century, contain some information drawn from sources much closer to the invasion age and can therefore provide illumination if used with care. The talented and rigorous English historian Bede, writing in the early eighth century, gives an account of the invasions that also seems to rest on earlier evidence, now lost, but there is much that Bede leaves out and much else that can be accepted only with reservations. For Bede, despite his remarkable historical skill, was centuries removed from the invasions themselves.

The few other written sources to which one can turn are fragmentary and still less trustworthy. Archaeological investigations have been helpful in providing additional insights into fifth- and sixth-century Britain, but the archaeologist is handicapped in investigating a society that built not with stone but with wood and other such perishable materials. Finally, patterns of Celtic and Germanic settlement have been investigated with considerable success through the study of place names. Scholars are able to identify particular names—and especially name endings—with particular peoples and thereby trace the advance of Germanic settlements and measure their intensity. A number of towns and settlements, for example, end in *ing* or *ingas,* which in Anglo-Saxon indicates that the original settlers were dependents or followers of a particular leader. Hastings derives its name from a group of early settlers called Haestingas, that is, the followers of a leader named Haesta, and we can conclude tentatively that a Germanic warrior of that name settled with his following in the vicinity of the present town. But place-name studies, valuable though they are, cannot be related to an exact chronological framework. Scholarly investigations of fifth- and sixth-century Britain have been pushed forward with great ingenuity; yet much remains uncertain and much unknown. The epoch has become a battleground of conflicting theories, many of which may never be positively proven or discredited.[5]

Before entering this historical wilderness it will be useful to establish, insofar as possible, the nature of the Germanic peoples as a whole and the significance of their invasions, not only of Britain but of the entire Western Roman Empire. Medieval European civilization was a synthesis of three distinct cultural traditions: the classical or Greco-Roman, the Judeo-Christian, and the Germanic. We have seen how classical culture in the closing centuries of the Roman Empire began to move toward a mystical, otherworldly outlook, thereby drawing closer to the Judeo-Christian tradition.

---

[5] On the early Anglo-Saxon period, see Sir Frank Stenton, *Anglo-Saxon England* (3rd ed., Oxford, 1971), Peter Hunter Blair, *An Introduction to Anglo-Saxon England* (Cambridge, 1956), and H. R. Loyn, *Anglo-Saxon England and the Norman Conquest* (New York, 1962).

At the same time, Christian theologians were interpreting Christian doctrine in terms of Greek philosophy, and the Christian Church was developing a political and legal organization that drew heavily from Roman administrative and judicial practices. Well before the demise of Roman imperial authority in the West, these tendencies had progressed to the point where classical and Christian cultures had fused. The making of medieval civilization was in essence the product of a prolonged tension, interpenetration, and eventual fusion between the classical-Christian tradition, fostered by the early medieval Church, and the Germanic tradition of the barbarian kingdoms that established themselves on the remains of the western Roman Empire.

Since the early Germanic peoples were illiterate, our knowledge of their culture must be drawn chiefly from the often tendentious testimony of occasional Roman observers. But a critical analysis of these writers provides, in broad outline, a reasonably trustworthy picture of the ancient Germans. They were organized for the most part into tribes, each of which had its own cultural peculiarities. Some tribes were nomadic, others sedentary and agrarian; many were in a process of transition from the first state to the second. Some tribes were far more deeply influenced by Roman civilization than others, and some were converted to Christianity during the course of the fourth century.

Certain broad generalizations apply more or less to all the tribes. To the Romans, the Germanic peoples were scruffy blond giants. Their custom of buttering their hair prompted the fifth-century country gentleman Sidonius Apollinaris to remark, "Happy the nose that cannot smell a barbarian." They devoted themselves chiefly to tending crops or herds, fighting wars, hunting, loafing, gambling, feuding, and drinking beer. They possessed slaves—war prisoners for the most part—but on occasion a free German might gamble himself into slavery. At the time of the invasions their key political unit was the tribe, ruled by a chieftain or king who from time to time sought the advice of a tribal assembly. Ordinarily, a new king was chosen by the assembly from among the sons and other close kinsmen of the former king. Kingship was hereditary but not strictly so, and an able younger son who had proved his skill as a warrior was often chosen over an incompetent elder son. The most honored profession was that of the warrior, and the warlike virtues of loyalty, courage, and military prowess were esteemed above all others.

The chief military unit within the tribe was the war band or *comitatus,* a group of warriors or "companions" bound together by their allegiance to the leader of their band. It was in the comitatus, above all, that the military virtues were cherished. The chief of the band was bound to set a high example of fearlessness and military skill, and his followers were obliged, should their leader fall in battle, to fight to the death in order to avenge him. The ethical foundations of the comitatus—honor, loyalty, courage—remained the norms of the English and continental warrior aristocracy for centuries thereafter.

Another, much older subdivision of the tribe was the kinship group or clan. Members of a clan were duty-bound to protect the welfare of their kinsmen. Should any man be killed or injured, his kinsmen would declare a blood feud against the wrongdoer and his clan. Since murders and maimings were only too common in the violent and honor-ridden atmosphere of the Germanic tribe, blood feuds were a characteristic ingredient of Germanic society. In order to keep their tribes from being torn apart by feuds, most of the Germanic peoples instituted a crude form of tribal justice. Early Germanic law was concerned primarily with *wergelds*—sums of money that wrongdoers might pay to their victims or their victims' kinsmen in order to appease their vengeance and forestall the feud (literally, the term *wergeld* means "man money"). In time, wergeld schedules became highly complex. Various sums of money were assigned for various injuries—so much for a severed finger, more for the loss of a hand, and so on. And murder wergelds varied, too, depending on the social status of the victim. In Anglo-Saxon England, for example, the wergeld of a free peasant was 200 shillings while that of a nobleman was 1,200 shillings.

The wergeld system mitigated the blood feud but by no means eliminated it, for there was no assurance that the alleged murderer would pay the required sum or even admit his guilt. Gradually the tribes developed bodies of customary law which were intended to determine guilt or innocence. Early Germanic law was exceedingly limited in its jurisdiction—many crimes of violence fell outside its scope. Its basic principle was the presumption of guilt. It was up to an accused man to prove his innocence, and he normally did so by submitting to an ordeal. Each of the several ordeals in Germanic law was regarded as an appeal to divine judgment. The accused man, for example, might be obliged to grasp a red-hot iron and carry it a prescribed distance, or to lift a stone from the bottom of a boiling cauldron. Several days thereafter the hand was examined carefully. If it was healing properly, the court concluded that the accused enjoyed divine favor and was innocent. But if the hand was infected, the accused was pronounced guilty. Similarly, the accused might be bound and thrown into a pond. If he floated, he was deemed guilty, for it was assumed that pure water would refuse to "accept" a guilty man. If he sank, he was judged innocent and was fetched from the water (presumably still alive) to enjoy the favorable verdict. It has been suggested that this last ordeal might actually have been effective in determining guilt or innocence. The accused, who believed firmly in the validity of the test, may well have had a subconscious compulsion to float or sink depending on his innocence or guilt, much as a modern defendant might betray himself by increased tension when answering falsely in a lie-detector test.

Germanic laws and institutions were crude indeed when compared with those of the Romans. Yet it was Germanic culture that dominated the barbarian successor kingdoms that arose on the ruins of the western empire. And the Germanic contribution to English history and Western civilization was by no means entirely negative. The Germanic peoples brought to Western Europe a rough but energetic spirit. Their ideals of loyalty and honor evolved gradually into the medieval notion of chivalry. Their respect for the sanctity of tribal custom, the advisory function of the tribal assembly, and the rough social equality among members of a war band faintly foreshadow later ideas of limited government, the rights of subjects, and the superiority of law over the royal will.

Nonetheless, it would be foolish to argue, as historians once did, that early Germanic institutions were protodemocratic. The sanctity of folk law and the prominence of tribal assemblies are found among many primitive peoples. Far from being politically precocious, the Germanic peoples were simply too crude and ignorant to create efficient despotisms. More than a millennium would pass before those ancient Germanic notions—mutual respect and honor within the comitatus, the inviolability of customary law, and the political role of the assemblies—evolved into anything resembling a coherent doctrine of limited representative government. The process of evolution is itself far more significant than the faint and ambiguous precedents in primitive Germanic custom.

On the continent, as we have seen, the fifth and sixth centuries witnessed the beginnings of a gradual fusion between the Germanic culture of the barbarian kingdoms and the classical-Christian tradition preserved and fostered by the Church. In Britain, on the other hand, the Germanic invaders remained immune to the Christian faith of the indigenous Britons. As British authority receded before the advance of the Germanic barbarians, Christianity receded with it. The failure of the Britons to Christianize their conquerors may perhaps be attributed at least in part to the profound hostility that developed between the two peoples and the consequent unwillingness of British missionaries to evangelize among the hated invaders. A century and a half elapsed between the first conquests and the beginnings of serious missionary work among the heathen Germanic settlers in Britain.

The Anglo-Saxon Conquest

According to the eighth-century historian Bede, three distinct Germanic peoples invaded England: the Angles, the Saxons, and the Jutes. Although repeated by historians and memorized by English schoolboys ever since, Bede's statement oversimplifies the actual situation. It would probably be more accurate to view the invasions as consisting of attacks—or sometimes peaceful settlements—by innumerable small Germanic war bands coming from various points along the long coastline of the North Sea between southern Denmark and the Netherlands. These bands included many warriors from among the Angle and Saxon tribes that had long been settled in northern Europe, but they also included Frisians, Swabians, and other Germanic peoples. On the continent the invaders came in large tribal groups bent on conquest and settlement; in Britain they came primarily as small marauding bands hungry for booty and land. The organization of the Germanic invaders into larger political units ruled by kings was a product of the decades following the original invasions.

The transition from Roman Britain to Anglo-Saxon England was gradual, complex, and prolonged. Roman Britain had long been subject to Germanic attacks, as the establishment of the Saxon Shore and the disaster of 367 make clear. And Rome had often invited Germanic warrior-mercenaries to settle within the empire—in Britain as elsewhere—to help defend the frontiers. This policy was continued in post-Roman Britain by the Roman-British aristocrat Vortigern [6] who rose to political leadership in southeastern Britain in about 425 and took upon himself the responsibility of defense against the sea raids of the Picts and Scots. Finding the Britons incapable of defending themselves adequately, Vortigern is said to have invited Germanic warriors to Britain, offering them lands in Kent in return for their military assistance. Gildas calls these warriors "Saxons" whereas Bede describes them as "Jutes" under the leadership of two chieftains named Hengist and Horsa. Many historians have followed Gildas in proclaiming Vortigern's decision an act of folly, but this is scarcely a fair judgment. Vortigern was simply following Roman tradition.

Nevertheless, Vortigern's invitation had disastrous consequences. The Germanic warriors, once settled, invited numerous kinsmen to join them, then rebelled against Vortigern's authority and spread devastation and terror across southeastern Britain.

This rebellion can perhaps be dated to the early 440s. During the next half century Germanic war bands came to Britain in large numbers, settling along the southern and eastern shores and penetrating deep into the interior, chiefly by means of eastern Britain's three great estuaries: the Thames, the Wash, and the Humber. The Britons appealed once again, vainly, to Rome: "The barbarians drive us to the sea; the sea drives us to the barbarians; between these two fatal threats we are either slain or drowned." [7] The statement is a self-evident exaggeration, but the Britons do seem to have been driven far westward and many emigrated across the Channel to the peninsula of Armorica, known in later years, appropriately, as Brittany.

After about 470, however, the British defense began to stiffen, and around the turn of the century the Britons won a major victory over the invaders at a site called Mount Badon. The inadequacies of our evidence regarding these events are well illustrated by the fact that historians are in complete disagreement as to both the site of this battle and its date. (Estimates range between 486 and 516.) On the authority of a ninth-century Welsh writer named Nennius, the great British victory at Mount Badon is associated with a leader named Arthur, who became the inspiration for the

---

[6] "Vortigern" is actually a title, not a name. It means, literally, "high king."
[7] The so-called "Groans of the Britons," addressed to the Roman *magister militum* Aëtius in about 446.

richly elaborated Arthurian romances of later centuries. Perhaps the original Arthur was indeed a hero of the British resistance against the Anglo-Saxons, but this tempting conclusion is far from assured: Nennius is an untrustworthy authority and wrote a good three centuries after the event. At any rate, Arthur's glittering court at Camelot, with its chivalrous knights who went on romantic quests, was an idealization of courtly society of the later Middle Ages and had nothing to do with the primitive, insecure world of early-sixth-century Britain.

For a half century after the British victory at Mount Badon, so Gildas tells us, the island enjoyed a period of relative peace and prosperity. The Anglo-Saxons were apparently forced to abandon some of the territories they had previously conquered, but they were by no means driven from Britain. The period of peace and British hegemony might be dated tentatively as the half century between 500 and 550. Gildas himself was writing in that period and provides eyewitness testimony to the relative security of the epoch.

The era between about 550 and 600 was far different. The Anglo-Saxons won a series of victories that ultimately drove the Britons into the mountains of Wales, Cumbria, and Devon-Cornwall. Those Britons who remained in the rich lowland zone, now almost completely under Germanic control, were obliged to acknowledge the Anglo-Saxons as their masters.

The details of the Anglo-Saxon invasions are far from certain. Even the broad pattern outlined here is hypothetical. But we do know that, although the Anglo-Saxon conquest was fitful and prolonged, it was, in the end, remarkably thorough. Roman-British culture was almost totally eradicated. Always a remote outpost of Roman civilization, Britain was the least successful of Rome's provinces in preserving vestiges of Roman culture into the Middle Ages. Insofar as any land can lose its past, Britain had lost hers, and the history of Anglo-Saxon England begins with a virtual *tabula rasa*. A new language superseded the old; German heathenism took the place of British Christianity; the square Celtic fields gave way to the long strip fields of the Anglo-Saxons; the Celtic family farm was replaced, for the most part, by the Anglo-Saxon village community; and Roman-British town and villa life vanished altogether. In a word, Britain was transformed into "Angle-Land," or England. And the Anglo-Saxons, who had neither the Roman past to build upon nor the Christian Church to teach them the ways of civilization, were ruder and more barbarous than any other Germanic people in the former empire.

Still, early Anglo-Saxon England began to move almost immediately toward political coherence, at least to a limited degree. As invasions turned into settlements, the warriors who had formerly commanded military bands now assumed the additional responsibility of territorial administration. They became important local aristocrats who, together with their military followers, constituted a warrior nobility sustained by the labor of subject peasants and slaves. English historians of the Victorian era were fond of describing

Anglo-Saxon England as a relatively egalitarian society, pregnant with democracy. Today most scholars regard this view as an illusion. Almost from the beginning, Anglo-Saxon society was dominated by an aristocracy of landed wealth and military prowess. And very early in the history of the settlements, war leaders of singular ability or luck began to assert their power over neighboring war bands, thereby beginning a movement toward political consolidation that resulted in the establishment of numerous territorial states ruled by royal dynasties.

England in A.D. 600

By the seventh century Anglo-Saxon England had resolved itself into about seven or eight major kingdoms and a number of less important ones— a political configuration that is traditionally called the Heptarchy. This term can be misleading, since it implies the existence of precisely seven states, all more or less equal in power. In reality the number of kingdoms fluctuated constantly and tended to diminish as political consolidation advanced. Moreover, the kingdoms of the Heptarchy varied in prestige and military might. Even by 600, if we may trust Bede, it was customary to accord one king the honor of pre-eminence among his royal colleagues by designating him *bretwalda*. This title was not permanently attached to a particular kingdom, but shifted from one dynasty to another with the varying fortunes of politics and war. The earliest bretwaldas were kings whose military strength enabled them to collect tribute from a few smaller neighboring kingdoms and whose fame had spread over much of England. Other important monarchs held the bretwalda in respect, but the degree to which they submitted to his commands is far from certain. Among the more powerful Anglo-Saxon kings his primacy seems to have been largely honorary. In later years, however, the authority of the bretwaldaship was destined to increase significantly and to play an important role in the ultimate unification of the realm.

The preeminent kingdom in Anglo-Saxon England around the year 600 was Kent, in the southeast corner of the island. Bede accords the Kentish king at this time the title of bretwalda, though it seems that Kent exerted authority only over the two neighboring kingdoms of Essex and East Anglia.

Kent is the one Anglo-Saxon kingdom whose conquest Bede attributes to the Jutes. Historians are still debating the questions of who the Jutes were and where they came from. It is quite true that Kent exhibits a number of peculiar features not found elsewhere in Anglo-Saxon England. Instead of the usual strip fields and agrarian villages, Kentish agriculture is characterized by consolidated fields and individual farms or *hamlets*. In its pottery, jewelry, burial methods, and legal customs, Kent differed from most of the remainder of England. On the other hand, its culture demonstrates marked similarities to that of the Franks, whose kingdom lay just across

THE EARLY
ANGLO-SAXON KINGDOMS
ABOUT 600 A.D.

Northern
Picts

Southern
Picts

Dumbarton

NORTH

Edinburgh

SEA

Old
Yeavering ● Bamburgh

GALLOWAY

N
O
R
T
H
U
M
B
R
I
A

BERNICIA

Carlisle

CUMBER-
LAND

DEIRA

● York

IRELAND

IRISH SEA

GWYNEDD ● Chester

● Lincoln

LINDSEY

MERCIA ● Lichfield

POWYS

EAST
ANGLIA

● Sutton-Hoo

DYFED

GWENT ● Gloucester

ESSEX

London ●

WESSEX

KENT ● Canterbury

Salisbury ●

SUSSEX

CORNWALL ● Exeter

English Channel

FRANCE

the Channel. It may well be that the Jutes of Kent were actually diverse peoples who achieved cultural unity only after their migration to Britain, and that their evolving culture was strongly influenced by their trade and intercourse with the Franks.

To the west and northwest of Kent lay three kingdoms associated by name with the Saxon migrations: the kingdoms of the South Saxons, the West Saxons, and the East Saxons, known respectively as Sussex, Wessex, and Essex. Of these Saxon states, only Wessex had the potentiality for future expansion westward at British expense, and in the centuries following A.D. 600 Wessex grew to become one of the three leading kingdoms of the land. Ultimately, Wessex became the nucleus of a united England, and the Wessex dynasty evolved into the English monarchy.

To the north of Kent lay the kingdom of East Anglia, whose inhabitants were divided into two separate groups—the North Folk and the South Folk—occupying the territories that would later become the shires of Norfolk and Suffolk. Subject to Kent in A.D. 600, the East Anglian monarchy acquired the bretwaldaship in the following generation. The wealth of the East Anglian kings in this epoch is attested dramatically by the richly laden royal burial ship dating from the mid-seventh century that was discovered at Sutton Hoo in 1939. The ship contains an abundance of gold and silver jewelry, plate, coins, and weapons, some of Frankish provenience, others from distant Byzantium. The discovery at Sutton Hoo leaves no doubt that the trappings of a great Anglo-Saxon monarch two centuries after the onset of the conquest could be splendid indeed.

PURSE COVER OF GOLD, ENAMEL, AND GARNET, C. 650
This piece was one of the many beautifully crafted artifacts discovered in 1939 in the Sutton Hoo Ship Burial in Suffolk. *British Museum.*

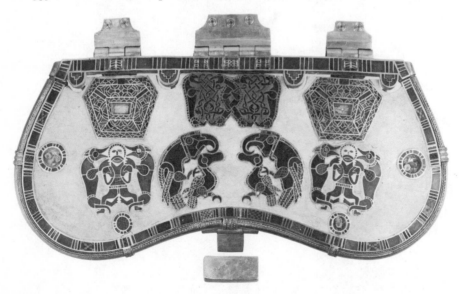

The English midlands were dominated by the kingdom of Mercia, which first emerges into the light of history with the accession of its great king, Penda, in 632. Like Wessex, Mercia could expand westward toward Wales at the expense of the Britons (or, as we should by now call them, the Welsh) and, like Wessex also, Mercia was destined to become one of the three dominant kingdoms of England in the centuries to follow. Indeed, throughout most of the eighth century the kings of Mercia were the most powerful monarchs in the land.

The third of these potentially dominant kingdoms was Northumbria —the land north of the Humber River. The kingdom of Northumbria took form shortly after A.D. 600 from the unification of two smaller, older, kingdoms, Deira and Bernicia, under a single dynasty. In the later seventh and early eighth centuries Northumbria became the setting of a splendid intellectual and artistic revival stimulated by a resurgence of Celtic culture and conversion to Christianity. Perhaps the greatest ornament of this Northumbrian renaissance was the historian Bede, whose writings have done so much to illuminate the dark epoch when his own savage forebears were ravaging and subduing Britain.

By the early seventh century the chaos of the invasion age had given way to a more stable regime dominated by reasonably coherent Anglo-Saxon kingdoms such as the seven described above: Kent, Sussex, Wessex, Essex, East Anglia, Mercia, and Northumbria. The splendor of Sutton Hoo demonstrates that the early Anglo-Saxons, even though cut off from the Roman past and isolated from the Church, were not without culture or resources. By A.D. 600, however, this isolation was ending. The new century was dominated by the momentous fact of England's conversion to Christianity. The Church returned to Britain at last, gradually winning the allegiance of the Anglo-Saxons and profoundly shaping their historical development.

Conversion and Unification

2 By the time of the British victory at Mount Badon (*c.* 500) Roman political authority had collapsed in the West. But although the Western Roman Empire was a thing of the past, Roman political institutions survived, in altered but recognizable form, in the organization of the Roman Catholic Church. Indeed, the Church has been regarded as a kind of transfigured Empire, its administration paralleling the old Roman civil administration with dioceses, provinces, parishes, and even a central authority in Rome. Where Roman emperors had once exerted political sway over the inhabitants of Western Europe, Roman popes now claimed responsibility for their immortal souls. And just as the emperor Constantine had established an imperial capital at Constantinople that rivaled Rome itself, so now an intense rivalry developed between the Roman pontiff and the patriarch of Constantinople.

Accordingly, the Church has been termed the ghost of the Roman Empire. To be sure, the ghost metaphor belies the very tangible ecclesiastical organization of the early Middle Ages and the significant impact of the Church on the lives of European Christians; yet there is some value in regarding the church, in the political sense at least, as an institutional legacy of the defunct empire.

The Celtic Church

In England, however, Christianity did not survive the Germanic invasions but receded with the Britons themselves into the mountains of Cornwall, Wales, and Cumberland (in northwest England).[1] In these rough

---

[1] For a good account of the early English Church see C. J. Godfrey, *The Church in Anglo-Saxon England* (Cambridge, 1962). Dorothy Whitelock, ed., *English Historical Documents,* I (London, 1955), provides a splendid and comprehensive selection of original documents in English translation from the period *c.* 500–*c.*1042.

lands the Britons found sanctuary against the military thrusts of the Anglo-Saxons, and here the British Church endured. Although several generations passed before Celtic Christianity made any headway against the heathen Anglo-Saxons, Celtic missionaries were spreading their faith in other directions. In the fifth century, the fabled British missionary St. Patrick (d. 461) had introduced Christianity to the Scots of Ireland, and other missionaries were undertaking the task of Christian conversion in Galloway (southwestern Scotland). Thus, although Christianity virtually disappeared from England with the completion of the Anglo-Saxon conquest, it continued to flourish in the lands that Englishmen call "the Celtic Fringe": Cornwall, Wales, Cumberland, Galloway, and above all, Ireland.

In the days of St. Patrick, the Celtic Church had been in contact with continental Christianity, but with the passage of time it became increasingly isolated. Despite its isolation—or perhaps because of it—the Celtic Church flourished remarkably, particularly in Ireland. During the sixth and seventh centuries it far exceeded the Church on the continent in the rigor of its scholarship, the depth of its sanctity, and the dynamism of its evangelical work. Irish monastic schools were perhaps the best in Western Europe at the time, and a rich Irish artistic tradition culminated in the illuminated manuscripts of the eighth century which were the wonder of their own age and still excite admiration in ours.

Because of its lack of contact with the papacy and continental Christianity, the Celtic Church developed certain practices and customs that were unique and, from the continental standpoint, suspicious. The tonsure of Celtic monks differed from that of continental monks; the Celtic method of calculating the date of Easter was at variance with the continental method. Matters such as these might well seem trivial today, but to a continental churchman of the early Middle Ages the Celtic celebration of Easter on the "wrong" day and the peculiar Celtic tonsure (the front half of the head was entirely shaved) seemed bizarre and even perverse.

More important, the Celtic Church differed from the continental Church in organization. On the continent the key unit in ecclesiastical administration was the dioceses, ruled by a bishop; in the Celtic Fringe it was the monastery, ruled by an abbot. The Celtic Church did have bishops, but their functions were spiritual and sacramental only. They had no administrative power at all, and they usually lived in monasteries under the authority of the abbot.

Celtic monastic life was peculiar, too, by continental standards. Celtic monks led simpler, harsher, but less regulated lives than their continental counterparts. The unique combination of profound dedication and relatively loose discipline does much to explain the wide-ranging and highly successful evangelical activities of the Irish monks. In the sixth and seventh centuries, they traveled far and wide across Western Europe, spreading the Christian faith into the remaining pockets of paganism and bringing the intense piety of Celtic Christianity to regions only nominally Christian. For our purposes, the most significant of these Irish evangelists was St. Columba (d. 597), who worked with great success toward the conversion of the Picts. In about 590, Columba founded a monastery on the island of Iona, off the west coast of Scotland; the monastery became a fountainhead of missionary activity among the Picts of Scotland and the English of Northumbria.

With the founding of Iona, the Celtic Church took up at last the immense task of converting the Anglo-Saxons. But, as it turned out, the Celtic spiritual penetration of Anglo-Saxon England from the north began almost concurrently with an entirely distinct Christian missionary endeavor from the south. In 597, the very year of St. Columba's death, a group of Christian evangelists sent by the Roman pope, St. Gregory the Great, and led by the Benedictine monk, St. Augustine, made contact with King Ethelbert of Kent. So it was that the seventh century saw Anglo-Saxon heathendom under spiritual assault from two independent and historically distinct Christian traditions.

The Roman Church and Benedictine Monasticism

As England was developing from the chaos of the early Anglo-Saxon conquests to the somewhat stabler Heptarchy, much larger Germanic kingdoms were forming on the continent. A powerful Germanic tribe known as the Franks had established a kingdom in Gaul and the Rhinelands; it was Catholic in religion but only superficially so, barbaric, poorly governed, and yet rather more sophisticated than the contemporary kingdoms of Anglo-Saxon England. The Germanic Visigoths had founded a loosely organized kingdom in Spain, destined to be overwhelmed in the early eighth century by the advancing Muslims. Italy, after a series of upheavals, was ruled in part by the Byzantine Empire, in part by a savage Germanic tribe known as the "Long Beards" or Lombards. In Rome itself the papacy maintained a precarious independence. Throughout these lands of Western Europe, scholarship was all but extinct, culture had sunk to a primitive level, the cities were moribund, and political and economic organization was rudimentary (except in Byzantine Italy). Germanic culture and institutions were everywhere in the ascendancy; and among the rough aristocracy of this epoch, fighting skill and loyalty to clan and lord were the appropriate virtues.

The taming of this crude, violent society by the intellectual and cultural values of antiquity and the teachings of Christianity was yet to be accomplished. The sixth-century Church, throughout much of the barbarian West, was little better than the lay society that surrounded it. Ineffective, ignorant, and frequently corrupt, it stood in desperate need of revitalization and reform. All things considered, isolation was by no means a disadvantage to the Celtic Church. Yet the continental Church of the sixth century had within it the strength to recover and to assume its great mission in the world. Its reform centered above all on two institutions: Benedictine monasticism and the papacy.

Christian monasticism arose in Egypt in the third century, but it did not become a significant factor in the life of the Church until the fourth. After the conversion of Constantine and his rise to power in 312, Christianity became a favored religion. Profession of the Christian faith was no longer the perilous and heroic act it had been in the days of the martyrs. As converts poured into the now-respectable fold, men of unusual piety began to seek a more rigorous Christian way of life—one that would enable them to withdraw from the sinful world and devote all their energies to communion with God. Many of them found what they were seeking in monasticism.

Traditionally, Christian monasticism was of two types: eremitic (hermit monasticism) and cenobitic (communal monasticism). During the fifth and sixth centuries increasing numbers of fervent believers became cenobitic or eremitic monks. The lives of the hermit monks were bewildering in their variety. Some established themselves atop tall pillars and remained there for many years; others retreated to the desert, living in a state of uncompromising austerity. And the monastic communities of the age tended to be equally diverse. Both hermit monks and cenobitic monks often carried the mortification of the flesh to extreme lengths, indulging in severe fasts, going without sleep for prolonged periods, wearing hairshirts, and whipping themselves.

The great contribution of St. Benedict (*c.* 480–*c.* 544) was the bringing of order to monastic life. A Roman of aristocratic background, his emphasis on the practical Roman virtues of discipline and organization transformed the monasticism of his day and infused it with new vigor. St. Benedict founded many monasteries in his lifetime, the most important of which was Monte Cassino, built on a mountaintop between Rome and Naples. But more important than his monasteries was the rule he created for their governance.

St. Benedict's rule was characterized by Pope Gregory the Great as "conspicuous for its discretion." The life of the Benedictine monk was austere, but not excessively so. He ate, slept, and dressed simply but adequately. His day was divided into a regular sequence of activities: there was a time for eating, a time for sleeping, a time for prayer, and a time for work. The Benedictine order had no central organization. Each monastery was autonomous (subject to the jurisdiction of the local bishop), and each was under the full and unquestioned authority of its abbot. On important matters the abbot was to consult the whole community of monks, but ultimately his word was final. Still, St. Benedict cautioned his abbots to respect the views of their monks, not to "sadden" or "overdrive" them or give them cause for "just murmuring." Here, as elsewhere, is the element of discretion to which Pope Gregory alludes and which was doubtless the chief reason for the rule's phenomenal success. St. Benedict tempered his sanctity with a keen knowledge of human nature. His monks had to submit to the discipline of their abbot and the authority of the rule; they had to practice poverty and chastity; they had to work as well as pray. Still, for all of that, the life St. Benedict prescribed was not for spiritual supermen alone, but one any dedicated Christian might hope to follow.

St. Benedict's rule transformed Western monasticism, revitalized the Church, and inspired many of the most prominent participants in the conversion of England. Benedictine monasteries became islands of peace, security, and learning in a sea of barbarism. They operated the best, often the only, schools of their day. Their extensive estates—the gifts of generations of pious donors—served as models of the most efficient agricultural techniques known in their time. They were the supreme civilizers of the early Middle Ages.

The other great invigorating institution in the early medieval Church was the papacy. For centuries the popes, as bishops of Rome and heirs of St. Peter, had claimed spiritual dominion over the Church, but they had seldom been able to exercise it until the pontificate of St. Gregory the Great (590–604). A man of humility and deep piety, St. Gregory was the first Benedictine pope. He was also the most powerful pontiff of the early Middle Ages. His pontificate represents, in effect, an alliance between the papacy and the Benedictine order.

Both parties profited from the alliance: Benedictine monasticism received a powerful impetus from papal support, and wherever the Benedictines went papal authority followed. When the Benedictines converted a heathen land, they converted it not merely to Christianity, but to Christianity as practiced and interpreted by the Roman Church. Hence, Benedictine evangelism was a potent factor in the spread of papal power and in the spiritual unification of Christendom.

The Benedictines in England

Pope Gregory the Great was a man of many talents. Like St. Benedict, he possessed in full the practical genius of his aristocratic Roman forebears and was a brilliant administrator as well as a sensitive pastor. He was a notable scholar too, by the standards of his day, and is traditionally grouped with the great fourth-century intellectuals—St. Ambrose, St. Jerome, and St. Augustine of Hippo—as one of the four "Doctors" of the Latin Church. Much of his theological writing failed to rise far above the level of his day, but his *Pastoral Care*—a handbook on the duties of bishops and priests— is a work of extraordinary practical wisdom; it became one of the most admired and widely read books of the Middle Ages.

Paradoxically, Gregory never set foot in England and yet is one of the central figures in early English history. Bede relates that, prior to his elevation to the papacy, Gregory encountered a group of fair-haired young boys from England who were being offered for sale as slaves. Asking the name of their race, he was told that they were Angles. "That is appropriate," he replied, "for they have angelic faces, and it is right that they should become fellow heirs with the angels in heaven." The story is hard to believe;

it seems unlikely that Gregory would risk his saintly reputation by indulging in such a deplorable pun. Bede himself is suspicious of the tale, but he includes it to illustrate "Gregory's deep desire for the salvation of our nation."

It was this deep desire that inclined Pope Gregory to send a band of missionaries to begin the conversion of the English. His devotion to the Benedictines prompted him to entrust the hazardous task to a group of monks of this order led by St. Augustine (not to be confused with the philosopher St. Augustine of Hippo). The ultimate effect of Augustine's mission was not only to win England to the Christian faith but also to enlarge enormously the scope of the Benedictine order and the authority of the papacy.

In 597 St. Augustine's mission arrived in Kent. This small kingdom was an ideal place to begin the work of conversion. It was the closest Anglo-Saxon kingdom to the continent; its king, Ethelbert, was momentarily the pre-eminent monarch of England and held the title of bretwalda. His queen, Bertha, was a Christian and a member of the Frankish royal family. At Queen Bertha's request, a Frankish bishop was residing in the Kentish royal household. Ethelbert received Augustine's mission courteously, permitted the monks to establish themselves in the royal town of Canterbury ("Kent City"), and in time became a convert to the new faith. Following Ethelbert, a great many Kentishmen were baptized, and significant progress made in converting the client kingdoms of Essex and East Anglia. Returning briefly to the continent, Augustine was consecrated by papal order as "archbishop of the English nation," thereby becoming the first in a line of archbishops of Canterbury that extends to this day.

In accordance with the sagacious instructions he received in letters from Pope Gregory, Augustine permitted his English converts to retain those aspects of their former heathen customs and rites that were not inconsistent with Christianity. Old heathen temples were neither abandoned nor destroyed, but were converted to Christian use. In general, Gregory and Augustine displayed a respect for the integrity of Anglo-Saxon folkways that would delight an anthropologist.

Almost from the beginning, St. Augustine was aware of the activities and potential rivalry of the Celtic Church. He attempted to secure its submission to his own archiepiscopal authority, but a series of unsuccessful summit conferences with leading Celtic ecclesiastics made it clear that the Celts would cling fast to their unique system of calculating Easter, their age-long independence, and their haircuts. The tension between Celtic and Roman-Benedictine Christianity was to continue for many decades.

It is no coincidence that Ethelbert of Kent, the first Anglo-Saxon monarch to become a Christian, was also the first to issue a series of written laws, or "dooms." The Dooms of Ethelbert are the first in a long series of Anglo-Saxon vernacular law codes running down into the eleventh century. They represent the first literary fruits of the encounter between Christianity and Anglo-Saxon culture. For although Ethelbert's Dooms are concerned largely with Germanic custom, they were undoubtedly committed to writing at the instigation of the Church, which was then the almost exclusive custodian of the written word. Indeed, the first doom in Ethelbert's list provides explicitly for the protection of ecclesiastical property. Other dooms deal with customary fines and wergeld rates: If a man cuts off another's ear he must pay twelve shillings; he must pay fifty shillings for an eye, six shillings for a front tooth, ten shillings for a big toe. In publishing these dooms, Ethelbert was not claiming the right to legislate but was merely specifying and clarifying the ancient customs of his people. In Germanic law the authority of the king was strictly limited by the customs of the folk.

The Conversion of Northumbria

Upon the death of Ethelbert in 616, Kent, Essex, and East Anglia underwent a heathen reaction. The bretwaldaship passed momentarily to East Anglia, but the center of evangelical activity shifted to the remote kingdom of Northumbria.

As we have seen, Northumbria came into being shortly after 600 through the unification of two northern kingdoms, Bernicia and Deira. The founder of Northumbria was a Bernician warrior-king named Ethelfrith (d. 616) who won a series of victories over the Celts, the Scots, and the Anglo-Saxon inhabitants of Deira, thereby establishing himself as the dominant power in the north and bringing the kingdom of Deira under his sway. The Deiran heir, a talented young warrior-statesman named Edwin, went into exile for a time at the East Anglian court; but in 616 Edwin's forces defeated and killed Ethelfrith and Edwin became king of Northumbria (616–632). Now it was the Bernician royal heirs who were driven into exile. They found refuge in Scotland where they fell under the influence of the Celtic monks of Iona.

Meanwhile, Edwin was proving himself a monarch of rare ability. He maintained a firm peace in Northumbria, led a highly successful military expedition against the Welsh, and even took his army on a triumphant campaign southward across the midlands into Wessex. Near his northern frontier he founded Edinburgh, which still bears his name. Edwin was a bretwalda of unprecedented authority, dominating his Anglo-Saxon contemporaries as no king before him had done. Even though his power rested on the ephemeral foundation of his own personal leadership and military skill, his reign represented an important step in England's long evolution toward political unity.

In the pages of Bede, Edwin's warlike prowess and successful statesmanship acquire a fundamental historical significance because of his conversion to Christianity. Like Ethelbert of Kent, Edwin had a Christian wife. Indeed, he was wed to a daughter of Ethelbert himself, Ethelberga, who took with her to Northumbria a vigorous chaplain named Paulinus. King

Edwin was subjected to Christian pressure from several quarters: from his devout wife, from Paulinus, and from the pope. In one of his letters to Ethelberga, the pope gave this counsel: "Persist, therefore, illustrious daughter, and to the utmost of your power endeavor to soften the hardness of his [Edwin's] heart by insinuating the divine precepts, etc." To King Edwin, the pope wrote,

> Hear the words of your preachers, and the Gospel of God which they declare to you, to the end that believing . . . [in] the indivisible Trinity, having put to flight the sensualities of devils, and driven from you the suggestions of the venomous and deceitful enemy, and being born again by water and the Holy Ghost, you may, through His assistance and bounty, dwell in eternal glory with Him in whom you shall believe.

After a time Edwin succumbed. At a royal council of 627 he and his counselors accepted Christianity in its Roman-Benedictine form. Bede tells of an episode in this council which, whether authentic or not, provides insight into the mood of the age. It is one of the most famous anecdotes of early English history—as familiar to English schoolboys as the story of George Washington and the cherry tree to Americans. According to Bede, one of Edwin's *Witan* (a member of his council), on considering the question of Christian conversion, advised his monarch as follows:

> The present life of man, O king, in comparison to that time which is unknown to us, seems to me like the swift flight of a sparrow through the hall wherein you sit at dinner in the winter, with your chieftains and ministers, and a good fire in the midst, while the storms of rain and snow rage without. The sparrow flies in at one door and immediately out at another. While he is within he is safe from the wintry storm, but after a brief interval of fair weather he immediately vanishes from sight into the dark winter from which he came. So this life of man appears for a brief interval, but we are utterly ignorant of what went before or what will follow. So if this new doctrine contains something more certain, it seems justly to deserve to be followed.

As the council concluded, the chief priest of the heathen gods is reported to have embraced the new religion and, with him, King Edwin himself. The Roman Church had won a notable triumph in a remote but powerful land.

The chagrin of the Christian party must have been great when, six years after his conversion, Edwin was killed in battle (632). His adversary, the heathen King Penda of Mercia (*c.* 632–654), laid waste to Edwin's kingdom, and as a result of the catastrophe Northumbria collapsed briefly into political and religious chaos. But with the fall of Edwin and the Deiran royal house, the two heirs of the Bernician dynasty, long in exile in Scotland, returned to claim their inheritance. These two princes, bearing the engaging names of Oswald and Oswy, brought with them the Celtic Christianity they had learned at Iona. Oswald, the older of the two, won the Northumbrian throne by defeating the Mercians and Welsh in 633. At this crucial encounter, known appropriately as the battle of Heavenfield, Oswald set up a wooden cross to symbolize his devotion to the new faith. But his victory must have evoked a mixed reaction among the Christians of Edwin's former court whose devotion to the Roman Easter and the Roman tonsure made it difficult for them to accept the alien ways of the Celtic Church.

Under the patronage of King Oswald (633–641) and his successor Oswy (641–669), Celtic Christianity established itself firmly in Northumbria. The Celtic missionary, St. Aidan, founded a monastery on the isle of Lindisfarne off the coast of northern Bernicia, which became a focal point of Celtic Christianity and culture. And in the middle decades of the seventh century Celtic missionaries carried the Gospel south of the Humber into Mercia and other Anglo-Saxon kingdoms.

But it was Northumbria, above all, that witnessed the collision and cross-fertilization of the Roman and Celtic traditions. The Celtic influence, radiating from Iona and Lindisfarne, was countered by the activities of Roman-Benedictine missionaries such as the fervent and uncompromising St. Wilfrid of Ripon (634–710). And despite the Celtic leanings of King Oswald and King Oswy, Roman Christianity, with its disciplined organization, its impressive ceremonial, and its majestic tradition, gradually advanced against the conservative and loosely administered Celtic Church.

The final victory of Roman Christianity in Northumbria was achieved at a synod held at Whitby in 663 in the presence of King Oswy.[2] Present were leading churchmen from all over England, representing both the Roman and the Celtic observances. The chief issue in question was the Easter date. Oswy, who had previously celebrated Easter according to the Celtic reckoning, was upset that his wife, who followed the Roman custom, should be keeping the Lenten fast while he was enjoying the Easter feast. The Easter issue symbolized a far more fundamental question: would England remain in isolation from continental Christendom by cleaving to the customs of the Celtic Christians, or would it place itself in the mainstream of European Christianity by accepting the guidance of the papacy and the customs of European Christianity? St. Wilfrid of Ripon saw the issue clearly when he addressed the Celtic churchmen at Whitby in these words:

> Although your fathers were holy men, do you imagine that they, a few men in a corner of a remote island, are to be preferred before the universal Church of Christ throughout the world? And even if you Columba—or may I say, ours also if he was a servant of Christ—was a saint of potent virtues, can he take precedence before the most blessed prince of the Apostles [St. Peter, whose vicar and representative the pope claimed to be] . . . ?

The synod of Whitby closed on an almost comic note, as King Oswy, determining that Peter possessed the keys to the kingdom of heaven, agreed to follow Peter's vicar, the pope, in all matters: "Otherwise, when I come to the gates of heaven, he who holds the keys may not be willing to open

---

[2] Sometimes dated 664. Bede's chronology is disputed.

them." Bede reports this statement in all seriousness, but another source reports that Oswy smiled as he uttered those words. Probably he had decided long before the synod opened to cast his lot with Rome. The question at issue was momentous, but the answer may well have been a foregone conclusion. For by the time of Whitby it must have been growing increasingly clear that the Roman way was the way of the future.

Celtic Christianity by no means expired with the synod of Whitby. It endured long thereafter, contributing much to Christian culture and the Christian life. But little by little it abandoned its separatist character. In 716 Iona itself submitted to the Roman observance, and in later years the churches of Wales and Ireland followed.

The Roman Church was quick to consolidate its victory. The acceptance of Roman authority and customs at Whitby was followed by a thorough reorganization of the Anglo-Saxon Church along Roman lines. The architect of this great administrative undertaking was St. Theodore of Tarsus, a distinguished scholar from Asia Minor who, having traveled to Rome, was sent to England by the pope to become archbishop of Canterbury. Theodore arrived in England in 669 at the age of sixty-six. He set about at once to divide the land into dioceses and selected devout, energetic bishops to rule them. The rational episcopal structure that Archbishop Theodore imposed upon the Anglo-Saxon Church was given unity and direction by a regular series of conciliar assemblies over which he presided. In the course of his twenty-one-year archiepiscopacy, Theodore succeeded in superimposing upon the multiplicity of Anglo-Saxon kingdoms a unified church, with clearly delineated territorial bishoprics, and with ultimate administrative authority centered at Canterbury. So it was that the English Church, shaped by the coherent political principles of the Roman papacy and, indirectly, the Roman Empire, achieved a degree of territorial coherence and administrative centralization that contrasted sharply with the instability of the Anglo-Saxon states. As the political unity of the Roman Empire underlay the spiritual unity of the Roman Church, so the unity Theodore imposed upon the English Church prefigured the political unity of England itself.

Theodore was a celebrated scholar who had earlier studied in Athens. He was accompanied on his journey to England by another scholar of eminence, a North African churchman named Hadrian. The Latin learning of Hadrian complemented the Greek scholarship of Theodore, and together they made Canterbury a distinguished intellectual center. Theodore established a school there which provided instruction in Greek and Latin letters and the principles of Roman law. The Roman legal tradition, which had virtually disappeared from Western Europe, was well known in Theodore's Byzantine homeland, and he was able to introduce it into England along with his native Greek tongue. Through their wide experience and broad culture, Theodore and Hadrian brought to seventh-century Canterbury the rich intellectual legacy of the Mediterranean world.

The Northumbrian Renaissance

But it was in Northumbria rather than at Canterbury that Anglo-Saxon ecclesiastical culture reached its highest degree of creativity. Here, at the northernmost edge of Christendom, the stimulating encounter between Celtic and Roman-Benedictine Christianity resulted in an intellectual and cultural achievement of the first order. In Northumbria during the later seventh and early eighth century, Anglo-Saxon culture—and perhaps the whole of Christian culture in the early Middle Ages—reached its climax.

One of the great patrons of this renaissance was a well-born Northumbrian named Benedict Biscop, a man of vigor and piety and a devoted Benedictine monk. Benedict Biscop made several trips to Italy and southern Gaul, and, indeed, was a companion of Archbishop Theodore and Hadrian on their journey from Rome in 668–69. In southern Europe Benedict experienced the ordered life of long-established Benedictine monasteries and collected large quantities of books and precious works of art, which he brought back with him to his native Northumbria. He founded two great Northumbrian monasteries of the strict Benedictine rule—Wearmouth (674) and Jarrow (681)—which he filled with his books and other treasures. These two houses became the foci of Roman-Benedictine culture in Northumbria, while the older establishment at Lindisfarne remained the center of Celtic culture.

Both cultures contributed to the renaissance in Northumbria. The impressive artistic achievements of the age seem to be predominantly Celtic in inspiration. The magnificently illuminated Lindisfarne Gospels are executed in the complex curvilinear style typical of Celtic art, although scholars have also detected an Anglo-Saxon influence in them. The Latin literature of the period is, of course, primarily Roman-Benedictine in inspiration; and it has been suggested that the same impulse that gave rise to the Latin writings of the Northumbrian renaissance also produced the written, vernacular version of the Germanic epic poem *Beowulf*.[3]

The achievements of the Northumbrian renaissance lay in many fields —in art, architecture, poetry, paleography, and manuscript illumination. But the supreme achievement of the age was the scholarship of the Venerable Bede (c. 673–735). In the writings of Bede, particularly his *History of the English Church and People*, the intellectual tradition of Western Europe attained a level unequaled since the fall of Rome.[4]

Bede was a product of the Roman-Benedictine tradition. He spent his life under the Benedictine rule at Jarrow, where he was an exemplary monk. He was also a superb scholar whose investigations were made

---

[3] The earliest extant version of *Beowulf* is from tenth-century Wessex, but philological evidence suggests that the Wessex text is based on an earlier version from central or northern England.

[4] Bede's masterpiece is most readily available in Leo Sherley-Price, tr., *A History of the English Church and People* (Baltimore, 1955).

ILLUMINATED PAGE FROM THE LINDISFARNE GOSPELS, C. 700
This most beautiful of early manuscript books is a product of the
Northumbrian Renaissance. *British Museum.*

possible by the fine library that Benedict Biscop had installed in the monastery in 681. Bede seems to have regarded his theological writings as his most important work, but his fame in later centuries rests primarily on his history. It was a pioneer effort, unprecedented in scope, and at the same time a work of remarkable maturity. Bede possessed a strong historical conscience—an acute critical sense that caused him to use his sources with scrupulous care, evaluating their reliability and often quoting them in full. Bede was by no means a scientific historian in the modern sense. His history is embroidered with numerous visions and other miraculous events, for he was a man of faith who accepted the possibility of miracles. But even in his miracle stories he demonstrates far greater caution—far more respect for the historical evidence—than was customary among his predecessors and contemporaries.

Bede's broad historical vision—his sense of structure and unity—sets his work apart from the dry annals and credulous saints' lives that typify the historical writing of his day. And his miracle stories fit logically into the basic structure of his work. For it was Bede's purpose to narrate the miraculous rise of Christianity in Britain and its crucial role of imposing coherence and purpose on the chaos of human events. In Bede's hands the history of the Britons and Anglo-Saxons and the rise of Christianity among them acquire shape and direction. In effect, Bede is recording the developing synthesis between the Germanic and the Christian cultures—the gradual softening of the savage, martial traditions of the primitive Anglo-Saxons by the peace, love, and humble labor characteristic of the Christian life. And of course, to Bede the Christian life *par excellence* is the life of the Benedictine monk. In one of the closing paragraphs of his history, Bede records—too optimistically—the triumph of monastic peace over Germanic violence:

> As peace and prosperity prevail in these days, many of the Northumbrians, both noble and humble, together with their children, have laid aside their arms, preferring to receive the tonsure and take monastic vows rather than study the arts of war. The result of this trend will be seen in the coming generation.

It is characteristic of this man who regarded Christianity as the supreme organizing force in history that he should be the first major historian to use the Christian era as his chronological base—to date events not in terms of kings' reigns or lunar cycles but in terms of Christ's birth.[5] Thus Bede's sense of chronology and historical development resulted in the division of history into the two eras, B.C. and A.D.

Finally, Bede gave to his contemporaries the concept of an "English people." At a time when England was divided into numerous individual kingdoms and loyalties were limited to one's clan or local lord, Bede conceived the notion of "Englishmen" and made it the subject of his history.

---

[5] Bede took the idea from a sixth-century scholar, the Roman monk Dionysius Exiguus.

Thus, Bede accomplished at the intellectual level what Archbishop Theodore had accomplished at the level of ecclesiastical organization. In the face of the savage particularism and petty struggles of Anglo-Saxon kings, both men saw England as one. It is fitting that later ages should honor the administrative genius of Theodore and celebrate Bede as "the first articulate Englishman."

The Return to the Continent

We have seen how the Benedictine order had its genesis in sixth-century Italy, how it was harnessed by Pope Gregory at the century's end to the task of converting the Anglo-Saxons, and how its encounter with Celtic Christianity in seventh- and eighth-century Northumbria evoked a cultural flowering. During the eighth century, the dynamic Roman-Benedictine Christianity of England was carried back to the continent by Anglo-Saxon missionaries and scholars to reinvigorate the Frankish Church and to spread civilization and the Gospel among the heathen Germans east of the Rhine. The greatest of these Anglo-Saxon missionaries was the Wessex monk, St. Boniface (d. 754). Working under the general direction of the papacy, and supplied with books and assistants by his Wessex countrymen, St. Boniface was the representative of three great dynamic forces of his day: the papacy, the Benedictine order, and the ecclesiastical culture of Anglo-Saxon England. During the 740s, with the cooperation of the Frankish kings, St. Boniface devoted himself to the reform of the Frankish Church, enforcing the strict observance of the Benedictine rule in monasteries and reconstructing Frankish diocesan organization on the same disciplined pattern that Theodore of Tarsus had earlier established in England. It was this reformed Frankish Church that provided the necessary environment for the impressive cultural achievements of Charlemagne's reign a generation later.

St. Boniface also devoted himself to the immense undertaking of Christianizing the heathen peoples of Germany. The task was far too great for a single man or a single generation, but Boniface made a promising beginning. Among the several Benedictine houses he founded in Germany was the monastery of Fulda, which, like Wearmouth and Jarrow in Northumbria, became a notable intellectual and evangelical center. Boniface devoted himself particularly to the conversion of the Saxons, Hessians, and Frisians, and it was at the hands of the latter that he died a martyr's death in 754.

Northumbria too participated in the work of evangelism on the continent. The fiery Northumbrian Benedictine, Wilfrid of Ripon, had been active in missionary work across the Channel long before Boniface undertook his mission. Much later, in the reign of Charlemagne (768–814), the Northumbrian scholar Alcuin of York, a student of a student of Bede's, was the leading intellectual at Charlemagne's court. A product of the Northumbrian renaissance, Alcuin became the chief figure of the later and better-known Carolingian renaissance.

In England itself, ecclesiastical culture declined from the summit attained in Bede's day, and in the ninth century it was virtually annihilated by the Vikings. Norse raiders sacked Lindisfarne in 793, Jarrow in 794, and Iona in 802. But before its demise in the north, this culture had spread its creative influence among the Franks and Germans. Having transformed the Anglo-Saxon world, the potent civilizing force of Benedictine evangelism now returned to the continent to provide the intellectual and spiritual foundations for Charlemagne's empire.

The Movement Toward Political Consolidation: Mercia

During the 220 years following the death of Bede in 735, the unity of England, foreshadowed in the ecclesiastical organization of Archbishop Theodore and in the historical work of Bede, was achieved at the level of secular politics. The chief historical theme of these years is the gradual trend toward political consolidation and, at length, the genesis of the English monarchy.

The progressive consolidation of royal power during the seventh and eighth centuries can be illustrated by the evolution of the bretwaldaship. Prior to the reign of King Edwin of Northumbria (616–632), a bretwalda might demand allegiance and collect tribute from one or two neighboring kingdoms, but elsewhere his pre-eminence seems to have been chiefly honorary. Indeed, the bretwaldas of southern England appear to have been ignored completely by Bernicia and Deira north of the Humber. Moreover, the bretwaldaship tended to flit from one kingdom to another—from Sussex to Wessex to Kent to East Anglia—never remaining in one place more than a generation. We are dependent on Bede for the names of the early bretwaldas, and it may well be that in attributing the bretwaldaship and its implied hegemony to these early kings, Bede was mistakenly injecting into a chaotic past the relative orderliness of his own day.

However this may be, the rise of Edwin of Northumbria to the bretwaldaship marks a new phase in England's political evolution. The smaller kingdoms of earlier years were gradually absorbed into the larger ones until, by the later seventh century, three kingdoms—Northumbria, Mercia, and Wessex—had come to overshadow all the others. To speak very generally, Northumbria was the leading Anglo-Saxon kingdom in the seventh century, Mercia in the eighth, and Wessex in the ninth and tenth.

The epoch of Northumbrian hegemony is celebrated in the pages of Bede's history, and the great days of Wessex are recorded in the writings of King Alfred the Great's court and in the *Anglo-Saxon Chronicle*. Mercia left to posterity no impressive scholarly works and no history of its age of greatness. The power of Mercia's eighth-century kings cannot be gainsaid, but local patriotism prevented both the Northumbrian Bede and the later

Wessex authors of the *Anglo-Saxon Chronicle* from portraying the rival Mercian state sympathetically. We must therefore use these sources with caution and beware of underestimating the statesmanship of the Mercian kings or the creativity of Mercian culture.

Mercia's political and military power was impressive indeed. Even Northumbria in its greatest days lived under an almost constant Mercian threat. Mercia's powerful heathen monarch, Penda, had challenged the Northumbrian hegemony more than once in the seventh century, defeating and killing King Edwin in 632 and King Oswald in 641 before being killed himself in battle against King Oswy in 654. During much of his reign, Penda exerted an authority over the kingdoms south of the Humber exceeding that of the earlier southern kings whom Bede called bretwaldas. By the end of his reign, he had vastly increased the extent of his kingdom—by absorbing a number of small neighboring states—and had exerted his supremacy over both Wessex and East Anglia. A remarkably effective heathen warrior-king, he is portrayed by contemporary Christian writers as something of a devil.

Penda's Christian son, King Wulfhere (657–674), resumed his father's drive for control of southern England, establishing dominion over Essex and the town of London, cowing Wessex, and winning the allegiance of Kent and Sussex. At his death he was endeavoring to subdue Northumbria itself. Had he succeeded, his authority over England would have been virtually uncontested.

The growth of Mercian power was interrupted for the half century after Wulfhere's death by a resurgence of Wessex, particularly in the reign of its able king, Ine (688–726). Sussex, Essex, and Kent passed for a time from Mercian into Wessex control. It was obvious by now that these smaller states were far too weak to maintain their independence, and the only question that remained was—which of the two "superpowers" would dominate them, Mercia or Wessex? During most of the eighth century Mercia not only successfully reasserted its dominion over these states, but usually managed to dominate Wessex as well.

Mercian supremacy in the eighth century resulted from the intelligent exploitation of its strategic position and considerable resources by two able and long-lived kings: Ethelbald (716–757) and Offa (757–796). Mercia under the leadership of these monarchs was a powerful state that dominated the midlands and exacted tribute and allegiance from the kingdoms to the south and east. Offa described himself in official documents as "king of all the English," and the royal boast was not too far from the truth.

The reality of Mercian power is well illustrated by a contemporary document known as the Tribal Hidage—a comprehensive assessment schedule that seems to have regulated tribute payments owed to the Mercian kings by various lesser kingdoms in southern and central England. In the early days of the Anglo-Saxon settlements the term "hide" had denoted a unit of land sufficient in extent to support the household of a single warrior.

By the time of the Tribal Hidage the hide had become the key unit of assessment. In the centuries to come, royal governments would exact taxes and military service from their subjects on the basis of the number of hides of land each subject owned. The fact that the eighth-century Mercian monarchy should produce a document enumerating the hides of most of the Anglo-Saxon peoples south of the Humber testifies to a far-flung administrative system and a central organization of unprecedented scale.

The reigns of Ethelbald and Offa witnessed not only an unparalleled degree of political power but also a resurgence of commercial activity. King Offa's minters produced considerable quantities of the silver pennies that remained the basis of the English currency for centuries to come. The very term "penny" was probably derived from the name of Offa's predecessor, King Penda. And the importance of commercial activities between the dominions of Offa and the empire of his illustrious contemporary, Charlemagne, is demonstrated by a remarkable treaty between these two monarchs. In it, Charlemagne addresses Offa in these words:

> You wrote to us about merchants. We extend to them our personal protection, as is the ancient custom for those engaged in trade. If treated wrongfully, let them appeal to us or our judges, and we will see that they have full justice. Similarly, should any of our subjects suffer injustice in your kingdom, they shall appeal to you for a just remedy, so that no trouble may occur between our subjects.

It is significant that English merchants were sufficiently active on the continent at this time to require a formal arrangement between two rulers, and perhaps even more significant that Offa should take such a broad view of his royal responsibilities as to intervene in behalf of English traders abroad. In Offa's hands, Anglo-Saxon monarchy was assuming new and larger dimensions.

Many details of Offa's reign are hidden from us by a lack of historical evidence. He has rightly been termed the most obscure great monarch of Anglo-Saxon England. As one historian recently wrote: "We can be sure that Offa was a crucial figure in the development of Anglo-Saxon institutions, without being able to find out exactly what he did." [6] Two centuries after Offa's death, King Alfred of Wessex spoke respectfully of his laws, but the laws themselves have since vanished. We have no contemporary account of his reign nor any celebration of his deeds. But we do know that Offa extended very considerably the limits of the Mercian kingdom and the scope of Mercian royal authority. He advanced his power westward at Welsh expense and delineated his western frontier by constructing a remarkable earthen boundary marker known as Offa's Dike, which has been called "the greatest public work of the whole Anglo-Saxon period." At his death, the venerable royal dynasties of Sussex, Essex, East Anglia,

---

[6] Eric John, *Orbis Britannae*, p. 35.

and Kent had ceased to rule, and the vague suzerainty of the earlier bretwaldaship was in the process of being transformed into a direct control and absorption of subject lands.

Offa's program for Mercian hegemony had the effect of temporarily subverting the hierarchical unity that Archbishop Theodore had earlier imposed on the English Church. Under Theodore, the archbishopric of Canterbury had stood unchallenged at the apex of the hierarchy; but in 735 a second archbishopric was established at York in Northumbria. It was inferior in prestige to Canterbury but nevertheless a potential rival. King Offa, it seems, demanded a separate archbishopric for Mercia, and accordingly in 787 a new archbishopric at Lichfield emerged. Shortly after Offa's death, however, it disappeared, and thereafter the English Church was dominated by its two remaining archbishoprics of Canterbury and York.

The Church was active during Offa's reign. General councils continued to meet, and, at a lower level, country parishes were gradually taking shape. The development of an effective parish system was of immense importance to both Church and society in the early Middle Ages. The Church had emerged from the highly urbanized Roman Empire with a diocesan organization based on the city. With the disintegration of Roman imperial society, the cities declined and the countryside came to the fore, but several centuries elapsed before the Church adjusted its organization to the needs of the rural society in which it worked. Peasants and small freeholders often were obliged to go many months without seeing a priest or attending mass. The answer to this unsatisfactory condition was found in the country parish, administered by a priest who was supported by the enforced tithes of his parishioners. The parish system developed only gradually, but in the eighth century, both in the empire of Charlemagne and in the kingdom of Offa, it was making significant progress.

In both ecclesiastical and secular affairs, Offa's reign marks a crucial stage in the development of the Anglo-Saxons. With the Northumbrian monarchy in the doldrums and Mercian power unchallenged south of the Humber, with a vigorous and statesmanlike monarch who could negotiate with Charlemagne on terms of equality, Offa's England attained a degree of stability such as the Anglo-Saxons had never before experienced.

The Movement Toward Political Consolidation: Wessex

The eighth-century Mercian kings gave England political coherence but fell short of giving it unity. With Offa's death in 796, competence departed from the Mercian royal line, and the leadership of southern England gradually passed to Wessex.

In the early Middle Ages sophisticated bureaucratic government was unknown to Western Europe, and whatever the resources of a state, its success in the ruthless political competition of the period depended heavily on the military and administrative talents of its ruler. Thus, Mercia prospered mightily under Ethelbald and Offa but declined under their less able successors. On the continent, the Carolingian Empire of the Franks declined similarly in the years following the death of Charlemagne in 814. Accordingly, the rise of Wessex in the early ninth century depended not merely on its wide extent and the relative abundance of its human and material resources, but also, and above all, on the skill of its monarchs.

It was the gifted King Egbert of Wessex (802–839) who won for his kingdom the hegemony that Mercia had so long enjoyed. At the battle of Ellendon in 825 he routed the Mercian army and won control of the lesser states of southern England—Kent, Sussex, and Essex. Shortly afterward he received the submission and allegiance of East Anglia and Northumbria, and for a brief time he ruled even in Mercia itself. Egbert's power was impressive, though less so than Offa's. But unlike Offa, Egbert had the good fortune to be succeeded by a series of remarkably able heirs. Egbert's reign was merely the beginning of a long epoch in which the Wessex monarchy, tempered by the fires of a terrifying Viking invasion, endured to become the sole royal power in the land. Egbert's descendants were to become the first kings of England.

The Viking Age and the Birth of the English Monarchy

The era of Mercian ascendancy corresponded approximately to the period in which Charlemagne and his gifted predecessors expanded the power of the Frankish kingdom to such an extent that it became virtually coterminous with continental Western Christendom. We have already noted the impressive intellectual upsurge at Charlemagne's court, and the role played by the Northumbrian Alcuin in this Carolingian renaissance. The hegemony of Wessex, on the other hand, was concurrent with the decline of the Carolingian Empire and the coming of the Viking Age. Traveling from their Scandinavian homeland in their long ships, the Vikings carried their activities of pillage and conquest far and wide across northern Europe and the Atlantic. They subjected the Franks and Germans to fierce harassment, established a powerful dynasty in Russia, raided Islamic Spain, settled Iceland, and even touched the coast of North America.

Although the reasons for the Viking outburst are a matter of considerable scholarly dispute, it is possible to suggest certain contributing factors. For one thing, a steady rise in population and political consolidation in Scandinavia may have prompted many adventurous spirits to seek their fortunes and satisfy their land hunger abroad. In addition, improvements in Viking shipbuilding seem to have added significantly to the mobility of these warriors. Charlemagne himself may have contributed unknowingly to the future debacle when he subdued and conquered the Frisians, a powerful maritime people who lived along the northern shore of Europe east of the Rhine. The Frisians had previously functioned as a buffer between Western Europe and Scandinavia, and, with their defeat, the barrier was removed. After Charlemagne's death in 814, Europe's defensive posture grew slack. Three decades later, in 843, Charlemagne's grandsons divided

The Gokstad Ship, an 80-foot Viking vessel, was found buried in Norway.
It could be sailed or rowed (by 16 pairs of oars) and carried as many as
70 people. *Universitetets Oldsaksamling, Oslo.*

his huge, unwieldy empire into three parts, creating thereby the nuclei of
modern France, modern Germany, and the long strip of intermediate lands
over which France and Germany have contested ever since. Although
Charlemagne's heirs were by no means weaklings, they represented a distinct decline in leadership, and the struggles among them created a political-
military vacuum that proved irresistible to the Viking raiders.

Neither Charlemagne nor Offa had possessed any navies to speak of,
and the English Channel had effectively separated the two powers. But to
the seafaring Vikings, the Channel was less a barrier than a boulevard. They
harried the lands on either side without partiality, plundering coastal settlements and sailing up rivers to bring havoc and terror deep into the interior
of England and the continent. Their first raids struck England, for they
found it expedient to ignore continental Europe until the passing of Charlemagne. It is said that the great Frankish emperor wept on seeing Viking
ships off the north Frankish coasts on their way to England, and Alcuin
wrote a letter expressing profound sympathies when the Danes sacked
Lindisfarne in his native Northumbria in 793.

The first Viking raid struck the Dorset coast of Wessex around 787.
The *Anglo-Saxon Chronicle* reports that on the arrival of three long ships,
the chief royal official of the threatened community—the port reeve—rushed
to the shore to inquire their business. The Vikings made emphatic reply,
killing the reeve and looting and sacking the town. It was a portentous episode, for in subsequent years countless other raiders came from Scandinavia

THE NORSE INVADERS
Carved decorations and sculpted figures such as this chieftain's head
are expressive of the rude vigor of the Norse peoples. *Universitetets
Oldsaksamling, Oslo.*

to devastate and plunder the land. When Wessex inherited the political hegemony that Mercia had formerly exercised, it also inherited the ominous and ever-increasing Norse threat.

Organized into small groups of ships' crews, the Vikings had the immense advantage of mobility and surprise over their more numerous, sedentary victims. At first confining themselves to plundering expeditions, they gradually conceived the idea of conquest and settlement. Norwegian Vikings attacked and overran Ireland, founded a state centering on Dublin, and remained in occupation of northern Ireland for generations thereafter. Another Viking band established a permanent settlement in northern Frankland at the mouth of the Seine. Its ruler, a Viking chieftain named Rollo, was converted to Christianity and was granted official recognition by the Frankish king, Charles the Simple, around 911. This Seine settlement evolved and expanded in later years into a powerful duchy known as Normandy, which gradually assimilated French culture, French institutions, and the French language, but retained the martial vigor of its Viking past. The establishment of the Norman duchy went unmarked in English annals, but Normandy was to play a crucial role in England's later history.

Midway through the ninth century, the Viking attacks on England began to change from plundering expeditions to campaigns of conquest. In 850 a large group of Danish Vikings spent the winter on the Isle of Thanet (off Kent) rather than return to their homeland at the close of the raiding season. In 865 a Danish host began a series of bloody and highly successful campaigns that shortly won them virtually all of England outside Wessex. The local kingdoms and subkingdoms that had survived the eras of Mercian and Wessex hegemony were destroyed, and of the monarchies of the ancient Heptarchy only Wessex endured.

In the wake of these lightning conquests came Danish settlers in such numbers as to change permanently the social and institutional complexion of large areas of England. These areas of Danish settlement and occupation, known later on as the "Danelaw," included: (1) Yorkshire (southern Northumbria), where the most intensive settlements occurred; (2) East Anglia; and (3) a large tract of central and eastern Mercia that came to be known as the "Five Boroughs" after its five chief centers of settlement—Lincoln, Stamford, Nottingham, Leicester, and Derby. For centuries these three Danish districts differed sharply from the remainder of England in their traditions and customs.

Alfred the Great

In 870 the Danish attack against Wessex began in earnest. It has seemed almost providential to English historians that in the following year there came to the Wessex throne a man of singular intellect and statesmanship, King Egbert's grandson, Alfred the Great (871–899). He was a monarch of many talents—a warrior, an administrator, a friend of scholarship, and a leader of men. With his reign the history of the English monarchy truly begins.[7]

Alfred's accession occurred at a desperate moment in Anglo-Saxon history. In 872 he was obliged to purchase a truce from the Danes in order to gain the time necessary to put his forces in order. During this brief, expensive intermission, he began a thorough military reorganization of his realm, which continued throughout his reign. His military reforms rested on three major innovations: (1) His army—or *fyrd* as it is called in the Anglo-Saxon documents—was divided into two halves, each serving for six months. Thus, when one half was at home, the other half was under arms, insuring that at no time would Wessex be defenseless. (2) Large fortifications known as *burghs* were built at strategic points to defend against Danish invasion and, later, to serve as forward bases in the reconquest of the Danelaw. An important tenth-century document known as the Burghal Hidage discloses that extensive and precisely delineated territories surrounding each burgh were responsible for its maintenance and defense, with responsibility assessed in terms of the hide of land. (We have already encountered the hide as the assessment unit of the eighth-century Mercian Tribal Hidage, and we shall encounter it again as the basis for military recruitment and tax assessment.) In later years many of the burghs of Alfred and his successors evolved into commercial centers, and the meaning of the term gradually changed from "fortress" to "town." (3) Recognizing more clearly than his predecessors or contemporaries, either in England or on the continent, that the Vikings must be challenged on the seas, Alfred established a fleet. His biographer, the Welshman Asser, reports that Alfred built numerous ships, both large and swift, "neither after the Frisian design nor after the Danish, but as it seemed to him that they could be most serviceable." This disclosure provides a clear illustration of the creative intellect and imagination Alfred applied to the problems of war.

His military reforms were far-reaching, but time was required to carry them out; and for Alfred time was all too short. In 876 a Danish chieftain named Guthrum led a host against Wessex; and again early in 878, catching Alfred off guard in the dead of winter, Guthrum led his army across the land, forcing the king to flee into the marsh country of Somerset. There he found refuge at a royal estate on the Isle of Athelney. For a time almost all of England was at the mercy of the Danes.

Athelney was England's Valley Forge. Alfred held out with a small group of followers throughout the winter, and in the spring of 878 he was able to rally the Wessex fyrd. (The Danish army was too small to occupy Wessex completely or to prevent the summoning of Alfred's army.) The armies of Alfred and Guthrum met in pitched battle at Edington, and Alfred

---

[7] On Alfred see Eleanor Duckett, *Alfred the Great* (Chicago, 1956). A biography of Alfred written by one of his own contemporaries is available in English translation: L. C. Jane, tr., *Asser's Life of King Alfred* (London, 1926).

won a total victory. As a consequence, Guthrum agreed to accept Christianity and to abandon Wessex forever. One may well doubt the depth of Guthrum's conversion, but the fact remains that he was the first important Viking to become a Christian. His baptism in 878 foreshadows the ultimate Christianization of the entire Viking world and its incorporation into the mainstream of Western European civilization.

In this age of warfare, skillful military leadership was essential to a king's very survival. Alfred, the ablest of all the Anglo-Saxon kings, was a military commander of the first order. In the years after 878 he was obliged to cope with repeated attacks by Danish raiding parties, and all of these he repelled. Indeed he was able, little by little, to drive back the Danish power. In 886 he recaptured London, and later in the same year he entered into a new treaty with Guthrum which defined the boundary between English and Danish authority. The frontier ran approximately northwestward, along the old Roman road known as Watling Street, from London to Chester on the Irish Sea. By this new agreement a large section of Mercia was freed of Danish control, and in that once powerful kingdom Alfred established a subking or *ealdorman* named Ethelred. The future allegiance of English Mercia was insured by a marriage between Ethelred and Alfred's daughter Ethelfleda, known as the "Lady of Mercia."

The struggle with the Danes continued to the close of Alfred's reign and well beyond, but by Alfred's death in 899 the crisis had clearly passed. Southwestern England was secure, London had been recovered, a successful military policy had been established, and the authority of the Wessex monarchy was supreme in non-Danish England.

Alfred was more than a warrior. The creative intelligence that he applied to military reorganization was equally effective in law and administration. Several of Alfred's predecessors had issued law codes or dooms. Ethelbert of Kent had been the first to do so, and he was followed by other monarchs such as Offa of Mercia (whose dooms are now lost) and Alfred's own distant ancestor, Ine of Wessex (688–726). But these earlier kings— Offa perhaps excepted—seem to have intended merely to clarify existing law and provide for new conditions. None went so far as to actually repeal old customs or, in the strict sense of the word, make new laws. Alfred interpreted his lawmaking authority more broadly than his predecessors had. Although he was hesitant to create new laws, he exercised considerable latitude in his selection or rejection of old ones, thereby placing his own imprint on the legal structure of his day. In the preface to his dooms, Alfred expresses himself in these words:

> Then I, King Alfred, collected these [laws] together and ordered that many
> of them which our forefathers observed should be written down, namely,
> those that I liked; and, with the advice of my Witan [council], I rejected
> many of those that I did not like and ordered that they be observed differently. I have not presumed to set in writing much of my own, because it
> was unknown to me what might please those who shall come after us. So

**ENGLAND
ABOUT 887 A.D.**

Scots

Picts

Tay R.

Firth of Forth

Lindisfarne
(Holy Island)

ENGLISH NORTHUMBRIA

Picts

Tees R.

Whitby

York

NORTH SEA

IRELAND

IRISH SEA

D A N E L A W

WALES

Trent R.

ENGLISH MERCIA

Severn R.

Ouse R.

EAST ANGLIA

London

Thames R.

SURREY

KENT

Canterbury

DEVON

WESSEX

SUSSEX

CORNWALL

English Channel

FRANCE

> I have collected here the dooms which seemed to me the most just, whether from the time of Ine, my kinsman, or of Offa, king of the Mercians, or of Ethelbert, the first of the English to receive baptism; I have discarded the rest. Then I, Alfred, king of the West Saxons, showed these to all my Witan who declared that they were all pleased to observe them.

In this significant passage we can glimpse the king at work, surrounded by his council as Germanic monarchs had been since their most primitive days, respectful of past custom as had always been the case, and yet injecting into his traditional royal role a novel element of creative judgment.

To Alfred the warrior and Alfred the statesman must be added Alfred the intellectual. Like Charlemagne a century earlier, Alfred was a patron of learning who drew scholars to his court from far and wide—the Welshman Asser, a Frankish scholar from Rheims, several Mercians (including one with the intriguing name of Werwulf), and a number of others. And Alfred himself made a far greater personal contribution to scholarship than the half-literate Charlemagne had been able to do.

The renaissance of Charlemagne's era had been less an outburst of creative genius than a salvage operation designed to recover and preserve a classical-Christian heritage that was in danger of vanishing in the West. Charlemagne's scholars were not original philosophers but gifted schoolmasters who reformed the script, purged the Bible of scribal errors, established schools, copied manuscripts, and struggled to extend literacy and to preserve a correct liturgy. These were humble tasks, but they were desperately essential. The Anglo-Saxon renaissance of Alfred's time, generally speaking, was of the same type. By the late ninth century the intellectual flowering of Bede's Northumbria had long passed. Latin, the linguistic vehicle of classical culture, was becoming virtually unknown in England. Priests could no longer even understand the Latin mass, much less study the works of Bede and the Church Fathers. And the Anglo-Saxon language, which everyone used, had only a very slender literary tradition behind it. Alfred himself described the decline of Latin in these words:

> So completely fallen away was learning now in the English race that there were very few on this side of the Humber who would know how to render their service book into English, and I doubt that there would be many on the other side of the Humber. There were so few of them that I cannot think of so much as a single one south of the Thames when I took the realm.

The king may be exaggerating, but probably not very much.

Alfred was determined to revive ecclesiastical culture in his land, and he did what he could to create a literate priesthood. The scholars he gathered around him created a notable school at his court. A few monastic schools were established, too, but a general monastic revival seems to have been out of the question in these turbulent times. Alfred's most original contribution to learning rose from his conviction that aristocratic laymen should be educated—that his administrators and military commanders should have some knowledge of the civilized heritage of Christendom. Such men were too preoccupied with the political and military hazards of their time to learn Latin, but Alfred hoped that they might be taught to read their native Anglo-Saxon. Accordingly, he and his court scholars undertook to translate into the vernacular some of the important Latin masterpieces of the day—Boethius' *Consolation of Philosophy,* Bede's *History of the English Church and People,* and Pope Gregory's *Pastoral Care.* A copy of the vernacular *Pastoral Care* was sent to every episcopal see in England in the hope that Alfred's bishops might be edified by Gregory's wisdom and common sense.

Alfred himself participated in the work of transition and often added comments of his own to the original texts. In the translation of Boethius, Alfred injects the revealing observation, "In those days one never heard of ships armed for war," and in the preface to the *Pastoral Care* he speaks nostalgically of the time "before everything was ravaged and burned, when England's churches overflowed with treasures and books." In passages such as these, one is reminded forcefully of the enormous disadvantages against which Alfred worked.

Associated with Alfred's reign is another literary monument in the English vernacular, the *Anglo-Saxon Chronicle.*[8] This important historical project, although probably not instigated by Alfred directly, was very likely inspired by the general surge of vernacular writing with which the king was associated. Around 892, an unknown Wessex chronicler wrote a year-by-year account of English history and its Roman and British background, running from the birth of Christ to 891. The account is based on earlier sources, most of which are now lost. The identification and reconstruction of these forerunners have occupied several generations of scholars, and many aspects of the problem remain obscure. In general, the early entries are characterized by extreme verbal economy:

> 634: In this year bishop Birinus preached Christianity to the West Saxons.
>
> 635: In this year Cynegils was baptized by Birinus, bishops of Dorchester, and Oswald [king of Northumbria] stood sponsor for him.
>
> 636: In this year Cwichelm was baptized at Dorchester, and the same year he passed away. And bishop Felix preached the faith of Christ to the East Anglians.
>
> 639: In this year Birinus baptized Cuthred at Dorchester and stood sponsor for him.

Copies of the 892 chronicle were sent to a number of important ecclesiastical centers of the time, and in some instances the early entries were expanded to include facts and traditions available in other portions of England. One manuscript was sent to Northumbria where the entry for 634, for example, was elaborated as follows:

---

[8] The *Anglo-Saxon Chronicle* is available in several modern English translations. One of the best is D. Whitelock, D. C. Douglas, and S. Tucker, ed. and tr., *The Anglo-Saxon Chronicle* (New Brunswick, N.J., 1961).

634: In this year Osric, whom Paulinus had baptized, succeeded to the kingdom of the Deirans; he was the son of Elfric, Edwin's paternal uncle; and
to Bernicia succeeded Ethelfrith's son, Eanfrith. Also in this year Birinus
first preached Christianity to the West Saxons under king Cynegils. That
Birinus came thither at the command of Pope Honorius, and was bishop
there until his life's end. And also in this year Oswald succeeded to the
kingdom of Northumbria, and he reigned nine years.

At several ecclesiastical centers the 892 chronicle was continued thereafter
on a year-by-year basis. In subsequent years copies continued to be exchanged and taken from one monastery to another, with the result that the
Anglo-Saxon Chronicle is a very complex document indeed. To be precise,
it is not one document at all, but a series of several related documents. Altogether, seven distinct manuscripts are extant, representing four more or
less separate chronicles. Of these, three end in the later eleventh century—
between 1066 and 1079—while the fourth continues to the accession of King
Henry II in 1154.

The various versions of the *Anglo-Saxon Chronicle,* written by many
different chroniclers in several religious houses over a number of generations,
are exceedingly uneven. At times they fail to rise above the level of bare
annals; at others, they provide fairly comprehensive accounts of the events
of their day, sometimes even attempting a degree of historical interpretation.
The chroniclers, like modern journalists, tended to pass over periods of
peace and cultural creativity with a few bare allusions to royal deaths and
accessions but became eloquent in times of upheaval and disaster. So little
is made of the fruitful reigns of Alfred's successors and King Canute, so
much is made of the second Danish invasions and the Norman Conquest,
that readers of the *Chronicle* are apt to be misled into regarding the period
of Anglo-Saxon England as one vast, sterile bore relieved by occasional
cataclysms. But whatever its shortcomings, the *Anglo-Saxon Chronicle* is a
unique phenomenon in the European vernacular literature of its day and
provides the modern student with an invaluable if sometimes aggravating
narrative of later Anglo-Saxon history. It is appropriate that from the reign
that marks the genesis of the English monarchy should come this remarkable
national history in the Old English tongue.

In many respects, then, Alfred's reign is the great watershed in the
history of Anglo-Saxon England. It represents the turning point in the
Danish invasions, the climax of the age-long trend toward political unification, and the first stage in the development of English royal government.
Alfred once described himself modestly as one who works in a great forest
collecting timber with which others can build. He was alluding to his efforts
toward intellectual revival, but the metaphor is equally relevant to his
military, administrative, and political achievements. As architect of the
English monarchy, he gathered the wood and also provided a preliminary
blueprint that would guide his successors in constructing a durable political
edifice.

Late Saxon England

King Alfred's work of reconquest and political consolidation was carried to its climax by his talented successors during the first three quarters of the tenth century.[1] At Alfred's death in 899, Wessex passed to his son Edward (899–924), whom later historians called Edward the Elder to distinguish him from a subsequent monarch of the same name. Edward the Elder and his sister Ethelfleda, Lady of Mercia, pursued an aggressive military policy against the Danelaw, strengthening Alfred's burghs and founding a number of new ones in the midlands to consolidate their conquests. One of the new burghs of this age was Oxford, a significant commercial and intellectual center in later years, whose name betokens its humble origin. By 918, all the Danish settlers south of the Humber had submitted to Edward the Elder's rule, and the death of Ethelfleda that year resulted in the permanent unification of Wessex and Mercia under Alfred's dynasty.

Edward the Elder was succeeded by his able son Athelstan (924–939), a skillful military leader who, turning back a major invasion of Yorkshire by Norse Vikings from Ireland, extended his sway across Northumbria to the Firth of Forth. By the time of Athelstan's death, virtually all England was under his control. His successors consolidated the conquest, put down revolts, and repulsed invasion until, by 954, England stood united under the Wessex dynasty of English kings.

---

[1] The works cited in Chapter 1, note 5, and Chapter 2, note 1 are also relevant to the present chapter. In addition, there are two very readable studies by Christopher Brooke: *The Saxon and Norman Kings* (New York, 1963); and *From Alfred to Henry III, 871–1272* (New York, 1961).

The Consequences of Political Unification

Yet the word "united" is perhaps too strong to describe England's situation in 954. The country was united politically (although with much local autonomy remaining), but not socially or culturally. The Anglo-Saxon inhabitants of northern Northumbria, who had managed to retain a precarious independence during the age of Danish invasions, had long been isolated from their brethren to the south and remained a people apart. And the numerous Danish settlers in Yorkshire, East Anglia, and the Five Boroughs remained socially and culturally distinct. The process of amalgamation between Dane and Englishman required several centuries to complete.

The immediate effect of reconquest and political unification was a generation of peace, well-being, and fruitful activity in the areas of royal administration and ecclesiastical reform. Anglo-Saxon England's happiest years coincided with the reign of King Edgar the Peaceable (959–975). In the words of the *Anglo-Saxon Chronicle,*

> His reign was marked by greatly improved conditions, and God granted that he lived his days in peace; he did his duty, and labored zealously in performing it; he exalted God's praise far and wide, and loved God's law; he improved the security of his people more than all the kings before him within the memory of man.

From another source we learn that Alfred's navy had developed by Edgar the Peaceable's time into a well-organized fleet that maintained constant coastal patrols, suggesting that Edgar was not only a man of God but also a vigorous and intelligent military strategist who took strong measures to protect his land from Viking assaults.

Edgar's reign also witnessed an impressive movement of monastic reform that paralleled reform movements occurring on the continent. Throughout its history medieval monasticism followed a pattern of decline and reform. Like all human institutions, it tended to decay with the passage of time from simplicity and fervor to luxury and complacency; yet over the centuries it proved capable of periodic revitalization through successive waves of reformist enthusiasm. The reinvigoration of continental monastic life brought about by the Carolingian renaissance had run its course by the tenth century, but the laxity of tenth-century monasticism was challenged by a religious movement centering on the new Burgundian monastery of Cluny. Founded in 910, Cluny developed, under the leadership of dedicated and long-lived abbots, into a vital center of ecclesiastical reform. The Cluniac monks followed an elaborated version of the Benedictine rule, but they abandoned the traditional Benedictine principle of autonomy. Instead, Cluny became the mother house of an ever-growing congregation of reformed monasteries subject to the direction and discipline of a single abbot.

The great champion of monastic reform in King Edgar's England was St. Dunstan, Abbot of Glastonbury, who became archbishop of Canterbury in 960.[2] Dunstan had no connection with Cluny, or with continental reform movements, but some of the other English reformers of his day were deeply influenced by the example of Fleury, a Cluniac house on the Loire. The English reformers worked with considerable success toward the strict enforcement of the Benedictine rule in English monasteries, but had no wish to associate formally with the Congregation of Cluny. As a result of their efforts, old monasteries were reformed and reorganized and a number of new ones were built. And the traditional Benedictine duties of poverty, chastity, and obedience were strictly enforced. King Edgar cooperated fully with his ecclesiastical reformers. Perhaps he recognized, as Alfred and Charlemagne had recognized long before, that a vigorous Church could contribute much to the political and social welfare of the realm. And he doubtless shared the belief of his times that the welfare of the Church was one of the major responsibilities of a Christian king.

The Development of Anglo-Saxon Institutions

Edgar's reign was followed by a second round of Danish invasions, the accession to the English throne of the Danish king, Canute (1016–1035), the re-establishment of the Wessex dynasty under Edward the Confessor, and, finally, the Norman Conquest of 1066. Before turning to these events it will be well to examine the development of political, social, and economic institutions in Anglo-Saxon England.

The kindom of Wessex in Alfred's day was subdivided into large territorial blocks called shires (or counties). It may be that the Wessex shires represent areas settled long before by individual West Saxon war bands. The Latin word *comitatus*, which originally meant a war band, became the medieval Latin word for "county"; our word "shire" is based on the Old English *scir*, which once meant the local war band or fyrd. Whatever its origins, by Alfred's time the shire had emerged as the administrative district within the kingdom of Wessex.

As the Wessex kings expanded their authority into Mercia and the Danelaw, these districts, too were organized into shires on the Wessex model. Some of the new tenth-century shires correspond to old kingdoms or sub-tribal districts—Norfolk, Suffolk, Kent, Sussex, and Essex, for example. Others were organized around important towns, after which they were named: Bedfordshire, Northamptonshire, Cambridgeshire, Worcestershire, and so on. Four of the Five Boroughs—Lincoln, Leicester, Derby, and Nottingham—became nuclei of new shires. The process of "shiring" the Danelaw was progressing rapidly in the late ninth and early tenth centuries, and it was virtually complete by the time of Athelstan's reign.

---

[2] See Eleanor S. Duckett, *Saint Dunstan of Canterbury: A Study of Monastic Reform in the Tenth Century* (London, 1955). Also, Eric John, *Orbis Brittaniae*, pp. 154–80.

THE ENGLISH SHIRES
Late Saxon England

SCOTLAND

NORTH
SEA

NORTHUMBERLAND

CUMBERLAND

WEST-
MORELAND

1 HUNTINGDON
2 BEDFORD
3 BUCKINGHAM
4 MIDDLESEX

UNSHIRED LANDS
ANNEXED TO
YORKSHIRE

YORK

IRISH SEA

IRELAND

BETWEEN RIBBLE
AND MERSEY

CHESHIRE

DERBY

NOTT-
INGHAM

LINCOLN

STAFFORD

LEICESTER

NORFOLK

SHROPSHIRE

WALES

WARWICK

WOR-
CESTER

NORTHAMPTON

CAMBRIDGE

SUFFOLK

HEREFORD

1

2

HERTFORD

ESSEX

GLOUCESTER

OXFORD

3

BERKS

4

WILTS

SURREY

KENT

SOMERSET

HANTS

SUSSEX

DEVON

DORSET

CORNWALL

English Channel

FRANCE

The shires of Alfred's time were governed by officials known as *ealdor-men*. It was the ealdorman who led the warriors of his shire to join the royal army or to defend the shire against sudden Danish attack. The ealdor-man was at once a royal official and a local aristocrat. He led the fryd and governed the shire in the king's name, and only at times when the monarchy was weak, did he assert a dangerous degree of independence. As time went on, one ealdorman began to exert authority over several shires, and administrative and military command of an individual shire then passed to another royal official known as the *shire reeve* or *sheriff*.

The chief officer of the shire, whether sheriff or ealdorman, presided in the king's name over the shire court, which convened twice yearly to try important cases. The personnel of the shire court consisted of important freemen of the district, who supplied relevant evidence and declared ancient custom. Guilt or innocence, however, was determined neither by the members of the court nor by the presiding sheriff or ealdorman but rather by the process of compurgation—the solemn oath of the accused assisted by the sworn testimony of kinsmen or friends known as oath helpers—or by recourse to one of the ancient ordeals. Run by local freemen and presided over by an official of the king, the shire court was at once a royal and a popular institution—an assembly in which monarchy and local freemen joined to provide justice (of sorts) for the land.

The late-Saxon shire was also normally divided into smaller territorial units called hundreds. Like the shires, the hundreds originated in Wessex and spread with the expansion of the Wessex monarchy. The hundreds too may have been military in origin, perhaps representing a group of one hundred warriors that served within the larger comitatus; but on this matter the evidence is far from clear. By the tenth century the hundred was a territorial administrative district centering on a hundred court. Similar in purpose and organization to the shire court—and presided over by a royal reeve—the hundred court met more frequently, normally once a month, and played a more intimate role in the affairs of the average freeman. Ordinarily, the hundred court, like the shire court, represented a mixture of royal and popular justice; but in time jurisdiction over many hundred courts passed into the hands of great private lords, both lay and ecclesiastical. These powerful landholders were granted by royal charter the rights of jurisdiction in their districts (contemporary charters refer to these jurisdictional rights as *sac* and *soc*), and their representatives took the place of royal officials as presidents of the hundred courts they controlled. The abbot and monks of Bury St. Edmunds, for example, gained jurisdiction over more than a third of the hundreds of Suffolk, and by the late eleventh century more than half the hundreds in Worcestershire were in the hands of three abbeys and a bishopric.

The hundred was typically (although by no means always) composed of one hundred hides. We have already seen that originally the hide was regarded as an estate sufficient to support the family of an individual warrior.

The late-Saxon hide, however, was not a unit of standard size, but an assessment unit on which fiscal and military obligations were based. Of two estates of identical area, one might be more productive than the other and therefore be assessed at more hides than the other. Moreover, hidage assessment was often erratic and unfair: some districts were assessed more severely than others, and sometimes, through royal generosity, an estate would have its hidage assessment diminished. A forty-hide estate might become a twenty-hide estate without being reduced by so much as a foot of land.

By the tenth century, and perhaps long before, the one-hide estate had come to be regarded as insufficient to provide the necessary economic support for a properly equipped warrior and was replaced by the estate of five hides. The profession of arms was the supreme aristocratic vocation in all Germanic societies, and the typical Anglo-Saxon aristocrat—the holder of a five-hide estate—was known as a *thegn*. In time of war, every five-hide unit was obligated to provide a fighting man for the army (or sometimes the navy), and although the owners of small estates within a five-hide unit might occasionally pool their resources to send a particularly well-equipped freeman as their representative to the fyrd, the normal five-hide warrior was a member of the thegnly aristocracy. The almost universally accepted relationship between status and arms in this violent age insured that the society of Anglo-Saxon England—influenced so deeply by the hard necessities of war—would be profoundly aristocratic.

Still, the varying military requirements of tenth- and eleventh-century England required, on occasion, the service of groups other than the thegns. In time of invasion every freeman was obliged to take up arms in defense of his locality. These ordinary freemen formed a motley but massive force around the nucleus of the five-hide warriors. At other times, the territorial five-hide fyrd proved insufficiently flexible or battle-ready and was augmented or replaced by full-time professional warriors. These might be simple mercenaries, or they might be landless household soldiers maintained on a permanent basis by the king or some great lord. In the course of the eleventh century these landless professionals became increasingly important. One such group, the "housecarles," who were instituted by Canute and retained by Edward the Confessor, formed the nucleus of the Anglo-Saxon army at Hastings in 1066.

Five-hide thegns, ordinary freemen, and landless professional warriors—these were the components of the Anglo-Saxon army. But a mere review of this organizational scheme fails to do justice to the powerful emotional factors that underlay the military structure of this age. In the tenth century, the ideology of the old Germanic comitatus was still very strong. Military prowess, absolute loyalty to lord, and honor among warriors remained the supreme aristocratic virtues. Indeed, in all Germanic literature the comitatus ideology is nowhere more powerfully illustrated than in a late tenth-century Anglo-Saxon poem, the *Song of Maldon;* it describes a fierce battle in 991 in which an invading Danish host defeated the fyrd of Essex led by its lord, the Ealdorman Byrhtnoth.[3] Toward the battle's end, Ealdorman Byrhtnoth was killed and the English nearly defeated. At this desperate moment,

> Then Byrhtwold spoke, he brandished his spear,
> raised up his shield; he was an old henchman;
> full boldly he taught the band of men:
> "Thought shall be the harder, heart the keener,
> mood shall be the more, as our might lessens.
> Here lies our earl, all hewn to earth,
> the good one, on the ground. He will regret it always,
> the one who thinks to turn from this war-play now.
> My life has been long. Leave I will not,
> but beside my lord I will sink to earth,
> I am minded to die by the man so dear."

Byrhtwold's speech is preceded by others in a similar vein. Inspired by these appeals to the traditional heroic ideal, the Anglo-Saxon attack the Danes, and in the midst of the fray the manuscript of the *Song of Maldon* breaks off abruptly. The author was doubtless embroidering his data and exaggerating Byrhtwold's eloquence. Nevertheless, the story reflects the highest aristocratic ideals of a people still tied to their bellicose past and dominated by the concept of lordship.

The development of Anglo-Saxon institutions can be understood as the gradual evolution of a Germanic warrior society toward territorial stabilization and administrative coherence. The fundamental element in this evolution was the rise of a centralized monarchy. Among a people to whom loyalty to one's lord was an almost holy virtue, the king endeavored to secure for himself the pledged allegiance not only of his ealdormen, sheriffs, and personal thegns, but of all freemen in England. In the dooms of King Edmund (939–946) it is commanded "that all, in the name of God . . . shall swear fealty to King Edmund, as a man should be faithful to his lord, without dispute or treachery, in public and in private, loving what he loves and shunning what he shuns." Thus the powerful bond of allegiance between an ealdorman and his thegns and household followers—attested so vividly in the *Song of Maldon*—was subordinated to the still higher duty of all free Englishmen to render loyalty to their monarch.

This principle of universal allegiance to the king was essential to the maintenance and progressive extension of royal control over England. The ealdormen must be royal officers, not independent potentates; and when they lead the fyrd of their shire they must do so—as Byrhtnoth did—in the king's name and in the king's service. Indeed, when the fyrd was summoned on a regional or national scale its normal leader was the king himself. As lord

---

[3] A modern English prose translation of the *Song of Maldon* is contained in Margaret Ashdown, tr., *English and Norse Documents Relating to the Reign of Ethelred the Unready* (Cambridge, 1930); the present excerpt is from the poetic translation by Kemp Malone.

of the Anglo-Saxons, he was necessarily the supreme war leader of the people in arms.

In time of war the king was expected to be braver and fiercer than any of the warriors he led, but in time of peace he sought to temper the violence of his people. In his coronation oath, Edgar the Peaceable made these commitments:

> In the name of the Holy Trinity I promise three things to my Christian subjects: First, that God's Church and all the Christian people of my realm shall enjoy true peace; second, that I forbid robbery and wrongful deeds to all ranks of men; third, that I exhort and command justice and mercy in all my judgments, so that the gracious and compassionate God who lives and reigns may grant us all His everlasting mercy.

In effect, Edgar is appealing from the militarism of Germanic culture to the pacifism of the Christian tradition. The Germanic king must lead his folk in war, but the Christian king must keep the peace.

The concept of the king's peace developed slowly. Anglo-Saxon England had no policemen, no professional lawyers or judges, no comprehensive legal codes; consequently, acts of private violence were much more common than today—the rule rather than the exception. Crimes of violence normally fell under the jurisdiction of the popular courts of shire and hundred, but almost from the beginning there existed the concept that violations of the peace committed in certain places or at certain times were subject to a direct royal fine. At first the king's peace extended only to the limits of the royal household, but in time it came to cover the shire and hundred courts, major roads and rivers, and churches and abbeys. Since the royal household had no permanent headquarters but was constantly on the move, the king's peace moved too, sometimes protecting one area, sometimes another. By the time of Henry I (1100–1135), the king's peace extended throughout the entire shire wherein the king was temporarily residing. And the king's peace was also gradually extended to cover all crimes of violence committed during the liturgical seasons of Christmas, Lent, Easter, and Whitsuntide. In the twelfth century, as we shall see, royal justice expanded significantly at the expense of popular and private justice and evolved ultimately into what Englishmen call the Common Law. The gradual spread of the king's peace in Anglo-Saxon times may be regarded as an early expression of this momentous legal concept of direct royal jurisdiction.

Anglo-Saxon law, like the law of most primitive societies, was far less precise, less logically constructed, more obscure, cumbersome, haphazard, and complex than the law of modern states. It was a patchwork of many local customs, varying from region to region, and only through the gradual expansion of the royal government did it achieve, long after the Norman Conquest, a degree of uniformity. Yet even in Anglo-Saxon times, the royal government endeavored, haltingly, to preserve and expand its area of jurisdiction. The power of the Anglo-Saxon kings was felt in the local courts of hundred and shire, made up of local worthies but presided over by the king's reeve. And the dooms, although far from comprehensive, constitute early efforts toward achieving a modicum of legal uniformity through the exercise of royal authority.

As the scope and functions of the Anglo-Saxon monarchy expanded, the royal administrative machinery became steadily more elaborate. In the earliest days, the retinue of an Anglo-Saxon monarch normally included a number of military followers or "companions" and some servants to look after the stables, maintain the royal wardrobe and bedchamber, supervise the food supply, and prepare the meals. The king's income was derived chiefly from the rents and harvests of his own vast estates—his demesne. Rather than transporting food to a central royal residence, the king traveled from estate to estate across his scattered demesne, consuming as he went. In these circumstances, the minimal administrative duties of the royal household could easily be handled by the chief servants.

With the passage of time, the royal treasury grew, royal military organization became more elaborate, and royal land gifts came more and more to be committed to writing. Moreover, it became increasingly desirable for the king to communicate with his regional officers by written rather than verbal messages. Since literacy remained largely a priestly monopoly, the growing secretarial duties were assumed by the royal chaplain and his priestly staff, which had been a part of every royal household since the conversion. In the eleventh century the king's chapel-secretariat came to be known as the chancery (from "chancel," the space in a church reserved for officiating clergy); and its chief officer, the chancellor, became in later years one of the chief officers of state.

The writing office of the late Anglo-Saxon kings was in some respects the most efficient royal chancery of its time in Western Europe. Like other chanceries, it prepared elaborate charters for the transfer of land and privileges. Its unique contribution to the history of administration was its invention of a type of short document known as a writ—a direct, economical statement of a royal command to a subject, usually written in English rather than Latin and (by the eleventh century) bearing an imprint on wax of the king's Great Seal to prove its authenticity. The writ was sufficiently short and simple to serve as a highly effective instrument in the everyday business of government:

> King Canute sends friendly greetings to Bishop Eadsige and Abbot Alfstan and Aethelric and all my thegns in Kent. And I inform you that my will is that Archbishop Aethelnoth shall discharge the obligations on his landed property belonging to his episcopal see now at the same rate as he did before Aethelric was reeve and after he was reeve up to the present day. And I will not permit that any wrong be done the [arch]bishop whoever may be reeve.

> King Edward sends friendly greetings to Bishop Stigand and Earl Harold and all my thegns in East Anglia. And I inform you that I have granted to

[the abbey of] St. Edmund, my kinsman, the land at Pakenham as fully
and as completely as Osgot possessed it.[4]

Writs were used much more commonly after the Norman Conquest than
before (and were normally in Latin rather than Old English), but they were
originated by nameless clerks in the chanceries of the Anglo-Saxon kings.
The idea of a brief, written, authenticated command seems obvious enough,
but in the largely illiterate society of Saxon England it was a new and powerful means of bringing literacy and precision to royal government.

Other offices of the royal bureaucracy developed out of various
branches of the household serving staff. The master of the stable—the
constable of later times—supervised the royal hunt and eventually became a
leading officer in the king's army. The chief servant of the royal bedchamber
and wardrobe evolved into the later chamberlain; and, since the king customarily kept his treasure in his wardrobe (or sometimes under his bed),
the chamberlain assumed important financial responsibilities. In the course
of the eleventh century the monarchy adopted the policy of leaving the bulk
of its treasure at Winchester, the chief town of Wessex, and carrying on its
travels only enough money to meet current expenses. The royal officer in
charge of the Winchester treasure came to be known, appropriately, as the
treasurer.

The chancellor, the constable, the chamberlain, and other household
officials such as the steward and the butler—although not known by those
names until after the Norman Conquest—rose in importance with the growth
of the Anglo-Saxon monarchy to become dominant figures in the royal ad-
'ministration. Besides performing their own special functions, they served
the king collectively as a trusted and intimate advisory body, accompanying
him on his endless perambulations through the country. Together with such
other magnates and important churchmen as might be present, they functioned as a pocket council, administering the king's justice and attending to
the varied and ever-growing business of royal government.

Occasionally when unusually important business arose—such as the
issuing of a series of dooms or the undertaking of a major military campaign—an Anglo-Saxon monarch would call many of the great magnates of
the realm, both lay and ecclesiastical, to join his normal household advisers
in counseling him or giving their formal support to his policies. We have
already encountered references to large councils of this sort on the occasion
of King Edwin's conversion in 627 and in King Alfred's statement that he
had shown his laws "to all my Witan who declared that they were all pleased
to observe them." The terms *Witan* or *Witenagemot* (council) might apply
to either the small household group or the larger and more formal assembly
of magnates. The Witenagemot, both small and large, probably had its

---

[4] Translated from Old English by F. E. Harmer, *Anglo-Saxon Writs* (Manchester, Engl.,
1952), pp. 184, 158.

roots in the primitive Germanic tribal assemblies; but the limitations of our sources prevent us from tracing its evolution with any precision until the tenth and eleventh centuries. We know from occasional references that it existed in early Anglo-Saxon England, but we can say little of such matters as its normal size, composition, or functions. Indeed, as the fuller sources from the late-Saxon period disclose, the Witenagemot, whether large or small, was an exceedingly flexible and informal institution. It was in no sense, of course, a representative assembly. It possessed no formal right of veto over royal policy, but was strictly advisory. It had no official members so far as we can tell, but simply included whatever important household officers and great men happened to be available and, on the more significant occasions, a miscellaneous group of lords. Still, the sources make clear that the Witenagemot played a crucial role in Anglo-Saxon government. Many historians today, in endeavoring to dispel the romantic myth of certain nineteenth-century scholars that the Witenagemot was a protodemocratic national assembly, have tended to underestimate its importance. To be sure, no Anglo-Saxon king was legally bound to follow his Witan's advice, but few monarchs were so foolish as to flout it. In an age lacking precise definitions of constitutional relationships, the deeply ingrained custom that the king was to govern in consultation with his Witan, implicit in almost every important royal document of the period, is sufficient to make the Witenagemot one of Anglo-Saxon England's fundamental political institutions.

The expanding monarchy of late-Saxon England was able to draw on an increasing variety of financial resources. The royal demesne remained the chief source of income, and, as the growing towns were normally regarded as belonging to the king's demesne, exactions from burghers poured into the royal treasury along with dues from the royal estates. The monarchy delegated responsibility for the fiscal exploitation of its demesne estates and towns to royal officials—reeves—who were assigned a fixed tax quota or "farm" to be collected from the districts they supervised. Any dues in excess of the quota belonged to them. As commerce quickened, it became increasingly common for the monarchy to receive a portion of its demesne dues in coin rather than in kind; for during the last several decades prior to the Norman Conquest, Anglo-Saxon England enjoyed a circulation of currency that was unusually brisk by continental standards.

Besides demesne revenues, the late-Saxon monarchy was enriched by a kingdom-wide land tax. What began as a symptom of military weakness and the monarchy's endeavor to purchase security from Viking marauders ultimately became one of the most important sources of royal income. In 991 King Ethelred, appropriately nicknamed the Unready, imposed a tax, the danegeld, to raise protection money against the Danes. This tax, like military service, was assessed on the basis of hides of land.[5] It was not re-

---

[5] Often at the rate of two shillings per hide.

stricted to the royal demesne but embraced all the lands of England. Eventually it became a significant source of strength to the English monarch, for in later years danegeld funds were used to hire soldiers and meet various other royal expenses. As the first general land tax in Western Europe since Roman times, the danegeld illustrates perhaps more vividly than anything else Anglo-Saxon England's progress toward royal centralization and administrative sophistication.

Continental monarchs, like English monarchs, employed agents to collect dues from demesne estates. And on the continent, as in England, central administrative bureaucracies were slowly evolving out of household staffs. But the late Anglo-Saxon royal administration was more coherent in organization and broader in scope than any other contemporary government in Western Christendom. In the centralization of its administrative structure, as in the relative efficiency of its tax system, England stood in the vanguard of a movement which, during the coming centuries, would transform the loosely structured Germanic monarchies that stretched across Christendom into well-organized states.

Town and Field

The century prior to the Norman Conquest was a period of accelerating commercial activity produced by the general political stability of the age. With commerce came the rise of towns, smaller at first than those of Roman times—and dirtier—but from an economic standpoint far healthier. Unlike the administrative and military towns of the western Roman Empire, which functioned as economic leeches on the countryside, the towns of late-Saxon England—and their continental counterparts—produced more than they consumed. It has already been suggested that many Saxon towns evolved out of the military burghs or boroughs of Alfred and his successors; but the rise of towns was an economic phenomenon, a product of England's wealth and vigorous commerce. A vast amount of urban development lay in the future —in the decades and centuries following the Norman Conquest—but evidence suggests that the elaborate guild systems of a later day were already in their formative stage in the late-Saxon period and that borough courts may have been functioning as early as the tenth century.

Typically, the town paid a regular tax to its local lord or to the king and received such privileges as the right to have its own court and to operate a market—a center of supervised buying and selling. The market became the commercial nexus not only of the town but of the neighboring countryside as well. Towns were a source of wealth to the monarchy, and, particularly in later years, the English kings favored them in many ways. Their emergence and growth were accompanied by slow but significant changes in the social and economic order. An economy based on exchange of goods gave way to a money economy, and the parochialism of the early Middle

Ages was eroded by the rise of international commerce. In the High Middle Ages—the twelfth and thirteenth centuries—the towns would become the foci of a rich, vibrant culture. Perhaps the greatest glories of high medieval civilization were the cathedral and the university, and both were characteristically urban phenomena.

But in the tenth century one could not know that the struggling urban communities had such a future before them or that they would one day be agents of momentous social change. They were still mere specks on an agrarian landscape—overgrown villages surrounded by walls. Probably fewer than ten Anglo-Saxon towns had more than 3,500 inhabitants. Norwich, Winchester, and Lincoln may have had 6,000 or more; York perhaps 8,000; only London—the chief commercial center—compared in size to a modern town. The townsmen went about their daily tasks; the aristocracy fought, trained, and dreamed of war; but the chief business of the Anglo-Saxons remained what it had been for generations past and what it would be for centuries to come: the raising of crops.

Among the romantic myths of nineteenth-century historical scholarship was the legend of the stalwart Anglo-Saxon farmer, communing with the good earth, fighting against invaders like a Massachusetts Minuteman, and laying the foundations of democracy by participating fearlessly and intelligently in village councils and hundred courts. Historians have since concluded that most Anglo-Saxon agricultural workers were probably slaves or inarticulate, semi-servile tenants. Men such as these were virtually ignored in contemporary documents, but without question they represented the majority of Englishmen in late-Saxon times and long afterward. They played no real role in local or hundredal administration; nor were they permitted to bear arms, for the possession of weapons was by tradition a mark of free status. Their influence on English constitutional development was minimal, but their contribution to the economy was vital. And their lives were hard beyond all imagining. An Anglo-Saxon writer of the late tenth century attributed these words to a fictional peasant of his times:

> I work hard. I go out at daybreak, driving the oxen to the field, and then I yoke them to the plow. Be the winter ever so stark, I dare not linger at home for awe of my lord; but having yoked my oxen, and fastened plowshare and coulter, every day I must plow a full acre or more. I have a boy, driving the oxen with an iron goad, who is hoarse with cold and shouting. Mighty hard work it is, for I am not free.[6]

Not all farm workers lacked personal freedom. At the top of the peasant hierarchy was a class of free farmers known as *ceorls*. It was this class the nineteenth-century scholars had in mind when they made their allusions

---

[6] *Aelfric's Colloquy*, G. N. Garmonsway, ed. (London, 1939), ll. 23–35.

to Anglo-Saxon grass-roots democracy. But the ceorls were neither as democratic nor as numerous as previously believed. Rather than being "typical Anglo-Saxon peasants," the ceorls were a peasant elite. They bore arms and, on occasion, fought in the fyrd alongside the aristocratic thegns. They usually owned their own farms, and most of them owned slaves. They enjoyed status before the law and were assigned a wergeld of 200 shillings. Beyond these few generalizations we cannot go, for the contemporary sources disclose very little about the free peasantry except to make clear that the term ceorl was applied rather loosely to agrarian freemen of widely differing economic levels.

At the next level up in the social hierarchy were the thegns, sharply differentiated by their 1,200-shilling wergeld but otherwise as heterogeneous as the ceorls. The thegns, as we have seen, constituted a warrior aristocracy; yet there is clear evidence that many of the lesser thegns were little better off economically than the wealthier ceorls. Some of them seem to have labored in their own fields as a matter of course, but ordinarily their involvement in agriculture was limited to supervising the labor of their subordinates.

Both ceorls and thegns participated in local administration and in the popular courts, and such experience was doubtless useful in later centuries in giving these classes a certain degree of political sophistication. But they made their chief contribution to the realm by defending it in battle and participating in the humble but essential task of food production.

The development of Anglo-Saxon agriculture was an immensely significant process. The Anglo-Saxons transformed the Romano-British agrarian system, with its squarish fields and single-family farms, into the system of communal agriculture, village communities, and strip fields that persisted throughout the Middle Ages and beyond. The key to this transformation was a new plow, far heavier and more effective than the light scratch plow used in Roman Britain and throughout most of the Roman Empire. The origins of the heavy plow are uncertain and have been much debated (it may have come westward from the Slavic inhabitants of the eastern European plains); we know only that it was widely used by the Germanic peoples who settled in the formerly Roman lands of northern Europe. In its fully developed form, the heavy plow was a wheeled machine with a large iron plowshare, a knife fixed in front of the share to direct the movement of the cut, and a device known as a moldboard that heaved the sod to one side, creating an artificial drainage pattern of ridges and furrows. The great virtue of the new plow was that it opened up to agriculture vast areas of rich clay soils and poorly drained lowlands that had defied the old Roman scratch plow. With these heavy plows, the Anglo-Saxons were able, for example, to till the fertile clay plains of East Anglia that had been wastelands in Roman times.

The heavy ploy required a large ox team to draw it—normally eight oxen, two abreast. And with the large team came a new, much more efficient harness than was commonly used in Roman times. Most important, the heavy plow and eight-ox team transformed the size and shape of the fields. The small, square fields of Roman Britain gave way to much larger fields, divided into narrow strips suitable to a plow and a team that was difficult to turn around. Since a single strip usually consumed a day's plowing (sometimes half a day's), the difficult process of reversing the plow's direction was minimized or avoided altogether.

The plow also prompted a shift from single farms to agrarian villages and communal agriculture. A single peasant family could seldom afford to own a heavy plow, much less an eight-ox team. Thus, ownership of plows and oxen came to be shared by a village community. Typically, the village was centered on a village green, or a well or pond, and was surrounded by great fields—divided into strips like the stripes of an American flag. These strips of land were not held in common by the village community but were apportioned among individual villagers. Since the various strips comprised a single agrarian unit, however, it was necessary for a village council (perhaps dominated by a local thegn) to make decisions on such matters as crop rotation, boundary disputes, and the apportionment of plows and oxen.

Accordingly, the village was the fundamental agrarian unit of medieval England; but alongside it there existed another, more artificial unit—the estate of the thegn or higher noble, in later days known as a manor. Normally a single village was a single manor. But occasionally a manor encompassed several villages, and a single village sometimes included parts of several manors. The village and the manor differed in that the village was an agrarian entity—a cluster of houses surrounded by fields—whereas the manor was a unit of lordship—an estate controlled by a single thegn.

The thegn usually exercised strong political, judicial, and economic authority over the peasants on his manor. He operated a manorial court to settle disputes and punish crimes. He often controlled the village water mill and charged his peasants for its use. He was entitled by custom to tax his peasants in various ways and to collect a portion of their crops (later commuted, in many cases, to a payment of money—a rent). And the lord had his own strips, called his demesne land, interspersed among his peasants' strips in the village fields. Peasants were normally obliged to labor on their lord's demesne for a certain number of days per week (the exact number depending on local custom, the season, and the peasant's status). The lord did not ordinarily do farm work himself, but depended for his income on the taxes and labors of his peasants.

The details of agrarian organization and class structure varied bewilderingly from one district to another. Kent remained throughout the Middle Ages a land apart, with family farms instead of the more usual village community. Throughout much of the Danelaw there were many more freemen than elsewhere. In Northumbria the manor was slow in developing. Other local variations existed, too numerous to discuss here. Whatever the details, however, the agricultural achievement of the Anglo-Saxons cannot be gainsaid: they transformed forests into fields, established the village community, fixed the peasant on his plot, and vastly augmented the bounty of the land.

Late-Saxon Art

In the arts, too, late-Saxon England demonstrated signs of a maturing civilization. No large Anglo-Saxon churches survive—most of them were torn down and replaced in the generation or two after the Norman Conquest—but descriptions by contemporary writers, confirmed by modern excavations, attest to the existence of spacious, well-designed cathedrals in episcopal centers such as Canterbury and Winchester. And there survive many village churches dating wholly or in part from Anglo-Saxon times. Although influenced to a degree by the styles of Carolingian France and, later on, the Rhinelands, they show in their proportions and in the rhythm of their textured surfaces a strong native originality. The church tower at Earls Barton, for example, is a bold, assured expression of a distinctive Anglo-Saxon style. The last great church of pre-Conquest England, Westminster Abbey, was built in the Norman Romanesque manner under the personal

EARLS BARTON CHURCH, NORTHAMPTONSHIRE
The towers are late 10th century; the battlements were added much later. _National Monuments Record._

RUINS OF JUMIÈGES ABBEY, NORMANDY, C. 1066
The original Westminster Abbey was built by Edward the Confessor
in a very similar style. *Rapho Guillumette*.

LATE ANGLO-SAXON ART
A crucifixion, from the
Gospel Book of Countess
Judith. *Pierpont Morgan
Library.*

supervision of Edward the Confessor (1042–1066). Although totally rebuilt
by Henry III in the thirteenth century (again in the style of contemporary
France), its original appearance can be imagined by looking at the majestic
ruins of the Norman abbey of Jumièges, built at about the same time and in
much the same style: vast and massive, its great round arches and heavy
columns convey a feeling of solidity and permanence.

Tenth-century English monastic reform, associated with such figures as
Dunstan and Edgar the Peaceable, produced an original body of religious
literature, written in the Anglo-Saxon language and intended for laymen as
well as churchmen. A number of manuscripts of the period are illuminated
in decorative styles that show the influence of both continental and earlier
Northumbrian traditions. Tenth-century Winchester was the center of a
highly original style of manuscript illumination that draws from Carolingian
models and yet is thoroughly distinctive in its fluid outlines of human and
animal figures, its fluttering draperies, and its soft pastel colors. In the
eleventh century, the Winchester style developed a degree of emotional intensity unparalleled in Europe. The poignant crucifixion from the Gospel

Book of Countess Judith (Winchester, c. 1050–1065) betokens a profound change in the mood of medieval piety—from the awesome to the human, from Christ in majesty to Christ suffering. Perhaps better than any other contemporary work of art, it shows the level of technical skill and emotional depth possible in the closing years of the Anglo-Saxon era.

The Second Danish Invasion

A century after Alfred turned the Danish tide at the battle of Edington, disaster struck England. It was a disaster that few at the time could have recognized as such, for in the year 978 England was apparently as prosperous and secure as it had been during the previous generation. Under Alfred and his able descendants the monarchy and the kingdom had made notable progress. But now, in 978, the crown passed to an incompetent heir—Ethelred the Unready (978–1016). The cataclysmic events that followed his accession proved once again the importance of adequate military and political leadership to a medieval state.

"The Unready" is really a mistranslation of Ethelred's nickname. The medieval term is *Unræd*, which means "no council" or "bad council." *Ethelred* itself means "noble council," and thus *Ethelred Unræd* makes a fine pun in Old English but a very obscure one in modern English. Some scholars have tried to compromise with "Ethelred the Redless," but that doesn't help much. We will stick with "the Unready," which catches the original punning spirit and makes some sense—even though it is not precisely the original sense.

According to the twelfth-century historian William of Malmesbury, Ethelred's troubles began early:

> Archbishop Dunstan, indeed, had foretold his unworthiness, having discovered it by a filthy sign: for when Ethelred was a tiny infant, just as he was immersed in the baptismal font, with all the bishops standing around him, he defiled the sacrament with a copious bowel movement. At this, Dunstan, being extremely angered, exclaimed, "By God and his mother, this will be a sorry fellow!"

Ethelred was timid, banal, and indecisive. He fell heir to the throne as a boy of ten, and although he reigned for thirty-eight years, he remained a child to the end. Like Peter Pan, he never really grew up. The kingdom he inherited was prosperous and well-governed by the standards of tenth-century Europe; but the long process of amalgamating the Scandinavian settlers of the Danelaw into the fabric of Anglo-Saxon society had barely begun, and the loyalty of these Anglo-Danes to the English monarchy was still tenuous. Without external pressures Alfred's dynasty would doubtless have survived Ethelred's incompetence, but the age of the Vikings was not yet passed. Within a couple of years of Ethelred's accession the raids resumed.

The early years of the reign were marked not only by Danish raids but also by the rising power of the Anglo-Saxon ealdormen at the expense of the royal government—an inevitable consequence of weak rule. As this trend toward decentralization progressed, the Danish raids steadily increased in intensity. The new raiders were often organized into tight military brotherhoods—war bands along the lines of the old comitatus but with stricter rules and more predatory goals. The Viking brotherhoods of this era seem to have been modeled on a warrior community which, according to Norse legend, was founded at Jomsburg near the mouth of the Oder in Germany by King Harold Bluetooth of Denmark.[7] The Vikings of Jomsburg—the Jomsvikings as they are called—had strict regulations regarding membership and conduct; these they enforced in their own military court. Under the general direction of the Danish monarchy, they often displayed fierce independence, undertaking plundering expeditions on their own or selling their services to the highest bidder. One of the most savage and bloodthirsty Danish raiders in Ethelred's reign, Thorkell the Tall, seems to have been a Jomsviking; and for a time Ethelred himself was able to purchase the services of Thorkell's band against the attacks of other Danes.

In spite of this independent spirit, England's second Viking invasions were far more closely governed by the Danish monarchy than the first. In Scandinavia, as in England, royal power had made impressive gains in the tenth century. When the invasions reached their climax they had become, in effect, an integrated effort on the part of the Danish monarchy to conquer England.

It would be a mistake to ascribe the success of the second Danish invasions, as is sometimes done, to an inherent weakness in the Old English state. The failure of the Anglo-Saxon military effort resulted from the disloyalty of the Anglo-Danes combined with the ill fortune of being ruled by an incompetent king. Contemporary writers dwell repeatedly on the wavering loyalties of the Anglo-Danish aristocracy; and the futility of Ethelred's leadership is illustrated vividly in the *Anglo-Saxon Chronicle:*

> And when they [the Danes] were in the east, the English army was kept in the west, and when they were in the south, our army was in the north. Thereupon all the counselors were summoned to the king, and it was decided how the country should be defended. But if anything was decided then, it did not last even a month. Finally there was no leader who would collect an army, but each fled as best he could, and in the end no shire would even help the next.

Desperate to forestall disaster, Ethelred adopted the expedient of appeasing the Danes with bribes. In 991, the same year that Ealdorman

---

[7] Many of the better known Vikings of this era were given nicknames: Swein Forkbeard, Eric Bloodaxe, Ragnar Hairy-Breeches, Halfdan the Generous with Money but Stingy with Food. An Icelandic musician was called Einar Jingle-Scale; a Norwegian poet, Eyvind the Plagiarist.

Byrhtnoth scorned the Danish demand for tribute at Maldon, King Ethelred paid the first danegeld. In later years danegelds were paid repeatedly; they served merely to emphasize to the fierce seamen the degree of England's weakness and the extent of its wealth.

In 1013, King Swein of Denmark, son and successor of Harold Bluetooth, threw all his resources into a campaign of conquest, and Anglo-Saxon England, now badly demoralized, fell quickly into his hands. The old Danelaw gave Swein its firm support, and the English, disgusted with Ethelred the Unready, offered only mild resistance. Ethelred fled to Normandy. His son, a skillful and courageous young prince named Edmund Ironside, fought on for a season but was killed in 1016, whereupon the Witan concurred in the accession of a Danish king to the throne of Alfred. Swein having died in 1014, his son Canute became the new king of England.

The Reign of Canute (1016–1035)

King Canute was a far better monarch than Ethelred the Unready. His contemporaries called him Canute the Wealthy; later generations knew him as Canute the Great.[8] A Norse saga writer provides a half-legendary description of him: he was tall and strong and had blond hair, keen eyes, and a long, narrow nose—slightly bent—that marred his good looks.

The new king was a product of civilizing forces that were just then transforming the Norse world. In 1016 Viking states from Iceland to Russia were in the process of embracing Christianity; and in Scandinavia itself the rise of royal power was bringing political coherence to the northern lands of Denmark, Norway, and Sweden. Accordingly, Canute ascended the Anglo-Saxon throne as a civilized man and a Christian. Alfred's dynasty was temporarily unseated, but in Canute's reign security and prosperity returned to England and the monarchy continued to grow in strength.

As it happened, Canute ruled Norway as well as Denmark, and his accession to the Old English throne made him master of a great empire girding the North Sea. It was an ephemeral empire, to be sure, held together by the fragile bonds of allegiance to a single man; but while he lived Canute was the dominant political figure in northern Europe.

England was by far the wealthiest and most civilized land in his empire, and Canute spent most of his reign there. Aware of the achievements of his Anglo-Saxon predecessors, he ruled in the Old English tradition, respecting old customs, issuing dooms, and supporting the Church. He won the vigorous support of the clergy by granting them land and treasure and providing them with an environment of peace in which to work. In the words of one contemporary observer, "Merry sang the monks of Ely as Canute the king rowed by."

---

[8] On the reign of Canute and his Anglo-Scandinavian "empire" see L. M. Larson, *Canute the Great* (New York, 1912).

KING CANUTE AND QUEEN AELFGIFU
The royal couple are shown presenting
a gift to the New Minster at Winchester, while Jesus, the Virgin Mary,
and St. Peter look down approvingly.
British Museum.

Canute succeeded far better than his Anglo-Saxon predecessors in
bringing unity to the land, for Englishmen and Anglo-Danes supported him
with almost equal enthusiasm. Indeed, perhaps only a Scandinavian king
could have won for the English monarchy the unquestioned loyalty of the
Danelaw. At a council at Oxford in 1018, Canute is described as formally
declaring peace between Danes and Englishmen and bringing an end to
their former strife. The king's Witan swore to uphold Christianity, to love
Canute, and to observe the laws of King Edgar.

King Canute was a Dane, and he acted as such. He divided his kingdom in Danish fashion into several large districts ruled by earls (a name
derived from the Old Norse *jarl*); and he brought to his court a bodyguard of
Scandinavian housecarles—a sizable group of trained warriors organized
along the lines of the Jomsvikings, with their own elaborate regulations and
their own judicial assembly. But in most other respects Canute ruled much
as an able Anglo-Saxon might have done. Hundred courts and shire courts
continued as before, towns grew even more rapidly through the stimulus of

an increased North Sea commerce, and agrarian life proceeded unaffected. Indeed, Canute carried his Anglo-Saxon traditionalism to the bedchamber by marrying Ethelred's widow, a strong-minded Norman princess named Emma, who quite clearly preferred her second husband to her first.

On Canute's death in 1035, his empire was divided between his two sons; they ruled England in turn, briefly and badly. When the last of them died without heirs, the Witan chose as its new king a member of the old Wessex dynasty, the long-exiled son of Ethelred and Emma. In 1042 the dynasty of Alfred was re-established peacefully in the person of Edward the Confessor.

The Reign of Edward the Confessor (1042–1066)

Edward, paradoxically, was even less an Englishman than Canute. Between the ages of twelve and thirty-six he had lived in exile in Normandy, the homeland of his mother. In these years he had become deeply Normanized. A pious man of limited political acumen, he spoke French by preference and installed Norman favorites in his court and kingdom. "When King Edward of holy memory returned from Francia," his biographer writes, "quite a number of men of that nation, and they not base-born, accompanied him. And these, since he was master of the whole kingdom, he kept with him, enriched them with many honors, and made them his privy counselors and administrators of the royal court." [9] Thus the Norman Conquest of England, although consummated on the field of Hastings in 1066, had its begining in 1042. Such, at least, were the feelings of many Englishmen of the time who loved Edward but not his Norman favorites or his Norman customs.

Under Canute the earls had been strictly controlled, but under the weaker Edward they began to assert their autonomy. Some of the great English earls became prime representatives of the growing Anglo-Saxon resentment against Norman infiltration. The most powerful of these magnates was Earl Godwin of Wessex, who managed to place his sons in several of the other earldoms and even engineered a marriage between his daughter Edith and Edward the Confessor.

The political tensions of the Confessor's reign reached their climax in 1051–52, when Earl Godwin and his allies briefly turned against the king in open rebellion. The affair may have arisen from a dispute over the succession. The Norman sources (which are not entirely trustworthy in these matters) indicate that in 1051 Edward, who was childless, designated as his heir Duke William the Bastard of Normandy, his relative and friend. It may be that Earl Godwin himself aspired to the throne and was driven to des-

---

9 *Vita Aedwardi Regis: The Life of King Edward,* Frank Barlow, ed. (London, 1962), p. 17. On the reign in general, see the excellent biography by Frank Barlow, *Edward the Confessor* (Berkeley, Calif., 1970).

perate measures by Edward's decision. Whatever the reasons, in 1051 Godwin rebelled against the king. The immediate cause was an incident that occurred at Dover, an important seaport in Godwin's Wessex earldom. A French lord, Eustace of Boulogne, was returning through Wessex from a visit to the royal court, possibly as an envoy from Duke William. When he came to Dover, the townsmen rioted and killed some of the knights in his retinue. King Edward demanded that Godwin punish the townsmen. Godwin refused and assembled an army, perhaps hoping to force Edward to dismiss his Norman coterie and change his succession plans. But Godwin quickly discovered that Edward had the backing of all the magnates except the Godwins, and the earl and his sons had to flee the country. In 1052, however, they returned, rallied support to their cause, overawed Edward with a show of military power, and forced him to reinstate them.

The Godwin clan had won an important bloodless victory. Edward was humiliated and, bowing to the wishes of the earl, sent home most of his Norman supporters. Among these was Robert of Jumièges, Archbishop of Canterbury, who was forced to abandon his see. Archbishop Robert was replaced by a creature of the Godwins named Stigand—a vainglorious popinjay of a man who presided over the English Church with a singular lack of distinction. From then on Edward became more and more a figurehead. The real power was exercised by Earl Godwin and, after Godwin's death in 1053, by his son Harold Godwinson, who succeeded to the earldom of Wessex.

Harold emerges from the writings of his age as a more attractive, less crassly ambitious figure than his father. Between 1053 and Edward's death in 1066, the king and the earl seem to have worked together on reasonably good terms. Harold behaved with proper deference toward Edward, did most of the necessary frontier campaigning, and left the monarch to his favorite pastimes—hunting, churchgoing, and directing the construction of the great Romanesque abbey at Westminster. Harold proved himself a man of political talent and exceptional generalship, and in the years of his power the kingdom flourished.

By the standards of mid-eleventh-century Western Europe, England on the eve of the Norman Conquest was prosperous and well-governed. The Church was thriving, the military organization was efficient, towns and commerce were growing, and money was circulating to a degree unknown on the continent. Despite enduring diversities in law and custom between one region and another, Anglo-Saxon England had achieved a genuine sense of national unity, which contrasted sharply with the state of political chaos and endemic private warfare that persisted throughout most of France. A vivid illustration of England's growing feeling of national cohesion is to be found in a passage from the *Anglo-Saxon Chronicle* under the year 1052. On Godwin's return from exile, both he and King Edward had large military forces behind them, and for a time there seemed every possibility of open battle. But, as the *Chronicle* explains, the chief military leaders on both sides decided against a test of arms: "It was hateful to them that they should fight against men of their own race, because very few worthy men on either side were not Englishmen." As this passage makes clear, Bede's vision of the English as a single people was by now shared by the laity.

The Reign of Harold and the Norman Conquest

King Edward the Confessor died in 1066. He is reputed to have remained chaste throughout his marriage to Godwin's daughter Edith; whether this is true or merely a pious excuse for a childless marriage, his death brought to a head the problem of the royal succession.

There were three serious candidates for the Confessor's throne. Earl Harold Godwinson had been the most powerful man in England for the previous thirteen years and had proven his capacity. Edward is alleged to have designated Harold his heir on his deathbed, and on the day after Edward's death the Witan chose the earl as king. In the absence of a royal son, Harold's position as heir designate of King Edward and his selection by the Witan gave him a strong claim. He also had a certain tenuous connection with the throne through his sister Edith, who was Edward's widow, although he was not himself of royal blood.

Duke William the Bastard of Normandy was distantly related to Edward through his great-aunt, Emma, the Norman wife of Ethelred the Unready and Canute. William also stood on his claim that Edward had earlier designated him heir to the English throne. It is quite possible, of course, that Edward had designated William in 1051 and Harold in 1066. Finally, William claimed priority over Harold Godwinson on the basis of a peculiar episode that occurred in 1064. Harold, visiting the continent, had fallen captive to a petty lord who had released him into Duke William's custody. William treated Harold as an honored guest, but it is by no means clear that the earl was free to leave the Norman court. At length, Harold took a public oath to support Duke William's claims to the English throne on Edward's death. Hence in 1066 William and his supporters regarded Harold as an oath breaker; and by both the Christian and the feudal ethics of the day the violation of a pledge was regarded with profound contempt.

Harold Hardrada, King of Norway, was an illustrious Norse warrior whose skill at arms had won him fame from Byzantium to Scandinavia. As ruler of Norway, he too claimed dominion over England as successor to Canute. Harold Hardrada's claim was perhaps the weakest of the three, but his immense military reputation must have made the English deeply apprehensive. It was clear that Harold Godwinson would have to fight for his new crown.

Beyond the rivalry of Harold Hardrada and William the Bastard, Harold Godwinson had two additional liabilities. In 1066 the papacy in Rome was in the process of reasserting its authority over the European

The Anglo-Saxon Kings

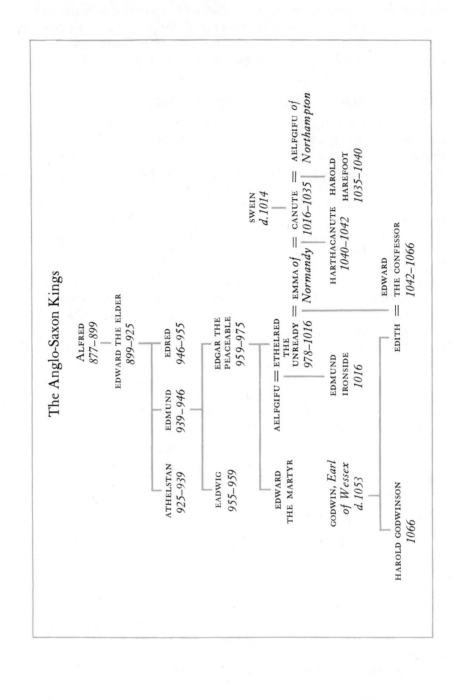

ALFRED
877–899

EDWARD THE ELDER
899–925

ATHELSTAN
925–939

EDMUND
939–946

EDRED
946–955

EADWIG
955–959

EDGAR THE
PEACEABLE
959–975

EDWARD
THE MARTYR

AELFGIFU = ETHELRED
THE
UNREADY
978–1016

EMMA *of* = CANUTE = AELFGIFU *of*
Normandy | 1016–1035 | *Northampton*

SWEIN
d.1014

EDMUND
IRONSIDE
1016

HARTHACANUTE
1040–1042

HAROLD
HAREFOOT
1035–1040

EDWARD
THE CONFESSOR
1042–1066

EDITH =

GODWIN, *Earl
of Wessex
d.1053*

HAROLD GODWINSON
1066

Church. As a jealous guardian of proper canonical processes, the papacy could not accept the deposition of Robert of Jumièges as archbishop of Canterbury in favor of Stigand. The appointment of a new archbishop before the old one was dead was a flagrant violation of canon law. Hence the papacy was hostile toward Harold Godwinson, who supported Stigand and whose father had engineered his usurpation. Duke William exploited this hostility, winning full papal support for his projected conquest of England. William's invading army was privileged to carry the papal banner which, together with the Norman claim that Godwinson was a perjurer, placed the duke in an exceedingly strong moral position and made his invasion a kind of holy war.

Harold Godwinson's second liability was his brother, Earl Tostig of Northumbria. Tostig was an unpopular lord who was overthrown by a Northumbrian revolt in 1065. The revolt appeared to have strong popular backing and was condoned by Harold; Tostig never forgave his brother. The Northumbrians chose as their new earl an important magnate named Morcar, brother of Earl Edwin of Mercia and unrelated to the Godwin clan. Harold's passive role in this affair seems to have won him the gratitude of the two powerful brothers, Edwin and Morcar; but Tostig, now in exile, was reasonably secure at home, but he had more than his share of dangerous enemies abroad.

Normandy, on the eve of the Battle of Hastings, was a well-organized feudal state whose duke controlled his vassals to a degree unmatched elsewhere in France.[10] During the century and a half since its establishment in 911, the Viking state of Normandy had embraced Christianity, absorbed French culture, adopted the French language, and based its military and political organization on the principles of French feudalism. Normandy in 1066 was a land of feudal castles and feudal knights whose cavalry tactics contrasted sharply with the infantry tradition of the Anglo-Saxon fyrd.

Evidence relating to pre-Conquest Norman history is far from abundant, but it is sufficient to suggest that the high degree of ducal control and centralization Normandy enjoyed in 1066 was to a considerable extent a product of William the Bastard's own statesmanship. Winning a significant victory over his rebellious barons in 1047, he spent the years thereafter subordinating the Norman nobility to the ducal administration and working toward the elimination of private warfare, which had long been endemic among the feudal baronage.

But strong as William was, he was not strong enough to win for Normandy a position of hegemony in northern France that would provide him with the necessary security to undertake a major invasion of England. He

---

[10] A thorough, highly technical account of eleventh-century Normandy is C. H. Haskins, *Norman Institutions* (1918). On the scope of Norman expansion in the eleventh century—into southern Italy, Sicily, and the Holy Land as well as England—see David C. Douglas, *The Norman Achievement* (Berkeley, 1969).

achieved this hegemony quite by accident when his two chief rivals, the count of the neighboring feudal state of Anjou and the king of France, both died in 1060. France fell to a child king, and Anjou entered a period of disputed succession. In the meantime William had insured the support of the prosperous neighboring county of Flanders by marrying the daughter of its count in 1053.

On Edward the Confessor's death, therefore, William was in a position to make good his claims to the English throne. Good fortune provided the opportunity, and William had the courage, imagination, and greed to grasp it.[11] The barons of Normandy agreed to the daring enterprise at a council early in 1066, and William set about to augment his Norman force with volunteers from all over Europe. Adventurous knights flocked to his standard from all quarters—from Brittany, Maine, Flanders, Aquitaine, central France, and even southern Italy—drawn by William's already formidable military reputation, by the generous wages he promised, and by the hope of treasure and estates in the conquered land. But despite the support of his duchy, the growing size of his army, and the moral backing of the papacy, William's projected invasion was an audacious gamble. England was far larger and wealthier than Normandy, and it was ruled by a warrior-king of ability and resolution.

Harold Godwinson, however, had a staggering task before him. Beset by enemies, he could not predict the place, the time, or the source of the first attacks against his kingdom. At it happened, the initial assault came from his brother Tostig. In May 1066, Tostig emerged from exile to begin harrying the coasts of southern and eastern England with a sizable body of followers. Tostig's men were turned back by local contingents of the fyrd, and he was obliged to retire to Scotland. Obviously incapable of doing serious damage on his own, he entered into an alliance with Harold Hardrada and merged his forces with those of the Norse king.

By midsummer, Duke William's army was ready for the invasion, and only the persistence of contrary winds prevented his crossing the Channel. Godwinson had meanwhile assembled the fyrd in southern England and had stationed a large fleet off the Channel shore. But week after week the winds remained contrary for William, and the English watched their coasts in vain.

Midway through September Godwinson was forced to dismiss his army and fleet. There is some evidence that service in the fyrd was limited by custom to two months. By mid-September the term had expired, provisions were exhausted, and the warriors wished to return home for the harvest. The

---

11 Much has been written on the Norman Conquest. Frank Stenton, *Anglo-Saxon England* (3rd ed., Oxford, 1971), contains a good summary; see also C. W. Hollister, *Anglo-Saxon Military Institutions* (Oxford, 1962), especially pp. 147–52, and H. R. Loyn, *The Norman Conquest* (London, 1965). On the background and aftermath of the Conquest see R. Allen Brown, *The Normans and the Norman Conquest* (London, 1969). A vivid contemporary account of the battle of Hastings is Guy of Amiens, *The Carmen de Hastingae Proelio*, Catherine Morton and Hope Muntz, eds. (Latin with English translation) (Oxford Medieval Texts, 1972).

contrary winds had served William after all, for Harold now had only his housecarles to guard the shore.

Immediately after disbanding his army, Godwinson received news that Harold Hardrada had invaded Yorkshire in northern England. Hardrada's army consisted of three hundred shiploads of Norse warriors, in addition to Tostig and his considerable following. The combined force moved toward the key northern city of York. On September 20, 1066, Hardrada's host encountered the northern fyrd led by the two earls, Edwin and Morcar, at Fulford Gate, two miles south of York. The battle of Fulford raged for the better part of a day, and in the end the local fyrd broke before the invaders. Receiving the submission of York, Hardrada then apparently conceived the idea of incorporating a number of Anglo-Danish Yorkshiremen into his army. He withdrew to a strategic crossroads called Stamford Bridge, seven miles east of York, to await hostages from the conquered city.

Godwinson reassembled his army as best he could on short notice and rushed northward. Five days after Fulford, on September 25, Godwinson's army arrived at Stamford Bridge, caught the Norwegian host by surprise, and after a long and savage battle succeeded in crushing it. Tostig and Hardrada were both killed, and the battered survivors of the three-hundred-ship host returned to Norway in twenty-four ships. Stamford Bridge was perhaps the greatest military triumph in Anglo-Saxon history. An ominous Scandinavian threat of twenty years' standing was removed, and the mightiest Viking warrior of the age lay in his grave.

Two days after the battle of Stamford Bridge the Channel winds changed at last, and the Norman invasion began. At nine in the morning on Thursday, September 28, the Norman fleet entered Pevensey Bay in Sussex, and William's army disembarked at leisure on an undefended shore. Immediately the Normans occupied the important port of Hastings and proceeded to build a castle there to protect their avenue of escape should the war turn against them. Modern historians, with the advantage of hindsight, have sometimes assumed that the Norman victory at the battle of Hastings was inevitable. But William, lacking the gift of foreknowledge, was far from certain of the outcome. Indeed, he could hardly have known at the time whether his enemy would be Harold Godwinson or Harold Hardrada.

On news of the Norman landing, Godwinson acted with almost frenzied speed. Within thirteen days he settled affairs in Yorkshire, pulled together his tired and decimated army, and marched 240 miles from York to Hastings. From the standpoint of military strategy, Harold's haste was a serious error. There was no real reason for it, since William was too cautious to proceed far from the Sussex shore until he had done battle with the English. Perhaps Godwinson was overconfident after his victory at Stamford Bridge; perhaps he was solicitous of the defenseless people of his former earldom of Wessex, who were being ravaged by the Normans. Whatever his reasons, he was obliged to face William with an exhausted army far below normal strength.

On Friday, October 13, William's scouts sighted King Harold's army,

THE BAYEUX TAPESTRY (LATE 11TH CENTURY)
The appearance of Halley's Comet alarms King Harold (center) and
his subjects. Harold's fear of the Normans crossing the Channel is
depicted by the ships on the lower border.

In this detail, the English foot soldiers atop their hill (right) are
successfully repulsing a charge of mounted Norman knights.

and on the following day there occurred the most decisive battle in English history. The battle of Hastings was fought on Saturday, October 14, from dawn to dusk. For the English it was the third major battle in less than four weeks. Edwin and Morcar and their troops had been too badly mauled by the Norsemen to join Harold on his southward march, and there had been insufficient time to summon the full complement of the southern fyrd.

Harold's army, depending on the traditional infantry tactics of the Anglo-Saxons to turn back William's cavalry, took a strong defensive position on the crest of a low hill, the forward line standing shoulder to shoulder in the form of a shield wall.[12] Repeated Norman cavalry charges were repulsed by this shield wall during the course of the day; and although the arrows of Norman archers took many lives, the Anglo-Saxon line remained firm. At one point in the battle the Normans fled in panic until their duke rallied them and ordered them to turn on a body of pursuing English, who were then savagely cut down. There is some evidence that on one or two later occasions the Normans feigned flight in order to draw more of the English out of their shield wall. At length King Harold himself was slain, and with the coming of dusk the shield wall broke at last. The English fyrd, now leaderless, fled into the Sussex forest.

William's triumph marks the end of Anglo-Saxon England and the beginning of Norman England. It remained for William to consolidate his conquest and establish firm rule over the kingdom. Hastings left England kingless, disorganized, and all but defenseless against the Norman host.

The great battle and its background have been described in some detail in order to see beyond the traditional view that Hastings represented the inevitable victory of an up-to-date continental feudal state over an effete, insular culture, exhausted of its inspiration and militarily antiquated. On the contrary, the Anglo-Saxon army gave a good account of itself under the most adverse conditions; and Anglo-Saxon civilization retained to the end its precocious political organization and rich cultural vitality. On the sturdy foundation constructed by Theodore of Tarsus, Alfred the Great, Edward the Elder, Edgar the Peaceable, and others like them, the Norman kings would build the most tightly organized Western European state since the days of the Romans.

---

[12] After the Conquest, William built Battle Abbey on this spot. The site is presently occupied by a school for girls.

DURHAM CATHEDRAL. *British Tourist Authority.*

II

THE EXPANSION OF
ROYAL GOVERNMENT
1066 to 1189

The Impact of the Norman Conquest

4 William the Conqueror was a gifted warrior-statesman, tenacious in the pursuit of his goals, cruel or magnanimous as it suited his purposes, and phenomenally energetic. A monk of the next generation described him in these words:

> He was tall, extraordinarily fleshy, with a fierce look, and a forehead bare of hair, with arms of such strength that nobody else could draw his bow, though he himself could bend it while his horse was at full gallop. He was majestic, whether sitting or standing—though the protuberance of his belly deformed his royal person—of robust health, addicted to the pleasures of hunting.[1]

Having won his gamble at Hastings, William moved unerringly toward the completion of his conquest. He knew that London was the key to England, and shortly after the great battle he advanced northward toward the city. Finding London Bridge too well defended to permit his crossing the Thames and assaulting the city directly, he led his army westward—devastating the countryside as he went—until he reached the town of Wallingford in Berkshire. Here he crossed the Thames and advanced eastward on London. Before he reached the city he was met by a number of London citizens and other notables—such as Archbishop Stigand and earls Edwin and Morcar—

---

[1] From William of Malmesbury, *Acts of the Kings of the English.* The most complete and satisfactory biography is David C. Douglas, *William the Conqueror* (Berkeley, 1964), which also provides an excellent account of pre-Conquest Normandy. Frank Barlow, *William I and the Norman Conquest* (London, 1965), is a good summary that presents William as a man with the values and talents of an able but essentially ordinary baron.

who made their submission to him and surrendered the city. On Christmas Day, 1066, Duke William was crowned king of England in the new Westminster Abbey, with all the pomp and ceremony that traditionally accompanied Anglo-Saxon coronations. All present, both Norman and English, promised their allegiance to the new king, and William, for his part, undertook to abide by the laws in effect during Edward the Confessor's reign and to rule in the tradition of the Wessex kings.

The Conquest Consolidated

To an extent, William abided by his promises, but it soon became clear that more than words would be required to pacify his new kingdom. In the months and years following the coronation many Englishmen continued to resist him or revolted against his rule at every opportunity. The Scandinavians too, despite their calamitous defeat at Stamford Bridge, continued to risk new invasions of England. To complicate matters, the kingdom of France and the county of Anjou were gradually recovering their former strength, and William had to devote much of his energy to continental campaigning to protect his Norman duchy. In short, William's new Anglo-Norman state was threatened by many hostile forces, both internal and external, and his energy was taxed to the limit in the defense of his far-flung domain.

During the five years following the Conquest, William and his lieutenants were kept occupied by a series of English rebellions, some of them coordinated with amphibious attacks from Scandinavia. William of Malmesbury, writing several decades later, comments on the savage measures the Conqueror took in defense of his crown:

> Perhaps the king's behavior can be excused if he was at times quite severe with the English, for he found scarcely any of them faithful. This fact so irritated his fierce mind that he took from the greater of them first their wealth, then their land, and finally, in some instances, their lives.

In the course of these revolts Edwin and Morcar turned against the Conqueror, and both lost their lives. A ruffian named Hereward entrenched himself against William on the Isle of Ely and plundered the surrounding countryside until he was at last suppressed by the Normans. Despite his savage sack of Peterborough Abbey, Hereward later became a glamorous figure in English patriotic legend.

William used both kindness and cruelty in consolidating his new realm, but in retrospect it was his cruelty that predominated. Obliged to besiege the town of Exeter, he allowed its citizens to surrender on generous terms. But he replied to a major revolt in Yorkshire by a campaign of ruthless devastation, transforming vast areas of that once-prosperous county into wastelands in order to break northern England's will to resist. Contemporary writers speak of hundreds of rotting corpses in the Yorkshire countryside and thousands of starving refugees.

ENGLAND
AND NORMANDY
AFTER 1066

SCOTLAND
Melrose
Jedburgh

IRELAND

IRISH SEA

Tynemouth
Newcastle
Durham
Tees R.
Richmond
Whitby

Tyne R.

Ouse R.
York
Gt. Stamford
Fulford Bridge
Ribble
Pontefract
ENGLAND
Chester
Rhuddlan
Degannwy
Lincoln
Nottingham
Shrewsbury
Montgomery
Crowland
Lichfield
Peterorough
Thorney
Elmham
Norwich
Thetford
WALES
Warwick
Huntingdon
Ely
Eye
Fakenham
Northampton
Cambridge
Hereford
Worcester
Evesham
Winchcomb
Clare
Severn R.
Usk R.
St. David's
Berkhamsted
Gloucester
St. Albans
Bristol
Dorchester
London
Thames R.
Wallingford
West-
minster
Malmesbury
Wells
Salisbury
Rochester
Canterbury
Bruges
Dover
Glastonbury
Ramsey
Winchester
Battle
Romney
Montacute
Bosham
Chichester
Wissant
St. Bertin's
Ghent
Sherborne
Hastings
Boulogne
Exeter
Selsey
Pevensey

FLANDERS

NORTH
SEA

Rhine R.

Meuse R.

Isle of Wight

English Channel

ARTOIS

St. Valéry

PONTHIEU

Rouen
Gisors
Bayeux
Dives
Oise R.
Caen
Coutances Falaise
Evreux
Mantes
Paris
NORMANDY
Avranches
Domfront
Alençon
Chartres
Seine R.
FRENCH
Dinan
Dol
Gael
Rennes
Bellême
ROYAL
BRITTANY
MAINE
BLOIS
Le Mans
Blois
DEMESNE
Angers
Tours
Loire R.
ANJOU
TOURAINE
FRANCE
POITOU
Poitiers
AQUITAINE

During these restless years William's task was rendered all the more difficult by the fact that he had to divide his time between England and Normandy. His ultimate success in subduing England was due to several interrelated factors: (1) English opposition was never properly coordinated. Almost from the beginning William was able to summon substantial portions of the English fyrd to fight in his behalf against English rebels. (2) While William was rising to power in pre-Conquest Normandy, he had won the firm support of a rising new feudal aristocracy; after the Conquest he could usually depend upon these powerful Norman aristocrats to defend his interests both in Normandy and in England. As holders of vast estates in the conquered land, they had both the power and the motivation to uphold the interests of the Norman monarchy. (3) William himself exhibited remarkable energy and resourcefulness in these years and demonstrated an almost uncanny ability to buy off his enemies, win their loyalty through generous terms, or terrorize them with his cruelty, as the occasion might demand. (4) Both William and his aristocratic followers built numerous castles in England. These fortresses, which had long been a characteristic feature of the Norman landscape, were smaller, tougher, and far more numerous than the Old English burghs. Although crude by later standards, usually consisting merely of an earthen mound surrounded by a wooden palisade and surmounted by a square wooden tower, they were nevertheless exceedingly difficult to capture by assault. Accordingly, they became bastions of Norman power and stark symbols of Norman authority in the conquered realm.

The Anglo-Saxon revolts ended around 1071. Thereafter the English were loyal to William and his successors, and in later years the Norman kings often employed Englishmen to help suppress rebellions by Norman barons. Nevertheless, even if the Conqueror did intend in 1066 to allow members of the Anglo-Saxon aristocracy to share the wealth and governance of England with his Norman followers, the revolts of 1066–1071 forced him to adopt a thoroughgoing policy of Normanization. As a consequence, the Old English aristocracy was virtually disinherited, and the spoils of the Conquest passed almost entirely to the king, his great Norman nobles, and other continental lords who had supported the invasion. Not only was the Anglo-Saxon secular aristocracy dispossessed; the great abbeys and bishoprics of England also passed, with few exceptions, into the hands of Norman prelates.

The effect of the Norman Conquest upon England has long been one of the most hotly contested issues in English medieval scholarship. That it resulted in a transformation of aristocratic society there can be no question, for it brought to power a French-speaking nobility accustomed to knightly cavalry warfare and castle building and different in many respects from the aristocracy of Anglo-Saxon times. But the aristocracy, powerful though it was, constituted only a tiny fraction of the population. What of the rest?

English towns were growing in size and economic importance before the Conquest and continued to grow after it; on the whole they seem to have been little affected by the dynastic and aristocratic revolution. If Scandinavian commerce declined, commerce with the continent increased. So, although the century or two following William's invasion witnessed an extensive growth in towns and commerce, this expansion was a product, not of the Norman Conquest, but of the vast economic changes that were affecting all Europe.

Peasant life, too, went on much as before. In the long run, the Norman Conquest probably tended to make the peasantry more uniform than in Anglo-Saxon times, raising the status of slaves and lowering that of freemen. Gradually, both were absorbed into the middle range of dependent farmers or serfs; they were bound to a manorial lord, tied to their land, and obliged to give a portion of their produce to their lord and to work certain days of the week on his demesne. But such changes occurred slowly, and they are difficult to trace with certainty. Eventually the buoyant economy of high medieval Europe seems to have resulted in a gradual elevation of the status of serfs, both in England and on the continent.

Architecturally, the Norman Conquest brought visible and impressive changes to the face of the land. Besides the numerous crude wooden castle towers built on artificial mounds, the Normans erected a few castles of monumental proportions—great square keeps with heavy stone walls, such as the Conqueror's Tower of London and the early-twelfth-century tower that now stands in ruins overlooking the cathedral at Rochester. Under the Conqueror and his sons there occurred a great program of church building in the Norman Romanesque style which had already been introduced into England in Edward the Confessor's Westminster Abbey. Almost every cathedral was rebuilt in the new fashion,[2] along with a great many village and abbey churches. In the early days the style was heavy and stark, but by the opening years of the twelfth century it was becoming more decorative. Complex geometrical designs were carved around portals and arches and sometimes—as at Durham—on the stout supporting columns. Interiors were dark but painted in bright colors and often decorated with frescoes, some of which survive at St. Alban's Abbey and elsewhere. As architects grew in skill and daring, wooden roofs gave way to stone vaulting. Much of this Norman construction still stands: in small churches, such as Iffley and Kilpec, and in large ones, such as Norwich, Gloucester, Durham, and Tewkesbury. Their thick walls, columns, and round-arched arcades—their solid towers and dominating proportions—evoke a feeling of strength unique in English architecture and bear witness even now to the power of the Normans.

Yet in architecture, as in so many other areas, major changes would have come to England even if Harold had won at Hastings. The Romanesque style was spreading across Western Europe in the later eleventh century, although not always with the massive proportions favored by the

---

[2] A cathedral is, technically, the headquarters church of a bishop and his diocese.

ROCHESTER CASTLE, KENT
Probably built by Gandulf
the Norman in 1077, this
immense example of Norman
Romanesque military architecture has walls twelve
feet thick. *National Monuments Record.*

Normans. It is important to remember that the Norman Conquest occurred
at the beginning of a notable epoch of European expansion—economic, political, military, religious, cultural, and intellectual.[3] This profound creative
upsurge has been termed "the renaissance of the twelfth century," but in
fact it affected the entire period between the mid-eleventh century and the
end of the thirteenth—the period conventionally called the High Middle
Ages. France was the core of this remarkable cultural development—the
source of Gothic architecture, the site of the great University of Paris, the
home of many of medieval Europe's most distinguished scholars and writers,
and the birthplace of the Crusades and military adventures that expanded
the frontiers of Western Christendom. It has been suggested that because
the culture of the High Middle Ages was pre-eminently French, the conquest
of England by a French duchy had the effect of making England much
more susceptible to the great creative trends of the era. This is an attractive
theory, but it is also a dangerous one. Ties with the continent had been

---

3 The bibliography on the High Middle Ages is immense. See in particular C. H. Haskins,
The Renaissance of the Twelfth Century (Cambridge, Mass., 1927); R. W. Southern,
The Making of the Middle Ages (New Haven, 1953); Friedrich Heer, *The Medieval
World: Europe, 1100–1350* (J. Sondheimer, tr., Cleveland, 1962); Christopher Brooke,
The Twelfth Century Renaissance (London, 1969); C. W. Hollister, *The Twelfth-Cen-
tury Renaissance* (New York, 1969); and Sidney R. Packard, *Twelfth Century Europe*
(Amherst, 1973).

THE NAVE OF DURHAM CATHEDRAL
Emphasizing strength and solidity, compound piers alternate with
sturdy columns carved with geometrical designs. *National Monuments
Record*.

NORMAN ROMANESQUE SCULPTURE
This ingenuous figure of St. Paul is on the Kilpec Church, Herefordshire
and dates from the mid-12th century. *Eric Hartmann, Magnum.*

strong ever since the conversion of England to Christianity; with or without the Norman connection England would have been deeply influenced by the culture of high medieval Europe. The effect of the Norman Conquest in this respect must remain imponderable.

We should keep this in mind as we turn to the problem of Norman influence on the English Church. William came to England with the blessing of the reform papacy on his head and holy relics around his neck. Harold's archbishop, the usurper Stigand, was offensive to the papacy, and in time William deposed him. Stigand's successor was a skillful ecclesiastical states-man named Lanfranc—a noted scholar, abbot of the newly founded Norman monastery of St. Etienne in Caen, and one of William's most trusted advisers. Under Archbishop Lanfranc the English Church began a thoroughgoing reform in keeping with the policies of the reform papacy. Simony, the buy-ing or selling of ecclesiastical offices, was banned, and the marriage of clergy-men, long uncanonical but widespread nevertheless, was expressly forbidden. New monasteries were founded, old ones were reformed, and cathedral clergy began to follow more stringent rules. Finally, William issued an ordinance that expanded the judicial authority of bishops in England, thereby contributing to the development in the following century of a highly organized system of ecclesiastical courts separate from the courts of shire and hundred.

One might well conclude that the Norman Conquest had a momentous effect on the English Church, bringing its practices closely in line with the notions of continental reformers. It could be argued, on the other hand, that Church reform would soon have come to England even without the Norman Conquest. The greatest of the eleventh-century reformers, Gregory VII, did not become pope until 1073; and it was not until his pontificate that the reform movement attained its full momentum. The reform ideas of Pope Gregory VII were bound to affect England, and the most that can be said of the Norman Conquest in this respect is that it hastened the process.

It should be added that King William and Archbishop Lanfranc were by no means as advanced in their concepts of church reform as Gregory VII. Pope Gregory and many of the reform cardinals who surrounded him were convinced that such evils as simony and clerical incontinence were products of a basic flaw in Christian society. To them, it was profoundly wrong that the appointment of clergymen should be in the hands of lay lords, as had long been the case in Western Europe. In the tenth and eleventh centuries it was customary for kings and dukes to select their archbishops, for counts to select their bishops, even for manorial lords to select their parish priests. Indeed, until the 1050s it was by no means uncommon for the Holy Roman Emperors to appoint popes. To lay lords, control of the Church seemed essential to their power, for the Church held vast tracts of land, and church-men often occupied key positions in the administrative and military systems of secular governments. To Gregory VII and his supporters, however, it seemed necessary that the Church should assume its proper position at the head of society. Spirit, they argued, is greater than matter, and the spiritual authority of the Church ought to take precedence over the worldly authority of kings and magnates. Accordingly, churchmen should judge laymen, not the reverse, and the Church should be supreme in the Christian commonwealth. Only then could Christian society assume its rightful order.

The gulf between papal and secular opinion on this crucial matter resulted in a protracted and often violent struggle. Pope Gregory VII, who had long contended against simony and incontinence, raised the explosive issue of lay control in 1075 by issuing a formal ban against lay investiture. This ban and the bitter Investiture Controversy that followed focused on the ceremony by which a bishop was invested in his see. Traditionally, a lay lord formally bestowed upon the initiate bishop a ring, symbolic of his marriage to the Church, and a staff, symbolic of his pastoral duties as shepherd of his Christian flock. Symbols had profound meaning in the Middle Ages, and in forbidding laymen to invest new bishops with the ring and staff, Gregory VII was in fact striking at the vital principle of lay control of the clergy.

Since Gregory's chief opponent in the Investiture Controversy was Henry IV, king of Germany and prospective Holy Roman Emperor, the fiery pope was not in a position to press the issue in England or Normandy. He could not fight all Europe at once. William the Conqueror, who had no intention of loosening his grip on the Anglo-Norman Church, was treated deferentially as a friend of the papacy and a sincere opponent of ecclesiastical corruption. The issue of lay investiture did not explode in England until a generation later; during the Conqueror's reign it remained dormant.

Nevertheless, certain tensions were bound to arise in Anglo-papal relations. William and Gregory VII were both dedicated to church reform, but they had radically different ideas on the question of ecclestical supremacy. Gregory, for example, assumed that the supreme spiritual position he claimed for the papacy carried with it broad secular powers. He succeeded in getting a number of important Christian princes to acknowledge that they were papal vassals—that the pope was their overlord. Indeed, he demanded the allegiance or "fealty" of the Conqueror himself, along with a request for the resumption of a papal tax known as Peter's Pence. William replied politely but firmly:

> Your legate, Hubert, Most Holy Father, coming to me on your behalf, has admonished me to profess allegiance to you and your successors, and to think better regarding the money which my predecessors were wont to send to the Church of Rome. I have consented to the one but not to the other. I have not consented to pay fealty, nor will I now, because I never promised it, nor do I find that my predecessors ever paid it to your predecessors.[4]

---

4 From the translation in *English Historical Documents*, II, ed. David C. Douglas and George W. Greenaway (London, 1953), p. 647.

With this assertion, the issue was abruptly closed. William and Archbishop Lanfranc continued to work toward the reform of the English Church, but the work was accomplished under strict royal supervision.

The Problem of Feudalization

The most vigorously contested scholarly problem relating to the Norman Conquest is the question of whether William the Conqueror introduced a "feudal revolution" into England—that is, whether the new Norman aristocracy established a network of feudal institutions in a previously nonfeudal land.[5] Many nineteenth-century scholars were inclined toward the view that feudalism developed gradually in eleventh- and twelfth-century England, and that the Norman Conquest merely hastened somewhat a development that was basically inevitable. During most of the present century, however, the opposite view has prevailed: feudalism was introduced by the Normans quite suddenly, pre-Conquest England was fundamentally unfeudal, and without Norman intervention it would probably have remained so. Today this feudal-revolution hypothesis is under strong attack by some scholars and is being stoutly defended by others.

In order to understand the problem, one must explore carefully the nature of medieval feudalism. At heart, feudalism consisted of a complex of personal and territorial relationships between members of a warrior aristocracy. It combined the old Germanic notion of the loyalty of a comitatus member to his lord with the early medieval concept of service in return for land tenure. In its developed form, feudalism involved a relationship between two aristocratic warriors—a lord and a vassal. The lord granted a parcel of land to his vassal and undertook to protect the vassal's interests. The vassal, in return, gave his allegiance (homage and fealty) to his lord and agreed to render him services of various sorts—most notably, knightly military service. The estate granted by the lord to his vassal was known as a fief or *feudum*—from which our word "feudal" is derived.

Feudalism was emerging in the Frankish kingdom during the eighth and ninth centuries, at a time when Frankish military tactics were placing increasing emphasis on the heavily-armed horseman. The cavalryman, or knight, required a fine horse, arms and armor, and above all a great deal of training in the art of mounted combat. In short, the rise of heavy cavalry

---

5 On this issue see C. W. Hollister, *The Military Organization of Norman England* (Oxford, 1965). The classical account of the Norman Conquest as "feudal revolution" is F. M. Stenton, *The First Century of English Feudalism, 1066–1166* (2nd ed., Oxford, 1961). Radically different views are expressed in H. G. Richardson and G. O. Sayles, *The Governance of Mediaeval England* (Edinburgh, 1963), pp. 22–135. All the various points of view are represented in *The Impact of the Norman Conquest*, ed. C. W. Hollister (New York, 1969). A good, recent summary is R. Allen Brown, *Origins of English Feudalism* (London, 1973).

necessitated the creation of an important and fairly numerous military elite. But this tactical change coincided with a time when money was in short supply. Some knights were simply fed and maintained in their lord's household; but gradually it became customary for a king or a magnate to "pay" his knights by granting them land in return for their service.

The practice of paying for service with land was by no means limited to the military sphere. The tenure-service relationship extended also to the fields of administration, justice, and even farming. A great landholder was expected, in return for his wealth in land, to assume the essential functions of public administration and to operate courts of law, as well as to provide knights for the army of his overlord. A peasant farmer, in return for his right to farm a particular plot, was required to contribute his labor on certain days of the week to the tilling of his lord's demesne land. Thus, in a money-poor society, wage service was secondary in importance to tenure service.

With the decline of central authority in Carolingian France during the Viking age, the desperate need for local defense against the lightning raids of the Norsemen resulted in an expansion and intensification of the lord-vassal relationship. Independent freeholders were forced to seek the protection of local lords, often becoming their vassals and giving them their lands. The lord would then return the land to his new vassal to be held as a fief in return for homage and fealty and knightly service. Or, if the freeholder was of the humbler sort and owned only a small farm, he might find himself sinking into the ranks of the dependent peasantry. It should be understood that the fief-holding vassal did not ordinarily labor on his own lands; he drew his wealth from the obligations of his serfs to pay him a proportion of the yield of their fields and to work on his demesne fields. There existed, therefore, an immense social chasm between the vassal and the serf; the serf was not directly involved in the network of relationships we call feudal, which principally concerned the aristocracy. But on the other hand, the feudal aristocracy depended ultimately on the toil of its serfs, and the entire feudal system rested on the economic foundation of peasant labor. Without serfs, a fief would be valueless.

During the Viking age there was a growing tendency for fiefs to become hereditary. This was particularly true of the extensive fiefs held by the great vassals of the Frankish kings—the dukes and counts. And although a powerful monarch like Charlemagne might expect the devoted loyalty of his chief vassals, it was far from certain that the sons, grandsons, or great-grandsons of these vassals would be equally loyal to Charlemagne's descendants. It is one of the characteristics of feudalism that loyalty tends to weaken with the passage of generations. This characteristic was aggravated during the Viking age, when the French kings often seemed helpless to defend their realm, and the great vassals were, from the military standpoint, on their own. Hence, the ninth and tenth centuries witnessed a steady disintegration of public authority. Administrative and judicial responsibilities and royal revenues passed increasingly into the hands of dukes, counts, and local warlords, who built castles, fought the Vikings, and ignored the sovereignty of the king. With the fractionization of sovereignty and the rise of small, semi-independent feudal states, it became increasingly common for feudal lords to fight one another when they were not fighting the Vikings. Private war became the curse of feudal society.

Every important feudal lord, even though a vassal of a higher lord, aspired to have a large army of his own. Hence, a vassal frequently divided a portion of his fief into smaller fiefs, which he granted to subvassals. This process, known as subinfeudation, sometimes went down through as many as twenty degrees, with subvassals functioning as lords of sub-subvassals who, in turn, were lords of sub-sub-subvassals, and so on down to the lowly vassal who held a single "knight's fee." And even the lowest vassal was a lord of sorts—a landlord over the serfs on his fee. Every vassal, therefore, was a lord as well; and every lord, except the king of France himself, was a vassal of some higher lord.

This description may seem sufficiently complex, and yet it is an over-simplified abstraction of the actual situation. Often a vassal had two or three lords, each for a different part of his holdings; should two of his lords go to war with one another, he was faced with the perplexing question of which one to serve. If a lord was dissatisfied with his vassal's service, or if a vassal was dissatisfied with his lord's protection, then lord and vassal might wage war against one another. There are even cases of a lord's receiving a fief from his own vassal, thereby becoming his vassal's vassal. The following charter may suggest some of the fantastic complexities that could occur in the feudal "system":

> I, John of Toul, affirm that I am the vassal of the Lady Beatrice, countess of Troyes, and of her son Theobald, count of Champagne, against every creature living or dead, excepting my allegiance to Lord Enjourand of Coucy, Lord John of Arcis, and the count of Grandpré. If it should happen that the count of Grandpré should be at war with the countess and count of Champagne in his own quarrel, I will aid the count of Grandpré in my own person, and will aid the count and countess of Champagne by sending them the knights whose service I owe them from the fief which I hold of them.

By the eleventh century, feudal France was beginning to regain a measure of coherence. The power of the French crown remained restricted to a modest territory in north central France embracing Paris and Orleans—the Ile de France—and the French monarchs exerted little or no authority over the lands of their vassals. But the great vassal states themselves were gradually becoming centralized and well governed. The counts and dukes of such feudal principalities as Anjou, Champagne, Blois, Flanders, Poitou, and Normandy were succeeding in bringing their own vassals under control. If they could not eliminate private war in their states, they could at least reduce it considerably; and through the establishment of networks of castles and exploitation of various feudal and nonfeudal revenues, they acquired the strength and wealth to dominate their lands.

It was only in the eleventh century that the obligations a vassal owed his lord became explicit. In Normandy, at least, the number of knights a vassal owed from his fief came to be specified exactly. In addition to supplying the stipulated number of knights, a vassal was obliged to join his lord's retinue on important ceremonial occasions and to serve in his court. Every important lord had a feudal court, in which he exercised jurisdiction over his vassals and heard appeals from subvassals. The vassal also owed his lord certain monetary payments known as aids. These were rendered on special occasions, such as the marriage of the lord's eldest daughter or the knighting of his eldest son. Vassals were also obliged to pay the lord's ransom should he be captured by an enemy.

The lord's authority over his vassal was further emphasized in four additional privileges: (1) the right to veto the marriage of a vassal's widow or heiress to his fief; (2) the right to occupy a fief during the minority of a deceased vassal's son and to serve as guardian of the young heir; (3) the right to collect a payment, known as "relief," when the fief passed from a deceased vassal to his heir; and (4) the right to repossess the fief should the vassal die without heirs. These rights are characteristic of the highly-developed feudalism of northern France in the eleventh and twelfth centuries. Although far from universal in their application, they are of particular interest to us because they became customary in post-Conquest England.

During the later eleventh and twelfth centuries, feudal obligations became increasingly exact. A vassal was now understood to owe his lord a certain number of knights to be used within a specified area (say, within the frontiers of Normandy) for a specified number of days per year (usually forty). Paradoxically, this tendency toward legal systematization appeared concurrently with two other tendencies that ultimately proved subversive to feudalism: strong centralized states and a money economy. As states grew in strength, feudal autonomy declined, and the authority of feudal courts was slowly undermined by the growth of royal justice. And with the expansion of commerce and monetary wealth, tenure service was gradually giving way to wage service and a new economic order was coming into being. From the standpoint of legal definitions the later eleventh and twelfth centuries are the "classical age of feudalism"; but from the political and economic standpoints they mark the beginning of feudalism's decline.

Prior to the Norman Conquest, the feudal customs described here were mostly limited to northern France. Even there, a bewildering degree of diversity prevailed, and a significant amount of territory remained outside the feudal structure altogether, being held unconditionally by free landowners. On the other hand, feudal institutions were already beginning to spread—into parts of southern France, eastern Spain, and the lands in southern Italy that Norman military adventurers were beginning to bring under their control. In the century after 1066 feudalism made its way into Germany, the

Crusader states of the Holy Land, and many other districts of Western Christendom; and each region exhibited its own peculiar feudal characteristics. Most scholars would add that the post-Conquest century witnessed the advent of feudalism in England. It is beyond doubt that post-Conquest England was a feudal state; but scholars differ as to whether the genesis of English feudalism was sudden or gradual, and whether or not post-Conquest English feudalism was anticipated significantly in the development of Anglo-Saxon institutions.

At first glance, one is struck by the fundamental differences between Anglo-Saxon England and feudal France. The shire and hundred courts, the danegeld, and the five-hide fyrd were all, basically, *public* institutions of a sovereign monarchy; whereas the feudal armies, feudal courts, and feudal aids were *private* in nature—products of a system in which privileges and responsibilities once exercised by a royal government had fallen into private hands. But it is unsafe to stress this dichotomy too strongly. The public orientation of Anglo-Saxon institutions had been strongly modified by the spread of private lordship. Great magnates and prelates received royal land charters granting not only extensive territories but also important jurisdictional rights. Many of the lords of Anglo-Saxon England operated the hundred courts within their territories and led their own contingents of the fyrd. But even so, the courts continued to function as units of a national legal system that remained fundamentally public; and the fyrd was still, both in theory and in practice, a national or royal army whose role was limited to the defense of the realm and the service of the king. One might cite certain exceptions to this statement—such as the military confrontation beween Earl Godwin and King Edward in 1052—but in general Anglo-Saxon lords did not lead their fyrds against one another; pre-Conquest England, unlike France, was remarkably free of private war. And even in Edward the Confessor's final years, when Harold Godwinson attended to the defense of the realm, the chroniclers often took the trouble to point out that Earl Harold led the fyrd "by the king's order."

The lord-vassal relationship of feudal France undoubtedly existed in essence in pre-Conquest England. The practice of thegns and other men promising their loyalty—"commending themselves"—to lords was widespread, and the intensity of such relationships is clearly demonstrated in the devotion of Ealdorman Byrhtnoth's men at Maldon. No French lord could ask for better vassals than these. In short, the personal relationship of lord to man was derived from a Germanic tradition shared by both England and France. But although the Anglo-Saxons had their own equivalent of the feudal vassal, it is doubtful that they possessed anything resembling the fief. The personal aspect of feudalism existed in Anglo-Saxon England; but the territorial aspect probably did not.

Even here, however, there is room for argument. Beginning in the tenth century, the bishops of Worcester are known to have granted "loan lands" to be held by tenants for life or sometimes for "three lives"—the life of the tenant, his heir, and his heir's heir. In return for the tenure, the recipients were obliged to perform a rather miscellaneous group of services to their lord, the bishop of Worcester. Among their obligations was military service, to be rendered at the normal rate of one man per five hides. The Worcester tenants were not knights in the strict sense of the word: they were not trained in cavalry warfare, they were ignorant of the art of castle building, and of course the bishop of Worcester would not have dreamt of leading them against a local enemy except in the service of the king. Still these loan lands might perhaps be described as fiefs if one is willing to define the word rather broadly. Whatever their differences from French vassals —and they were many—the Worcester tenants did, after all, hold their lands conditionally from their lord in return for service. It has been argued that the Worcester loan lands were not typical of Anglo-Saxon landholding; other scholars would reply that the existence of loan lands elsewhere in England is hidden from us by the disappearance of relevant records. Thus the argument goes on. It is interesting up to a point, but ultimately the question of whether Anglo-Saxon England was feudal depends on how broadly one is willing to define the word. "Feudalism," like "democracy," though useful in some respects, is a fuzzy term.

One might wish to say that William the Conqueror established feudalism in England, or perhaps simply that he instituted a far more thoroughgoing feudal regime than England had known before. He and his great barons dotted England with castles and introduced the private feudal court alongside the older courts of hundred and shire. He introduced the highly significant concept, unknown in either Anglo-Saxon England or pre-Conquest Normandy, that all the land of England belonged either directly or indirectly to the ruler. Operating on this philosophy and angered by the protracted English rebellions, he confiscated immense tracts of land. Much of this land he added to the royal demesne—the territory controlled directly by the crown. The remainder he granted as fiefs to trusted military followers. In the course of this vast process of redistribution, the lands of several thousand thegns were consolidated into large fiefs held by about 180 great Anglo-Norman barons—tenants-in-chief who held their land directly of King William. Most of these fiefs consisted of widely scattered estates rather than compact territorial blocks; and although the scattering of baronial estates had the effect in later years of attenuating local particularism, William apparently had so such object in mind when he distributed the lands. On the contrary, the scattering seems quite accidental, arising from the fact that pre-Conquest estates themselves tended to be scattered and from the further fact that the distribution was made in piecemeal fashion as the estates of one rebellious Anglo-Saxon lord after another fell successively into the king's hands.

By the 1070s William had assigned arbitrary quotas of knights' service to virtually all the lands outside the royal demesne, whether held by secular or ecclesiastical vassals. These quotas were sufficient to provide the king with a total force of about 5,000 knights. Aside from a handful of exempt abbeys, every English tenant-in-chief now owed a specific number of knights to the crown and was obliged to perform many of the additional feudal duties already exacted in Normandy. In the years that followed, William's great vassals undertook to support the knights they owed the crown by creating smaller fiefs from portions of their larger ones. Thus, the process of subinfeudation occurred in England much as it had at an earlier time in France. English aristocratic society soon took the form of a complex chain of lord-vassal relationships.

Feudalism in Norman England, being the product of a single will, was far more orderly and thoroughgoing than its French counterpart. Above all, it was rigorously subordinated to the interests of the ruler, who was at once sovereign king and chief lord at the apex of the feudal pyramid. This lord-king—*dominus rex* as he was called in contemporary documents—exerted a control over his potentially turbulent vassals such as feudal France had never known. In part, this authority was a product of the Conqueror's own forceful personality, but it also owed much to his skillful use of Anglo-Saxon traditions. He preserved the danegeld, as one might expect, and exploited it thoroughly as a unique and highly lucrative source of royal revenue. He also preserved the Old English fyrd and summoned it to his service on occasion. He tempered the centrifugal forces of feudalism by calling upon the Old English custom of universal allegiance to the crown. In England, the sub-vassal owed primary loyalty not to his immediate lord but to the supreme overlord—the lord-king. In 1085, William summoned the more important landholders of England to a great assembly at Salisbury in order to receive their oaths of allegiance. In doing so, he was following a venerable English tradition that had been exemplified long before in the oath King Edmund demanded of his subjects. Further, William permitted his great vassals to build castles, as they had been accustomed to do in Normandy; but recognizing that these fortresses were potential centers of insurrection as well as strong points in England's defensive system, he allowed them to be built only by royal license. Finally, and still following Anglo-Saxon tradition, he took much of the fun out of feudalism by refusing to permit private war. The knights of England, like the soldiers of the Anglo-Saxon fyrd, were to serve the king alone.

Thus, Norman England was deeply influenced by the royal centralization achieved by the Anglo-Saxons; yet it was more cohesive under William the Conqueror than it had been in Anglo-Saxon times. In a very real sense, the Anglo-Norman monarchy was greater than the sum of its parts, for the English and Norman traditions on which it was built were strengthened and enlarged by the Conqueror himself. William's claim to ultimate ownership of all English land, which went far beyond the claims of any lord in feudal France, was equally unprecedented in England. It is far from certain that fiefs were normally regarded as hereditary under William the Conqueror; and even though they were usually passed on from father to son, the Norman kings denied their vassals the security of *legally* hereditary tenure by charging arbitrary and exceedingly high reliefs when the fief passed to an heir. In effect, these monarchs allowed a son to succeed his father only by royal sufferance, and at an exorbitant price.

Feudalism had arisen long before to meet the needs of a money-poor, intensely particularistic society. It was now adapted to a society ruled by a relatively strong monarchy—a society that enjoyed a vigorous commercial life and an expanding money economy. Thus, the feudalism of Norman England gave way increasingly, as time went on, before the steady growth of royal government and the progressive substitution of wage service for tenure service. The Conqueror himself had made good use of mercenary soldiers in his great invasion, and as the decades passed, mercenaries became steadily more important to the English military system. Furthermore, before the end of the eleventh century it was becoming customary for some tenants to pay money to the crown in lieu of feudal military obligation; and this military tax—known as scutage—was usually employed by the post-Conquest kings to pay the wages of mercenaries. With the development of scutage, the fundamental feudal obligation of knightly service was converted into a new source of royal revenue. The feudal structure persisted—the feudal aristocracy remained powerful throughout the Middle Ages—but the basic principle of tenure service was gradually dissolving.

The Administrative Contributions of William the Conqueror

With a vastly augmented royal demesne, with danegeld revenues flowing in regularly, and with a tight control over a loyal feudal aristocracy, William ruled England with unprecedented authority. And like his Anglo-Saxon predecessors, he ruled with the advice of a royal council. The council of the Norman kings—the *curia regis*—represents a drawing together of two parallel institutions: the ducal court of Normandy and the Anglo-Saxon Witenagemot. William's counselors are described in the *Anglo-Saxon Chronicle* as his Witan; like the Old English Witenagemot, the Anglo-Norman curia regis could be either the small and more or less permanent council of household officials and intimate friends or the larger and more formal council of great magnates. But it would be profitless to argue that the curia regis was more English than Norman. The councils of England and Normandy were similar, and William's large, formal councils, attended by the greater tenants-in-chief, were predominantly Norman in personnel and feudal in mood. They represent neither a violent break with the Anglo-Saxon past nor a conscious accommodation to it.

While on their numerous visits to Normandy, the Norman kings left the administration of England in the hands of some trusted subordinate who was necessarily empowered to act in the king's name. William the Conqueror delegated his authority to different men at different times—to loyal magnates, to some trustworthy household official, or to a powerful churchman such as Archbishop Lanfranc. In later reigns, this vice-regal authority came to be assigned permanently to a particular individual who, in the twelfth century, assumed the title *justiciar*. But the Conqueror, with his boundless energy, preferred to rule for himself or to delegate authority on an ad hoc basis. With the possible exception of Lanfranc, no one person shared William's authority for any significant time.

The power and vigor of English royal government under William the Conqueror, unmatched in Western Christendom, is illustrated vividly in William's greatest administrative achievement: the Domesday survey. As the *Anglo-Saxon Chronicle* describes it,

> the king had important deliberations and deep discussions with his council about this country, how it was peopled and with what sorts of men. Then he sent his men all over England into every shire and had them determine how many hundreds of hides there were in each shire, and how much land and cattle the king himself had in the country, and what annual dues he ought to have from each shire. He also had recorded how much land belonged to his archbishops, his bishops, his abbots, and his earls, and— though I relate it at too great length—what and how much everybody had who was a landholder in England, in land or in cattle, and how much money it was worth. So very thoroughly did he have it investigated that there was not a single hide or virgate [a quarter of a hide] of land, or even (it is shameful to record but it did not seem shameful to him to do) one ox or one cow or one pig which was omitted from his record; and all these records were afterwards brought to him.

The Domesday survey, later consolidated into two large volumes known as Domesday Book, would have challenged any modern government. For its age it was altogether unique. Although by no means free of errors and omissions (London and several other towns are left out), it is nevertheless an essentially trustworthy and immensely valuable historical source. It is organized by shires and, within each shire, by the estates of the royal demesne and the fiefs of royal vassals. Although cows and pigs were omitted from the final record, Domesday Book undertakes to list the name of every manor, its assessment in hides, its value both in 1066 and at the time of the survey (1086), and the number and social status of its tenants. Any social, economic, or institutional history of Saxon or Norman England must begin with this astonishing survey.

The Conqueror died in 1087. Injured while in the midst of a continental campaign, he was brought to Rouen, the chief city of Normandy; there he settled his affairs, made his last confession, and died. He had planned originally to leave England and Normandy to his eldest son, Robert Curthose ("Short-boots"). But Curthose had rebelled against his father and was, indeed, in rebellion at the time of the Conqueror's death. William would probably have left both England and Normandy to his second son, William Rufus ("red-faced"), but friends of Curthose persuaded the dying king to abide by the Norman custom of primogeniture and leave the Norman duchy to the eldest son despite his rebellion. Thus, reluctantly, William the Conqueror split his dominions, leaving Normandy to Robert Curthose and England to William Rufus—King William II. To his youngest son, Henry, the Conqueror granted a treasure of £5,000 (the equivalent of several million dollars today). The struggles of these three sons over the next two decades resulted finally, as we shall see, in the reunification of England and Normandy.

Of William the Conqueror's ability there can be no question; but judgments of his character have varied widely. He enforced justice and kept the peace, but he was avaricious and could be savagely cruel. A modern biographer describes him as "admirable; unlovable; dominant; distinct." [6] A similar ambivalence is to be found in the judgment of a well-placed contemporary observer—an Anglo-Saxon monk who had once lived at William's court:

> This King William of whom we speak was a very wise man, and very powerful and more worshipful and stronger than any king before him. He was gentle to those good men who loved God, but stern beyond all measure to those who resisted his will.... And he was such a stern and violent man that no one dared go against his will. Earls who resisted him he placed in chains, bishops he deprived of their sees, abbots of their abbacies, and thegns he imprisoned.... Among other things we must not forget the good order he kept in the land, so that an honest man could traverse his kingdom unharmed with his bosom full of gold. No one dared kill another, however much he had wronged him, and if any man raped a woman he was immediately castrated.
>
> He ruled over England and by his cunning it was so investigated that there was not one hide of land in England that he did not know who owned it, and what it was worth, and then set it down in his record.... Certainly in his time people had much oppression and very many injuries:
>
>> He had castles built
>> And poor men hard oppressed.
>> The king was very stark
>> And took from his subjects many a mark
>> Of gold and more hundreds of pounds of silver,
>> That he took by weight and with great injustice
>> From his people—with little need for such a deed.
>> Into avarice did he fall,
>> And loved greediness above all ...
>> Alas! Woe, that any man should go so proud,
>> And exalt himself and reckon himself above all men!
>> May almighty God show mercy on his soul,
>> And grant unto him forgiveness for his sins.
>
> These things we have written about him, both good and bad, that good men imitate his good points and entirely avoid the bad, and travel along the road that leads us to the kingdom of heaven.[7]

---

[6] D. C. Douglas, *William the Conqueror* (Berkeley, 1964), p. 376.
[7] From the *Anglo-Saxon Chronicle*, A.D. 1087.

Norman England: William II, Henry I, and Stephen

5 As the Conqueror lay dying at Rouen, William Rufus—William the Red-faced—left for England with his father's blessing. Through the good offices of Archbishop Lanfranc, he received the customary approval of a council of magnates and was crowned in Westminster Abbey on September 26, 1087.[1]

The Reign of William Rufus

William Rufus was even a greater puzzle than his father. The monk William of Malmesbury describes him as

> squarely built, with a reddish complexion and yellow hair, and open countenance and multi-colored eyes, varied with glittering specks—of astonishing strength, though not very tall, and his stomach stuck out.

Elsewhere, Malmesbury remarks,

> When he was in public, and in large assemblies, he wore a haughty look and darted his threatening eyes on those around him, and with pretended severity and fierce voice he would assail those who conversed with him. From fear of poverty and of the treachery of others, presumably, he was excessively devoted to money and to cruelty. In private, when he was

---

[1] For the period from William Rufus through John, see A. L. Poole, *From Domesday Book to Magna Carta* (2nd ed., Oxford, 1955). A comprehensive selection of sources in English translation is to be found in D. C. Douglas and G. W. Greenaway, tr., *English Historical Documents, 1042–1189* (London, 1953). The best of several fine medieval historians is William of Malmesbury, *History of the Kings of England* (J. A. Giles, tr., London, 1847).

dining with his intimate companions, he gave himself over to joking and mirth.

To illustrate Rufus' extravagance, Malmesbury tells of how he exploded in anger at a chamberlain for buying him a pair of boots worth only three shillings:

> "You son of a whore! Since when has the king worn such cheap boots? Go and bring me a pair worth a silver mark." The chamberlain went, and bringing the king a much cheaper pair than before, told him falsely that they cost as much as he had commanded. "Yes, indeed," said the king, "these suit the royal majesty!"

Rufus was said to have "feared God but little, man not at all." He scorned religion (except at such times as he feared imminent death), and he exploited the Church ruthlessly, demanding that prelates render him large gifts of money in order to retain the royal favor. Not surprisingly, Rufus earned a bad press among the monastic chroniclers. His itinerant court was described as a sort of traveling den of iniquity: the courtiers looted food, drink, and property from the people of the countryside through which they journeyed, took liberties with local wives and daughters, stole the goods of villagers (later selling them), got drunk on stolen liquor and, when they could drink no more, washed their horses with what was left or poured it onto the ground. Rufus' courtiers dressed in the height of fashion, with

> flowing hair and extravagant clothes; and a new kind of shoes was introduced, with points that curled upwards. Then the model for young men was to rival women in delicacy of person, to walk with mincing steps and loose gesture, half naked.... Troops of effeminate men and gangs of harlots followed the court.

On the other hand, even Rufus' enemies conceded that he was an excellent soldier and was as loyal to his trustworthy vassals and his knightly followers as he had earlier been to his father. Although remorseless in his financial exploitation of the English Church and people, he was generous to his military companions and prodigal in the wages and bounties he gave to his numerous mercenary knights. He demonstrated a deep moral commitment to the ancient Germanic notion of loyalty among men-at-arms.

Rufus' saving virtue was the strength of his iron rule. For by inspiring fear in his subjects and maintaining the devotion of his soldiers, he managed generally to keep peace in his land. The *Anglo-Saxon Chronicle* was perhaps biased when it branded Rufus as a man "hated by almost all his people and odious to God," but other writers of the period were scarcely more sympathetic. William of Malmesbury described him as a man much pitied by churchmen for losing a soul they could not save, beloved by the mercenary soldiers for his innumerable gifts, but unlamented by the people because he brought about the plundering of their property.

Rufus' reign had scarcely begun when, in 1088, he was faced with a rebellion of many of his barons in favor of Duke Robert Curthose of Normandy—a weaker, more amiable man than his royal brother. The rebels sought, through armed force, to reunite the Anglo-Norman state under Robert's genial rule. But Rufus kept the loyalty of the English Church, some of the barons, and the articulate classes of the English people. In view of the above appraisals of his character, it may well be wondered why the Church and the English stood by him. They did so for two reasons. First, the reign was young, and Rufus had yet to make his abhorrent impression. He won the English with lavish promises of just taxes and good government, which he did not keep. Second, the Church and the English consistently favored strong government, however harsh, over the terrible prospect of baronial anarchy. Accordingly, the English fyrd, the military tenants of the bishoprics and monasteries, and the remaining loyal barons rallied to Rufus' side and enabled him to crush the rebellion. A much smaller feudal insurrection in 1095 was suppressed in similar fashion, and thereafter Rufus reigned in peace.

As the Anglo-Saxon chronicler observed, Rufus, even more than his father, claimed ultimate control of all the English lands—"he claimed to be the heir of every man, cleric or lay." Accordingly, he denied the security of a normal succession to laymen and churchmen alike. A baronial heir could succeed to his father's estates only after paying, as a relief, whatever sum the king might demand—and Rufus' reliefs were notoriously high. He exploited the feudal privilege of vetoing the marriage of a vassal's widow or female heir by literally selling the hand of the noble lady to the highest bidder, or forcing her to pay him generously for the privilege of selecting a husband of her choice. He abused the right of wardship by taking possession of the estates of minor heirs and milking them dry before the heirs came of age. He behaved in much the same way toward church lands, keeping abbacies and bishoprics unfilled for scandalously long periods after the deaths of their former incumbents, in the meantime diverting their revenues into the royal treasury.

Indeed, he was not hesitant to deal in this manner even with the archbishopric of Canterbury itself. At Lanfranc's death in 1089, Rufus took the vast archiepiscopal lands into his own hands and left the archbishopric empty for some four years. It might well have remained vacant still longer had it not been that in 1093 Rufus suffered a near-fatal illness. Fearing death, he responded to the pressures of his lay and ecclesiastical subjects—pressures that had been building up ever since Lanfranc's death—and appointed to the archbishopric of Canterbury the saintly and scholarly Anselm, a distinguished Italian churchman who had spent many years in Normandy as monk, prior, and abbot of Bec.[2]

It is ironic that such an irreligious king should appoint such a notable

---

[2] R. W. Southern, *Saint Anselm and His Biographer: A Study of Monastic Life and Thought* (Cambridge, 1963), is a thoughtful, perceptive study.

archbishop. St. Anselm was not only a man of profound piety; he was the supreme intellectual of his age and perhaps the finest Christian philosopher since St. Augustine of Hippo. St. Anselm's philosophical and theological works constitute the initial achievement in the intellectual awakening of the High Middle Ages. As the first great scholastic philosopher, he stood at the beginning of a remarkable intellectual movement that culminated in the thirteenth century in the works of such men as St. Bonaventure and St. Thomas Aquinas.

We are concerned here not with Anselm the philosopher but with Anselm the ecclesiastical statesman. A man of integrity, sympathetic with the revolutionary notions of papal supremacy and ecclesiastical independence that had been pioneered by Pope Gregory VII, Anselm brought the Investiture Controversy to England. A man in his early sixties at the time of his appointment, he claimed to have accepted the archbishopric reluctantly, remarking that he was like a weak old sheep being yoked to an untamed bull. But as archbishop of Canterbury he was far from sheepish in his defense of the new reform ideology, and king and archbishop soon found themselves at odds on a multitude of issues. Anselm wished to go to Rome to receive the pallium—the symbol of his spiritual authority—from the reform pope, Urban II. Rufus refused to let him out of the kingdom and for a time refused to recognize the claims of Pope Urban over those of an antipope supported by the Holy Roman Emperor. At length, late in 1097, these and other difficulties forced Anselm to abandon the kingdom for exile in Italy and France, and Rufus resumed his control of the revenues of the see. Anselm returned to England early in the next reign, but for the time being the Norman monarchy was rid of its troublesome saint.

Rufus' ruthless financial exactions were carried out by a loyal subordinate and thoroughly unscrupulous churchman, Ranulf Flambard, whom the king had made first a royal chaplain and later bishop of Durham. Flambard was Rufus' man Friday. He was the ubiquitous agent of the royal administration whom Rufus employed for a variety of executive and legal tasks. He served as the king's regent in England when Rufus was overseas. His primary function, however, was the raising of revenues for the king, and he performed this task with such ingenuity that he was soon roundly hated. On one occasion he summoned the English fyrd to Hastings for service overseas, collected ten shillings from every soldier, and sent them directly home.

Rufus was a man of inordinate ambitions who needed every penny that Flambard could collect. Once secure in his kingdom he undertook to conquer Normandy; but his campaigns and machinations against Duke Robert Curthose met with only partial success. He brought portions of Normandy under his control but could not win it all. In 1096, however, Robert was seized with crusading fervor in response to Pope Urban's eloquent appeal to the warrior nobility of Western Christendom to drive the Muslims from the Holy Land. Having determined to participate in this First Crusade, Robert was hindered by a lack of money to support a worthy knightly retinue on the lengthy journey. Accordingly, a bargain was struck between the two brothers in 1096: Robert pawned Normandy to Rufus for three years in return for 10,000 marks of silver, which the king obtained by levying a double danegeld on his kingdom. Robert was enabled to go crusading well financed, and William Rufus had Normandy at last.

Rufus quickly transformed Robert's casually governed duchy into a centralized, tax-ridden state on the English pattern. He defended Normandy's frontiers and endeavored to expand them; and shortly before his death he seems to have been bargaining to receive Aquitaine in pawn from its crusade-bound duke. One contemporary writer suggests that Rufus even aspired to the throne of France.

But these schemes went unfulfilled. On August 2, 1100, Rufus was fatally wounded by an arrow while hunting in the New Forest—a vast royal hunting preserve in southern England that the Conqueror had established by cruelly evicting a number of peasants and imposing severe restrictions on those who remained. The New Forest had become a symbol of the Conqueror's tyranny, and it was regarded as fitting that his son should meet his death there.

The Reign of Henry I (1100–1135)

Rufus was in his early forties when he was killed. His abrupt death brought about a crisis in the royal succession. Since he had remained unmarried and left no children, the kingdom might well have passed to his elder brother, Robert Curthose. But Robert was only now returning from the Crusade, whereas the Conqueror's youngest son, Henry, was on the scene. Henry had been a member of Rufus' fatal hunting party; some historians have suggested that Rufus may have been deliberately murdered at Henry's instigation, but this is a wild guess, unsupported by evidence or by the slightest hint of fratricide in the contemporary sources.[3]

At Rufus' death, Henry moved swiftly and surely. He dashed to nearby Winchester, seized the royal treasure, won the approval of a rump royal council, and then hastened to London where he was crowned at Westminster Abbey on August 5, a mere three days after the shooting.[4] In preparation for Robert's return, Henry did everything in his power to win the

---

[3] See the entertaining but wrongheaded reconstruction of the event, *The Killing of William Rufus,* by Duncan Grinnell-Milne (Newton Abbott, Devon, 1968), which interprets the killing as a political murder plotted by Henry I. Still more unlikely is Margaret Murray's theory that it was a ritual slaying in accordance with the rites of witchcraft and done at Rufus' request (*God of the Witches,* London, 1951). The question is re-examined in C. W. Hollister, "The Strange Death of William Rufus," *Speculum,* XLVIII (1973):637–53.

[4] Henry's seizure of the throne is often described as an act of usurpation. But the custom of the eldest son succeeding was by no means a fixed rule at this time. It had occurred only rarely in England over the previous 250 years, and was directly violated in the successions of such kings as Alfred the Great and William Rufus.

support of his subjects. He sought to appease the barons and the Church by issuing an elaborate coronation charter, known in later years as the Charter of Liberties, in which he promised to discontinue the predatory practices of William Rufus. Among other things, Henry promised to

> neither sell nor put at farm nor, on the death of an archbishop, bishop, or abbot, take anything from a Church's demesne or from its vassals during the interval before a successor is installed. . . . If any of my barons or earls or other tenants shall die, his heir shall not redeem his land as he did in my brother's time, but shall henceforth redeem it by a just and lawful relief. . . . And if the wife of one of my tenants survives her husband . . . I will not give her in marriage unless she herself consents.

Henry did not keep these campaign promises. It has been estimated that they would have cost him four or five thousand pounds a year—perhaps a quarter of the total royal revenue under Rufus—and Henry was at least as money conscious as his predecessors. The coronation charter was neither a prelude to constitutional monarchy nor an open act of royal generosity, but simply one of several gambits that Henry employed to gain needed support in the oncoming crisis.

To win Anglo-Saxon and Scottish backing, the new king married a Scottish princess named Matilda, who happened to be a direct descendant of the Old English royal family. He courted popular opinion still further by imprisoning the detested Ranulf Flambard. But early in 1101, Flambard escaped from the Tower of London and crossed to Normandy to join Robert Curthose, who had now returned from a distinguished career on the First Crusade and was eager to wrest England from his younger brother. Alarmed by the growing threat, Henry sent letters into every shire confirming his coronation oath and requesting that all his free subjects swear to defend the land against all men and especially against Robert of Normandy.

In late July, 1101, Robert Curthose led a large force across the Channel to Portsmouth, where he was joined by many Anglo-Norman barons who longed for the reunion of the two lands and the easier rule of the Norman duke.[5] Meanwhile Henry had assembled a sizable army of his own, consisting chiefly of episcopal contingents, common knights, and a large force of native Englishmen. Some barons were present in the royal army, but the loyalty of many of them was uncertain. Henry seems to have placed great confidence in the English, and we are told that he took pains to instruct them in the techniques of fighting against mounted knights. One contemporary writer asserts that Henry's army would have quickly driven Robert's forces out of the country, but as it happened the issue was settled by negotiation. "The more discreet on each side"—evidently the barons—arranged a truce, realizing perhaps that a decisive royal victory would weaken their own posi-

---

5 On Robert Curthose see C. W. David, *Robert Curthose, Duke of Normandy* (Cambridge, Mass., 1920), a skillful work of technical scholarship.

tion. Henry, for his part, was happy to avoid the uncertainty of battle, and Curthose was obliged to settle for what he could get. The duke recognized Henry's royal title in return for an annuity of two thousand pounds (which Henry discontinued two years later).

With the settlement of 1101, the great crisis of the reign had passed, and Henry's throne was secure. One further rebellion, centering on the earldom of Shrewsbury on the Welsh frontier, was put down without great difficulty in 1102; thereafter Henry ruled England unchallenged until his death in 1135. Indeed, his vast confiscations of land in the wake of the 1101 and 1102 rebellions served as an invaluable source of royal revenue in the years to come.

Having secured England, Henry turned his attention to the conquest of Normandy. Paving his way with bribes to Norman barons, he campaigned in Normandy in 1104 and 1105. At length, on September 28, 1106, his army met Duke Robert's in open battle near the Norman castle of Tinchebray and won an overwhelming victory. Robert Curthose himself was captured and languished in prison until his death in 1134.

Contemporaries noted that the battle of Tinchebray was fought forty years to the day after William the Conqueror's landing at Pevensey Beach. By this "English conquest of Normandy," Henry became master of the duchy, reuniting the Anglo-Norman state the Conqueror had forged. Thenceforth Henry spent a good part of his time in Normandy. Occasionally he was obliged to defend the duchy against rebellion or invasions by the king of France and the count of Anjou. But for the most part, Normandy remained at peace under his firm rule.

By the time of Henry's victory at Tinchebray, another great crisis of his early years was nearing resolution. At the beginning of his reign Henry, in keeping with his conciliatory policy, had invited the exiled Archbishop Anselm to return to England. But Anselm's long exile had only served to sharpen his commitment to the papal campaign for a church free of secular control, and Henry and Anselm were soon at odds from the first. The king was willing to concede all the issues that had divided Anselm and Rufus, but Anselm raised new issues. Henry expected Anselm to render him the customary feudal homage for the Canterbury estates (which owed him sixty knights), but the archbishop—who had earlier rendered homage to Rufus— now took his stand on a recent papal ban against churchmen doing homage to laymen. Anselm also objected vigorously to the practice of lay investiture in England (which he had tolerated under Rufus). Neither party would relent, and at length, in 1103, Anselm returned to exile, and Henry confiscated the Canterbury revenues. But negotiations continued through the period of exile. They reached a crisis in 1105 when St. Anselm threatened Henry with excommunication during the king's Norman campaign against Curthose. The threat forced Henry to compromise, and after lengthy negotiations an agreement was ratified in 1107 between the king, the archbishop, and the pope. Henry agreed to relinquish lay investiture but was permitted, reluctantly, to continue receiving homage from his ecclesiastical tenants-in-chief. (Anselm himself, however, was never obliged to render homage to Henry I.) The English Church was never again quite so completely under royal control; but the king's authority over his churchmen remained substantial, and he was usually successful in controlling appointments. He had agreed to allow his clergy the privilege of free canonical elections; but free elections and strict royal management were by no means incompatible, as is demonstrated by a royal writ from King Henry II to the monks at Winchester in the later twelfth century: "I order you to hold a free election, but nevertheless I forbid you to elect anyone except Richard, my clerk, the archdeacon of Poitiers."

Henry I was a very different sort of king from William Rufus. He was quieter and more calculating and less given to explosions of anger—or of mirth. He was less reckless, less emotional, and considerably more intelligent. William of Malmesbury describes Henry in these words:

> He was taller than short men but shorter than tall ones. His hair was black and fell over his forehead; his eyes were sweetly serene, his chest muscular, his body fleshy. He was witty at appropriate times, nor did the press of business cause him to be any less genial when he mixed in company. Disinclined toward personal combat, he verified the saying of [the ancient Roman general] Scipio Africanus, "My mother bore me to be a general, not a common soldier." Thus he was second to no modern king in wisdom, and it might almost be said that he easily surpassed all his predecessors on the throne of England.... He was plain in diet ... never drank but to quench his thirst ... slept soundly and snored lustily; his speech was informal, not oratorical—easy-paced, not rapid.

Henry was, in short, altogether less flamboyant than Rufus. In one respect, however, he stands out among all kings of English history: insofar as the facts are known, he holds the record for illegitimate royal offspring, having sired more than twenty bastards. For this exploit, Henry has been severely reprimanded by a number of nineteenth- and twentieth-century historians; but the monastic writers of Henry's own time, thankful for his peace and strong government, did not hold his bastards against him. Indeed, William of Malmesbury sprang to Henry's support with this ingenious defense:

> He was free, during his whole life, of all lewd desires, for—as we have learned from those who know—he lay with women not for the gratification of lust, but for the sake of issue; nor did he give in to amorous delights except when he could effectively send forth the royal seed. Thus he was the master of his passions, not the passive slave of lust.

Another contemporary monk, Orderic Vitalis, describes Henry simply as "the glorious father of his country."

Despite Henry's reconciliation with Anselm, his reign was not, on the whole, a great age of Christian reform. In view of his personal life, he could hardly have been a dedicated proponent of clerical celibacy. He did agree to the official prohibition of clerical marriage but was lax in enforcing it. On more than one occasion, he simply assessed moderate fines against married clergy, as a device to increase royal revenues. Henry's most powerful and trusted administrator, Roger, Bishop of Salisbury, made no secret of his mistress; and Roger's nephew Nigel, Bishop of Ely, had a wife. Among Henry I's other bishops known to have had either wives or children (or both) are the bishops of Worcester, Lincoln, Chester, London, and two successive bishops of Durham, the second of whom served for a decade as Henry's chancellor. Moreover, Henry often kept bishoprics and abbacies unfilled for years at a time in order to enjoy their revenues—though in this regard he was less culpable than Rufus. When Archbishop Anselm died in 1109, Henry kept see of Canterbury vacant for five years.

If the reign of Henry I is not noted for ecclesiastical reform, it is exceedingly significant from the standpoint of royal administration. Henry was known as the Lion of Justice, and although this title is not altogether in keeping with other facets of his behavior, nevertheless his rule was firm and, when his interests were not involved, just. He was not a kindly or easy man. His defense of the Anglo-Norman state required a flow of revenue for building castles, bribing barons and neighboring feudal princes, and hiring mercenaries to curb rebellion and defend the frontiers. Henry and his ministers exploited the wealth of England to the fullest, although with more discretion and less gusto than had been customary in Rufus' reign. Henry's severity is a recurring theme in the *Anglo-Saxon Chronicle:*

> 1104. . . . It is not easy to describe the miseries this land was suffering at the time because of various and different injustices and taxes that never ceased or diminished. . . .

> 1110. . . . This was a very severe year in this land because of the taxes that the king collected for the marriage of his daughter.

> 1116. . . . This land and people were also this year often severely oppressed by the taxes which the king collected both in and out of the boroughs.

> 1118. . . . England paid dearly . . . because of the various taxes that never ceased during the course of all this year.

> 1124. . . . It was a very troublous year; the man who had any property was deprived of it by harsh taxes and harsh judgments at court; the man who had none died of hunger. etc. etc.[6]

The customary laws of Henry's time were harsh, and on occasion Henry could enforce them without pity. In 1125, discovering that his minters were producing adulterated coinage, the king had them castrated and deprived of their right hands. Yet, paradoxically, the *Anglo-Saxon Chronicle* observed of

---

[6] Apart from 1110, these years of exceptional taxation are also, and by no coincidence, years of major military campaigning in Normandy.

Henry on his death, "He was a good man, and people were in great awe of him. No one dared injure another in his time." In short, despite his severity —or perhaps because of it—he enforced justice and kept the peace. And justice could be lucrative to an English monarch. Judicial fines added to the royal revenue, and by extending the scope of the king's justice, Henry was increasing the flow of money into his treasury. But more important, effective royal enforcement increased the king's authority over his realm and contributed to the general peace by discouraging crime and encouraging the peaceful settlement of private disputes.

Henry's reign witnessed a significant growth in the royal judicial system and the royal administration. While local justices were appointed in each shire to assist the sheriffs in judicial business, the most important legal cases were judged by the king and his great men at the royal court. Since it was often difficult for suitors to get to court (which was always on the move), the practice gradually developed of sending royal justices to various parts of England to hear pleas. These itinerant justices, or justices in eyre, acted in the king's name. By hearing important cases in the shires, they greatly enlarged the scope of the king's justice, often diverting cases from the baronial courts or dealing with pleas that otherwise might not have been heard at all. When one of Henry's itinerant justices was present, the shire court was transformed temporarily into a royal court; and ordinary country people were for the first time brought face to face with the judicial authority of the crown. During the reign of Henry I the judicial tours seem to have been spotty and unsystematic; but they were a vital beginning of what would become, by the later twelfth century, a comprehensive, regularized practice.

Henry's chief instrument of command over the considerable areas he ruled was the royal writ. We have already traced the origin of the writ to Anglo-Saxon times in Chapter 3; under the Norman kings it was employed much more commonly than before. It was a brief royal command or statement, written in Latin on a strip of parchment, witnessed, and authenticated by the attachment of the royal seal. Ordinarily a writ would be addressed to the local sheriff, or to the baronial or ecclesiastical lord of an area, or to all the king's officials and faithful men of a particular shire or group of shires:

> Henry king of the English to Hugh of Bocland and Robert of Ferrers and William sheriff of Oxford and Nicholas of Stafford, greeting. I order that you justly and immediately cause all fugitives of the abbey of Abingdon to return there with all their goods, wherever they are, so that I may hear no further complaint on the matter for lack of right; and in particular, restore to Abingdon the man who is on the land of Robert of Ferrers, and with all his goods. Witness: Robert fitz Richard. [issued] At Wallingford.

Some 1500 such writs have survived from Henry I's reign (as compared with about 300 from William the Conqueror's), and we can be certain that those that have survived constitute only a small fraction of the original total pouring out of Henry's chancery. They deal with an immense variety of judicial and administrative matters: grants or confirmations of lands and privileges, orders of restitution, commands to act in some way or to cease acting in some way, exemptions from certain taxes, or freedom from tolls. Taken together, they convey a powerful impression of the scope and authority of royal government under Henry I. England had never before been so thoroughly administered. There were some who complained about the emergence of big government. But for most, Henry's administration was a welcome contrast to the conditions of civil strife and local violence and thuggery that characterized most of Europe in the early twelfth century.

When Henry traveled to Normandy he left a regent in England to hear important legal cases, issue writs, and head the administration. During the first half of the reign his English regent was usually Queen Matilda, assisted by such seasoned administrators as Roger, Bishop of Salisbury. After Matilda's death in 1118, Roger of Salisbury himself acted as regent in Henry's absence—as a kind of English viceroy.[7] Roger was one of medieval England's most gifted administrators, and even when Henry was in England he dominated the royal administration. Roger had no official administrative title, but similar viceroys-administrators of later reigns were called "chief justiciars." Bishop Roger's main responsibilities seem to have been in the area of the royal finances, and it was probably he, more than anyone else, who forged the powerful instrument of fiscal accounting known as the exchequer.

In later generations the exchequer became an important department of state. In the beginning, however, under Henry I, it was not a department, but a twice-yearly audit of the royal income from the shires. All the sheriffs of England were required to come to the treasury at Winchester to report their revenues to a group of auditors. Some of these auditors were officials from the Winchester treasury; others were trusted barons from the king's court. The audit was usually presided over by Roger of Salisbury himself. The term *exchequer* is derived from the table around which the auditors worked. On the table was a checkered cloth, resembling a checkerboard, divided into columns representing various denominations of money. Markers were placed on these columns to represent the accounts of sheriffs who reported in. The method of accounting was based on the principle of the abacus and the decimal system of arithmetic, which had only recently been introduced from the Islamic world. The exchequer accounts were recorded on long rolls of parchment known as pipe rolls—now precious historical sources. Unfortunately, only one of Henry's pipe rolls has survived (from 1130), but we have a continuous set of these annual records from 1156 on.

The exchequer served as an important control of the activities of the

---

[7] Conversely, when Henry was in England, his Norman administration was governed by one or more Norman regents—usually a royal steward and an administrator-bishop.

king's sheriffs. These royal agents were by no means faceless professionals in the Anglo-Norman period. Only a person of wealth and stature could protect the royal interests in the turbulent countryside of early feudal England, and the sheriffs were normally recruited from the ranks of the high Anglo-Norman nobility. Indeed, many sheriffs seem to have grown too powerful for the king's good; often they abused their positions to enrich themselves and their families and sought to make their positions hereditary. The exchequer audits restrained them to a degree, but Henry I was obliged to take further measures to insure his control over his local officials. Old sheriffs were deposed and new ones appointed from among the king's own trusted subordinates. The new sheriffs were often men from obscure families of the smaller landholding class, men who had risen in the royal service and hoped to rise still further, who attached their hopes—and their unswerving loyalty —to the crown. Not uncommonly, such a man might be given shrieval authority over a large block of counties, thus extending his own power while simplifying royal governance.

Henry I's reign marks the coming of age of the royal administration; some historians have seen it as the beginning of the modern state. The functions of the royal household officials were growing in importance and degree of specialization. The exchequer provided Henry with the first remotely modern accounting office known to the medieval West. And the tightly controlled sheriffs and itinerant justices were forging the essential links between the royal administration and the countryside. Northern Europe had known no such coherent administrative machinery since Roman times, and no northern monarch was as wealthy as Henry I. For Henry had discovered that a positive relationship existed between the efficiency of his administration and the size of his revenues. He was fully alive to the fact that strong government was good business. And, conversely, he well understood that a king could not be strong if his treasury was empty.

Henry's regime contained many nonfeudal elements, and his powerful administration limited the scope of his feudal aristocrats. Still, Henry cannot be described as an antifeudal king. The disasters of the later reign of King John should be sufficient to convince anyone that a medieval English monarch could not succeed without support from his barons. And Henry proved himself adroit in winning the allegiance of a number of English nobles through a kind of patronage system. For those who demonstrated their loyalty and won his favor, he provided tantalizing opportunities to advance their careers and fortunes in the royal service. Such men were given an inside advantage in acquiring forfeited lands, wealthy wives, lucrative wardships, danegeld exemptions, shrievalties, and the various other spoils at the crown's disposal. In this way, great baronial families flourished if they were loyal to the king, while a number of lesser aristocrats rose to high position, and men of still lower station ascended into the prosperous middle levels of the aristocracy. To be sure, these royal favorites had to pay the king for every privilege he gave them—in Henry's government nothing was cheap—

and they seldom rose to high position overnight. Nevertheless, they were fully aware that they owed their success to the king's favor and that their future service in his behalf would continue to be rewarded. Through his astute use of patronage, Henry created a royalist core in the aristocracy. Royal patronage was to be a central and enduring element in English politics and society for many centuries thereafter; under Henry I it made its first appearance as a fully articulated system.

Henry's government was complex, sophisticated, and to a degree impersonal; yet it depended ultimately on the existence of a strong, fear-inspiring king. Accordingly, Henry devoted much attention to the problem of the royal succession. Although he had a score of illegitimate offspring, he produced only two legitimate heirs: a daughter named Matilda and a younger son named William, who was carefully groomed for the throne. It is the supreme tragedy of Henry's reign that William was killed on the eve of his manhood, in 1120, by the sinking of a vessel that was carrying the prince and a distinguished but intoxicated party of aristocratic associates from Normandy to England. This catastrophe, known as the disaster of the White Ship, threw the royal succession into a state of chaos. Henry, whose first wife had died, promptly remarried, but the second marriage was childless. Finally, in 1127, Henry secured oaths from his barons to accept his daughter Matilda as the royal heir.

Matilda had earlier been married, at the age of eleven, to the Holy Roman Emperor Henry V, but by 1127 she was a widow. Having secured the pledges of his barons, Henry arranged a fateful marriage between Matilda and Count Geoffrey of Anjou. This was a bold stroke of policy, for it promised to end the long struggle between Normandy and Anjou for hegemony in northern France; but it also gave rise to a myriad of problems. For one thing, some of the Anglo-Norman barons were doubtless uneasy over the prospect of being ruled by a woman, and particularly by a woman of Matilda's fiery personality. For another, Matilda and Geoffrey were poor mates. Matilda was a widow of twenty-five, whereas Geoffrey was a boy of about fifteen. Their personalities clashed, and after a year of marriage they separated and Matilda returned to her father in England. At length, however, Geoffrey and Matilda were reconciled, and in 1133 Matilda bore her husband a son, the future King Henry II. For a brief time Henry I relaxed, enjoying the pleasures of being a grandfather and the security of having obtained a male heir at last. But Matilda, now reconciled with her husband, drew Geoffrey into a quarrel with her father. Matilda claimed a number of castles as her promised dowry; Henry refused to yield them, and in mid-1135 a small-scale frontier war broke out. Henry's armies triumphed once again, but in December the old king—now in his late sixties—died of acute indigestion. He was at odds with Matilda at the time of his death, and the succession was thereby thrown into confusion. Henry's peace died with him, and Matilda's untimely quarrel with her father cost her the English crown.

The reign of Henry I was long and significant. He had reunited the

HENRY I'S BAD DREAMS

In A.D. 1130, Henry I was said to have had three nightmares in a single
night. In the first, angry peasants threatened him with their tools; in the
second, knights approached him with their weapons; in the third,
churchmen attacked him with the points of their staves. Such dreams
were the psychological penalty for the building of a powerful centralized
government with a ruthlessly efficient system of taxation. *President and
Fellows of Corpus Christi College, Oxford.*

Anglo-Norman state, kept the peace in England, successfully defended his far-flung frontiers, and instituted notable administrative advances. A perceptive modern scholar speaks of the reign in these words: "Looking to the future, it is here, we feel, that the history of England begins—a history which is neither that of the Norman conquerors, nor that of the Anglo-Saxons, but a new creation." [8]

The Reign of King Stephen (1135–1154)

When Henry I died, his grandson was a child of two whose ambitions did not yet extend to duchies and kingdoms. The English barons had sworn to accept Matilda, but their enthusiasm was dimmed by the fact that they had been fighting on Henry's side against her in 1135. Hence, the great English landholder Stephen of Blois, a son of the Conqueror's daughter and a nephew of Henry I, acting with the same dispatch that Henry himself had demonstrated in 1100, was able to seize the throne. Matilda had perhaps the better hereditary claim, but hereditary right was not everything in the making of an English king. Indeed, it had been nearly a century since an English

---

[8] R. W. Southern, "The Place of Henry I in English History," *Proceedings of the British Academy*, XLVIII (1962), 128–29.

The Norman Kings

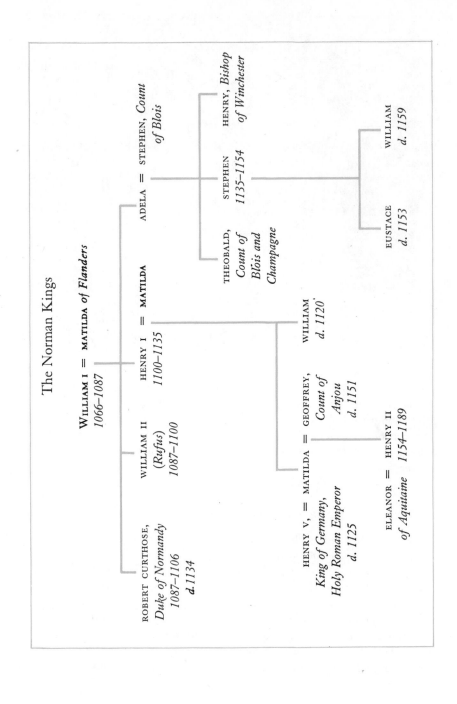

WILLIAM I = MATILDA *of Flanders*
1066–1087

ROBERT CURTHOSE,
Duke of Normandy
1087–1106
d.1134

WILLIAM II
(*Rufus*)
1087–1100

HENRY I = MATILDA
1100–1135

ADELA = STEPHEN, *Count*
of Blois

THEOBALD,
Count of
Blois and
Champagne

STEPHEN,
1135–1154

HENRY, *Bishop*
of Winchester

WILLIAM
d. 1120

HENRY V, = MATILDA = GEOFFREY,
King of Germany,
Holy Roman Emperor
d. 1125

Count of
Anjou
d. 1151

ELEANOR = HENRY II
of Aquitaine   *1154–1189*

EUSTACE
d. 1153

WILLIAM
d. 1159

monarch had been succeeded by his eldest offspring, and the claims of all the Norman kings thus far had been clouded.[9]

Stephen had long been a loyal follower of Henry, and Henry had showered him with lands and privileges. At Henry's death, only one other Anglo-Norman landholder could compete in wealth with Stephen of Blois. That person was Earl Robert of Gloucester, King Henry's favorite bastard son.

Stephen was the most genial and least competent of the Norman kings. Erratic and lacking in firmness, he was in many respects Henry's opposite. In the words of the *Anglo-Saxon Chronicle,* "he was a mild man, and gentle and good, and did no justice." During the first two years of his reign he squandered Henry's treasure on lavish bribes and wages for mercenaries, and managed more or less to keep the peace. In 1138, however, Count Geoffrey of Anjou attacked Normandy, Earl Robert of Gloucester rebelled in favor of his half-sister Matilda, and the king of Scots (Matilda's uncle) took up her cause by invading England. Stephen succeeded in defending himself against these threats only to be faced with an invasion by Matilda herself. The next decade witnessed a seesaw battle between Stephen and Matilda, accompanied by a general state of baronial anarchy. The warfare and turbulence of these years was by no means universal—it was limited to particular areas and particular times—but it was terrifying nonetheless and left a deep impression on contemporaries. The twelfth-century historian Henry of Huntingdon, commenting on the horrors of Stephen's reign, remarks that "whatever King Henry had done, whether in the manner of a tyrant or that of a true king, appeared most excellent in comparison."

Perhaps the most vivid descriptions of the anarchy are to be found in the *Anglo-Saxon Chronicle.* While the chronicler's picture of general and total chaos is doubtless exaggerated, his specific impressions are probably authentic:

> Every powerful man built his castles and held them against the king, and they filled the country full of castles. They oppressed the wretched people of the country severely with their castle building. When the castles were built they filled them with devils and wicked men. Then both by night and day they took those people that they thought had any goods, men and women alike, and put them in prison and tortured them with indescribable tortures to extort gold and silver from them—for no martyrs were ever so tortured as they were. They were hung by the thumbs or by the head, and armor was hung on their feet. Knotted ropes were placed around their heads and twisted until they penetrated to the brains. They put them in prisons where there were adders and snakes and toads, and killed them in that way.... Many thousands they killed by starvation.

I have neither the ability nor the power to tell all the horrors and all the

---

[9] R. H. C. Davis, *King Stephen* (Berkeley, 1967), and H. A. Cronne, *The Reign of Stephen* (London, 1970) are both excellent modern studies.

torments that they inflicted on the wretched people of this land. And all this lasted the whole nineteen years while Stephen was king, and it was always going from bad to worse. They levied taxes on the villages at intervals, and called it "protection money." When the wretched people had no more to give, they robbed and burned the villages, so that you could easily go a whole day's journey and find nobody occupying any village, nor any land tilled. . . . Some lived by begging, who had once been rich, and others fled the country. . . .

They respected neither church nor churchyard, but took all the property that was inside, and then they burned the church and everything together. Nor did they respect bishops' lands nor abbots' nor priests', but robbed monks and clerics, and everyone robbed somebody else if he had the greater power. If two or three men came riding to a village, all the villagers fled from them; they expected that they would be robbers. The bishops and learned men were always excommunicating them, but they thought nothing of it, because they were all utterly accursed and perjured and doomed to perdition.

Wherever cultivation was done, the ground produced no grain, because the land was all ruined by such doings. And they said openly that Christ and his saints slept.

At length, the dynastic struggle settled into an uneasy truce. In 1148 Matilda retired from England in defeat; but in the meantime her husband, Count Geoffrey, had conquered Normandy. The two contending parties were separated by the English Channel, and baronial unrest diminished in England.

But now Henry I's grandson, Henry of Anjou (or Henry Plantagenet), was approaching manhood and was preparing to undertake an energetic struggle to make good his inherited claims. County Geoffrey died in 1151, and two years later the young Henry—Count of Anjou and Duke of Normandy—invaded England.

This ambitious young man of nineteen was already the greatest feudal magnate in France. In addition to Normandy and Anjou and their satellite provinces, Henry Plantagenet had won the extensive duchy of Aquitaine in southern France by marrying its vivacious heiress, Eleanor.[10] He came to England as a man of great substance and significant resources, and as duke of Normandy he was in a position to terrify the English barons by threatening to confiscate their Norman fiefs. Henry's campaign in England progressed with middling success, but Stephen resisted doggedly—not so much for himself now as for his son and chosen successor, Eustace. At Eustace's sudden death in August 1153, Stephen lost his spirit and submitted to the

---

[10] Eleanor of Aquitaine had recently divorced King Louis VII of France. Amy Kelly, *Eleanor of Aquitane and the Four Kings* (Cambridge, Mass., 1950, paperback edition, 1959), is a highly readable account of her career and her relationships with her two husbands, Louis VII and Henry II, and her two royal sons, Richard the Lion-Hearted and John.

growing sentiment for compromise. He and Henry entered into an agreement known as the Treaty of Westminster. Stephen was to rule England unmolested until his death, but was to make Henry Plantagenet his heir. Baronial partisans on both sides were guaranteed their lands and were promised immunity from punishment. England was to return at last to a state of peace. Nine months after the Treaty of Westminster King Stephen died, and Henry Plantagenet acceded unopposed to the English throne as King Henry II. With his coronation the Norman age of English history comes to an end, and the Angevin age begins.[11]

The troubled reign of Stephen is traditionally described as an epoch of feudal anarchy, a reaction against the strong government of Henry I, and an age when a good but pliable king was exploited unmercifully by greedy barons. As a result of recent research this interpretation requires modification. For one thing, Stephen was not so openhearted or simpleminded as he has sometimes been described. He was a cheerful man, by and large, but he could also be sly and treacherous. In particular, he had a habit of arresting his barons and administrators by surprise and without good cause. His arrest of Henry I's great administrator Roger of Salisbury in 1139, together with Roger's son and two nephews, made a shambles of the royal administrative machinery. His peremptory arrests of two of England's most powerful barons, Geoffrey de Mandeville and Earl Ranulf of Chester, prompted both of them, once released, to revolt against their king.

Many barons had grievances, not only against Stephen but against the whole Anglo-Norman tradition of centralized royal government. Throughout the Norman age hereditary feudal tenure had been persistently compromised by the royal doctrine of ultimate ownership, a doctrine that had been manifested repeatedly in arbitrary and excessive reliefs, royal abuse of the feudal rights of wardship and marriage, and widespread forfeitures. By Stephen's time a vast number of disputes had arisen over rights to land, and very often two contending claimants to a particular fief would be found fighting on opposite sides in the struggle between Stephen and Matilda. There was evidently a deep desire on the part of the feudal aristocrats to make their precarious holdings secure and to win the unquestioned right to hereditary succession on their own fiefs.

The Treaty of Westminster and the subsequent accession of Henry II constitute a victory for the hereditary principle both on the royal and the baronial level. Henry succeeded in part by the approval of the council, in part by the designation of his predecessor—as kings had done over the past century—but above all, and unlike the Norman kings, he succeeded by

---

11 The Angevin dynasty (1154–1399) is so called because Henry II and his successors were descendants in the male line of Count Geoffrey of Anjou. From about the fifteenth century onward the Angevin kings were often termed the "Plantagenets" after the broom flower native to Anjou—the *plante genêt*—which Count Geoffrey used as his emblem.

hereditary right, as eldest grandson of Henry I. And from that day to this with very few exceptions, hereditary right based on primogeniture has governed the succession of English monarchs.

It has also governed the inheritance of English lands. Henry II and his successors recognized fully the right of an eldest son to succeed to his father's estates. Forfeitures to the crown became rare—only three are recorded in the half century following Henry's coronation. Stephen's own younger son was permitted to keep his extensive estates, and most of the earlier baronial land disputes were settled by compromise. Thus Henry II's succession marks a vital stage in the development of feudal land tenure. In the words of one modern scholar, Stephen's magnates "demanded that the King should recognize their hereditary right in specific and unambiguous terms. . . . That is what the barons fought for in Stephen's reign, and that is what they won." [12]

---

[12] R. H. C. Davis, "What Happened in Stephen's Reign, 1135–54," *History,* 49 (1964): 12.

The Age of Henry II

Henry II reigned for thirty-five years (1154–1189), almost exactly as long as his grandfather, Henry I.[1] The two reigns are similar in many other respects, for Henry II undertook quite deliberately to revive Henry I's policies and strove to rule in his imperious tradition. Yet the new king was a vibrant personality in his own right. His contemporaries regarded him as a fear-inspiring, peacekeeping monarch—mercurial, lecherous, always on the move, and altogether overwhelming in personality. One writer of the time described him as

> a man of reddish, freckled complexion, with a large, round head, grey eyes that glowed fiercely and grew bloodshot in anger, a fiery countenance and a harsh, cracked voice. His neck was poked forward slightly from his shoulders, his chest was broad and square, his arms strong and powerful. His body was stocky, with a pronounced tendency toward fatness, due to nature rather than self-indulgence—which he tempered with exercise.

Henry was astonishingly energetic. At the end of a hard day he would refuse to sit down, before or after dinner, but instead would "wear out the whole court by continually standing." The scholar Peter of Blois, who spent some time at Henry's traveling court, describes it as a scene of fantastic confusion. Henry I had planned his itineraries carefully, but Henry II's movements through the countryside seemed to depend on no prearranged schedule but on the royal whim. "If the king promises to spend the whole day somewhere," Peter of Blois complained, "you can be sure that he will leave the place bright and early, and upset everyone's plans in his haste." Then everybody will be "rushing madly about, urging on the pack-horses, hitching the teams to their wagons, everyone in total

---

[1] The best biography of Henry is W. L. Warren, *Henry II* (Berkeley, 1973).

confusion—a perfect portrait of hell. . . . And I believe our plight added to the king's pleasure." The harassed scholar eventually elected to resign from the royal entourage: "I shall dedicate the remainder of my days," he concludes, "to study and peace."

But Peter of Blois' portrayal of a vast yet directionless royal effort is surely exaggerated. Henry knew where he was going, even if his followers did not. And it is significant that a scholar of Peter of Blois' sort should be in the royal household at all. Henry II was the best educated English king since the Norman Conquest, and he delighted in associating with scholars and patronizing their works. As Peter of Blois himself said of Henry, "Whenever he can get breathing space in the midst of his business cares, he occupies himself with private readings or endeavors to work out some difficult intellectual problem with his learned clerics. . . . With the king of England it is school every day, constant conversation among the best of scholars, and discussion of problems."

EFFIGY OF HENRY II IN FONTEVRAULT ABBEY, ANJOU, FRANCE
The figure is highly idealized and shows Henry as a much younger man than he was at the time of his death. *Caisse Nationale des Monuments Historiques, Paris.*

Twelfth-Century Civilization

In this respect, as in others, Henry II was a child of his times. The twelfth century had witnessed an impressive intellectual revival, in England as elsewhere in Western Christendom. The University of Oxford was in the process of formation and was destined to develop within a century into one of Europe's most distinguished intellectual centers. Archbishop Theobald of Canterbury, whose archiepiscopate (1139–1161) spanned the reigns of Stephen and Henry II, became the head of an important scholarly circle at Canterbury; it included for a time such notable figures as the great twelfth-century English humanist, John of Salisbury, and the future archbishop, St. Thomas Becket. The English historian William of Malmesbury, writing in the first half of the twelfth century, practiced his craft with an elegance and insight almost worthy of Bede, and the historical works of William of Newburgh in the next generation are no less impressive. Nor were these historians isolated figures. Others scarcely less talented were writing at the same time.

The twelfth-century revival of historical writing was accompanied by a resurgence of philosophical and scientific thought. Adelard of Bath, a younger contemporary of Henry I, was a pioneer in bringing the Greco-Arabic scientific tradition into Western Europe. A great traveler, Adelard came into contact with Greek and Islamic science. He introduced several works of major importance to Western Christendom by translating them into Latin—Euclid's *Elements,* for example—and also wrote important scientific treatises of his own. There is evidence suggesting that Adelard may have participated for a time in Henry I's administration; he wrote an important treatise on the abacus, and may possibly have been associated with the early development of the English exchequer. Adelard was by no means the only Western scholar of his age with keen scientific interests, nor even the only Englishman working in the fields of mathematics and science. He and others like him represent the genesis of the rich scientific tradition of medieval England which culminated in the works of Robert Grosseteste in the thirteenth century and William of Ockham and Thomas Bradwardine in the fourteenth.

The revival of intellectual creativity was one of the essential factors underlying Henry II's fruitful reign. Another factor of equal importance was the growth of towns and commerce. Town life, centering on the supervised town market, was still rustic and parochial by later standards, but it was growing steadily more vigorous, and money was becoming more and more abundant. Increasingly, town government was dominated by merchant guilds or by market guilds—those within and without the town who were privileged to sell goods in its market. Towns such as Bristol, Newcastle, Northampton, and, above all, London were becoming significant commercial centers. The monarchy, recognizing their importance, granted them charters containing valuable privileges, such as the right to operate a borough court, freedom from taxes and tolls, and various commercial monopolies. Henry I had granted his Londoners the privilege of appointing their own sheriff, and by the early thirteenth century they were allowed to elect their own mayor —which they have been doing ever since. In general, English burghers (townsmen) were recognized as a class apart, free of the obligations and tenurial complexities of feudalism: "A burgher can give or sell his land as he pleases and go where he wishes, freely and undisturbed." [2]

London under Henry II was becoming one of Western Europe's great commercial centers. The contemporary writer William fitz Stephen describes it in language that would rouse the envy of a modern chamber of commerce:

> Among the noble and celebrated cities of the world, London, the capital of the kingdom of the English, is one that extends its glory farther than all others, and sends its wealth and merchandise more widely into far distant lands. It lifts its head higher than all the rest. It is fortunate in the healthiness of its air,[3] in its observance of Christian practice, in the strength of its fortifications, in its natural situation, in the honor of its citizens, and in the modesty of its matrons. It is cheerful in its sports, and the fruitful mother of noble men. . . .

> It has on the east the Palatine castle [the Tower of London], very great and strong. The keep and walls rise from very deep foundations and are fixed with a mortar tempered by the blood of animals. On the west there are two castles very strongly fortified, and from these there runs a high and massive wall with seven double gates and with towers along the north at regular intervals. London was once also walled and turreted on the south, but the mighty River Thames, so full of fish, has with the sea's ebb and flow washed against, loosened, and thrown down those walls in the course of time. Upstream to the west there is the royal palace [Westminster Palace, built by William Rufus, and still standing] which is conspicuous above the river, a building incomparable in its ramparts and bulwarks. It is about two miles from the city and joined to it by a populous suburb. . . .

> Those engaged in business of various kinds, sellers of merchandise, hirers of labor, are distributed every morning into their several localities according to their trade. Besides, there is in London on the river bank, among the wines for sale in ships and in the cellars of the vintners, a public cook shop. There daily you may find food according to the season, dishes of meat, roast, fried and boiled, large and small fish, coarser meats for the poor and more delicate for the rich, such as venison and big and small birds. . . .

> To this city from every nation under heaven merchants delight to bring their trade by sea. The Arabian sends gold; the Sabaean spice and incense. The Scythian brings arms, and from the rich, fat lands of Babylon come oil of palms. The Nile sends precious stones; the men of Norway and Russia, furs and sables; nor is China absent with purple silk. The French come with their wines.

---

2 From the customs of Newcastle at the time of Henry I.
3 Actually, London had a smog problem even in the twelfth century.

William fitz Stephen goes on to describe the entertainments and sports of the metropolis: religious plays showing the miracles of saints and martyrs; the festivities of the annual Carnival Day—cock fights, and ballplaying in the fields outside the city, with teams representing various London schools and guilds competing with one another. "On feast days throughout the summer the young men indulge in the sports of archery, running, jumping, wrestling, slinging the stone, hurling the javelin beyond a mark and fighting with sword and buckler." And in winter

> swarms of young men issue forth to play games on the ice. Some, gaining speed in their run, with feet set well apart, slide sideways over a vast expanse of ice. Others make seats out of a large lump of ice, and while one sits on it, others with linked hands run before and drag him along behind them. So swift is their sliding motion that sometimes their feet slip, and they all fall on their faces. Others, more skilled at winter sports, put on their feet the shin-bones of animals, binding them firmly around their ankles, and, holding poles shod with iron in their hands, which they strike from time to time against the ice, they are propelled as swiftly as a bird in flight.[4]

Not everyone found London so delightful. The chronicler Richard of Devizes quoted a French merchant as giving this advice to a friend who was about to visit England:

> If you come to London, pass through it quickly.... Whatever evil or malicious thing that can be found anywhere on earth you will find in that one city. Do not associate with the crowds of pimps; do not mingle with the throngs in eating houses; avoid dice and gambling, the theater and the tavern. You will meet with more braggarts there than in all France; The number of parasites is infinite. Actors, jesters, smooth-skinned lads, Moors, flatterers, pretty boys, effeminates, pederasts, singing and dancing girls, quacks, belly dancers, sorceresses, extortioners, night wanderers, magicians, mimes, beggars, buffoons: all this tribe fill all the houses. Therefore, if you do not want to dwell with evildoers, do not live in London.[5]

The life of the peasant in the twelfth century remained grim by modern standards. A year or two of drought, cattle plague, or excessively heavy rains could bring on widespread starvation. In 1125, for example, the *Anglo-Saxon Chronicle* reports that "many villages were flooded and many people drowned, and bridges collapsed, and grain and meadows utterly ruined, and famine and disease among men and cattle. And there was more bad weather for all crops than there had been for many a year."

---

4 The description is translated in full in *English Historical Documents*, II:956–62.
5 *The Chronicle of Richard of Devizes*, John T. Appleby, ed. (London, 1963), pp. 65–66. Other English cities fare almost as badly in Richard of Devizes' pages: At Bristol "there is nobody who is not or has not been a soap maker." York "is full of Scotsmen, filthy and treacherous creatures—scarcely men." Exeter "refreshes both men and beasts with the same fodder." Bath, lying amidst "exceedingly heavy air and sulphureous vapor, is at the gates of hell." "Ely stinks perpetually from the surrounding fens."

Even so, conditions were gradually improving. Agrarian slaves, who still survived as a small but distinct minority at the time of Domesday Book (1086) had vanished by the time of Henry II. They had risen into the semi-free class of landholding villeins, bound to their land and subject to their manorial lord, but possessing their own strips in village fields. According to the laws of the time, "no lord can eject his cultivators from their land as long as they can perform their due service"; on the other hand, those "who leave the estate on which they were born" are to be arrested and sent back.[6] Most peasants cherished their lands, and the ban against leaving them was not as intolerable as it might seem today. Still, there had been considerable numbers of peasants in pre-Conquest England who were free to go where they pleased, and under the Norman and Angevin kings most of these free peasants lost their liberty. They descended into the villein class at the very time the slaves were ascending into it.

The twelfth-century peasantry, in short, tended to be a much more uniform group than the peasantry of former times. A twelfth-century peasant was characteristically of villein status, subject to his manorial lord, living in an agrarian village, tilling his strip fields with heavy plow and eight-ox team, and devoting certain days to the cultivation of his lords demesne fields. His life was tied to the agricultural calendar of plowing, sowing, and harvesting. He ground his grain in his lord's flour mill and had it baked into loaves in his lord's bakery. He dwelled in a one-room hut in the village along with his wife, children, parents, and domestic animals. When he was not working in the fields he tended his oxen, pigs, and chickens, raised vegetables in a kitchen garden next to his hut, and occasionally broke the routine of work with church festivals and country dances, religious celebrations and "church-ales" (where everyone got drunk in the village church).

But the uniformity of the twelfth-century peasantry must not be over-stressed, for there remained immense diversity in agrarian life and organization. In certain areas—such as Kent—the single-family farm persisted. Regions of less fertile soil were devoted to cattle or sheep raising. Some manors had no demesne strips at all, and their lords lived off the rents and taxes of their peasants; other manors consisted entirely of demesne strips, worked by hired laborers. In general, manors varied widely in the relative proportions of peasants' strips and demesne strips. There was wide variation, too, in the authority that a lord might exercise over the peasants on his manor. And in some of the more remote portions of England there was no manorial organization at all: the villagers pursued their routine under only the loose authority of a distant lord.

Whatever the local customs and conditions might be, life for the average peasant would have seemed almost changeless from year to year.

---

[6] *Leis Willelme,* 29.1, 30.1 (*c.* 1090/1135).

But the economy of twelfth-century England was in fact becoming steadily more active and prosperous. The work of forest clearing and swamp draining, begun by the Anglo-Saxons, was now reaching its climax. And with the growth of commerce and the increased circulation of money, it became possible for farmlands to produce for profit rather than for mere subsistence. The Cistercians, an austere monastic order that rose to great prominence in twelfth-century Europe, established many abbeys in England—often in remote wilderness areas—and began to raise sheep on a large scale.[7] Wool production had long been important to England, but it was now pursued at an unprecedented level of efficiency. Neighboring Flanders had developed a vigorous textile industry, and in the course of the twelfth century, England became Flanders' chief source of wool. A large-scale trade developed between the two lands, and Henry II was able to turn the situation to his own diplomatic advantage by threatening the count of Flanders with suspension of the trade if he did not cooperate with English royal policies.

Grain production also became more efficient. The traditional system of dividing manors into two fields farmed in alternate years, had been giving way over the past several centuries to a more complex and more productive three-field system of crop rotation. Field 1 would be planted in the fall (with wheat or rye), field 2 would be planted the following spring (with oats and barley), and field 3 would be rested all year, to be planted the following fall—and so on around. The effect was that two-thirds of a village's arable lands could be planted and harvested each year rather than half as under the two-field system. Three-field agriculture was possible only in the more fertile regions, however; and the two-field system continued to be used in parts of England throughout the Middle Ages. Indeed, a single manor might rotate part of its land on a three-field basis and part on a two-field basis. Nevertheless, three-field agriculture contributed much to the productivity of medieval agriculture.

The English agrarian economy was also benefiting from the increased use of mechanical power. Water mills were widely used in Anglo-Saxon times—over five thousand are recorded in Domesday Book—and before the end of Henry II's reign the windmill had made its debut in the English countryside. These innovations are difficult to trace—the historians of the age give them scant attention—but their importance is incalculable. For despite the surge of commercial activity, grain production remained the fundamental economic enterprise of medieval England, and significant improvements in agrarian technology were bound to have a buoyant effect on the prosperity of the realm. These innovations were by no means the products of English inventive genius but were appearing at the same time on the continent. Hence the economic surge of twelfth- and thirteenth-

---

[7] See below, p. 144.

century England was shared by France, Germany, and indeed almost all of Western Christendom.

Military, Administrative, and Legal Reforms Under Henry II

Still, in certain respects, England was in the vanguard of the twelfth-century boom. This was particularly true in the area of political administration. Under Henry II, as under Henry I, England was more thoroughly and efficiently governed than any other state in the West.

Henry II began his reign by endeavoring to revive in all its fullness the royal authority exercised by his grandfather. He was not always able to do so. The principle of hereditary feudal succession, for example, was now established beyond question. Nevertheless, Henry II undertook to undo, insofar as possible, the disintegrative work of Stephen's reign. He destroyed a great many unlicensed castles that barons had hastily erected during the height of the anarchy, and he was stingy in granting new licenses for castle building. He worked energetically, first to rebuild the powerful government of Henry I and later to expand it. Three areas of the royal government received Henry II's particular attention: the military organization, the administrative system, and above all the legal structure.

Henry II's military reforms are well illustrated by two important documents from his reign: the *Cartae Baronum* (Baronial Charters) of 1166 and the Assize of Arms of 1181. The first is a series of written statements from all the tenants-in-chief of the realm, both lay and ecclesiastical, in response to a royal inquest relating to knights' service. The tenants-in-chief were required to tell the king: (1) how many knights they had enfeoffed prior to Henry I's death in 1135; (2) how many they had enfeoffed between 1135 and 1166; and (3) to what degree—if any—the enfeoffments fell short of the knightly military quotas the monarchy had imposed on them. The knights that the tenants-in-chief had enfeoffed were to be identified by name. The *Cartae Baronum* of 1166 constituted the first general survey of knights' service to be undertaken by the king since the establishment of the quotas by William the Conqueror. Henry II may well have been interested in discovering the extent of his feudal military resources, but he seems also to have had two very specific reasons for the inquest: First, he wished to identify all the knightly subvassals of England who had not yet rendered him their formal allegiance so that he might secure their oaths in the near future. Second, on the basis of the data supplied by the *Cartae Baronum*, he attempted to obtain additional scutage from those vassals whose enfeoffments exceeded their royal quotas.

The Assize of Arms of 1181 was far more radical in its implications than the *Cartae Baronum*. Coming at a time when the Anglo-Saxon fyrd had ceased to function and the feudal military obligation was tending to become a mere excuse for the levying of scutage, the Assize of Arms marked the first of a series of attempts—running through the thirteenth century—to reorganize the English military obligation on the basis of wealth.

Henry II divided the English military force into four categories. The first corresponded to the feudal army: the holder of each knight's fee was to have a shirt of mail, a helmet, a shield, and a lance. The second and third categories roughly paralleled the old five-hide fyrd, but the basis of the obligation was shifted from the number of hides in a man's possession to the annual income from his land and the total value of his movable possessions. Every free layman with movables and rents of sixteen marks or more (second category) was to have a shirt of mail, a helmet, a shield and a lance—the equipment of a knight. Every free layman with movables and rents of ten marks or more (third category) was to have a hauberk, an iron cap, and a lance. The fourth category embraced all freemen with chattels and rents of less than ten marks: they were to have quilted coats, iron caps, and lances. Finally, all four of these groups were to swear fidelity to Henry II and bear their arms in his service according to his command.

The Assize of Arms established a graded hierarchy of military obligations based on a single recruitment system extending from knightly service down to the general military duty of all freemen. It preserved the knight's fee of earlier times but equated it with an estate of sixteen marks or more. This equation between a knight's fee and an estate of some specified monetary value constitutes the beginning of a long process that tended to incorporate the older system of arbitrary private feudal tenures into a larger and radically different structure—a standardized national system of military assessment.

Henry II's Assize of Arms of 1181 was merely the first of a series of such ordinances. Similar ones were issued by Henry III in 1230 and 1242 and by Edward I in his Statute of Winchester in 1285. These later ordinances increased the number of categories of nonknightly military service from three to five, incorporated the nonfree peasantry into the military system, and provided for new military classes, such as archers and light horsemen. And beginning in the thirteenth century, the monarchy sought to bring knights' service still more closely into line with the new system by requiring all men with estates of a certain annual value (usually twenty pounds) to become knights.

The shift from hides to annual income as the basis of land assessment is just as evident in the tax system. By Henry II's reign the ancient hidage assessment was becoming anachronistic, for it no longer served as an adequate indication of changing land values, and it failed to reflect the growing wealth of the townsmen. Thus the annual land tax based on hides, was abolished under Henry II. In its place there emerged a new tax, levied only occasionally to meet emergencies, and assessed at some percentage of a subject's annual rents and chattels. Taxes levied on this new basis continued through the subsequent reigns of Richard I, John, Henry III, and long thereafter, paralleling the fundamental changes in the military recruitment system that were initiated by the Assize of Arms. From the standpoint of both taxation and military service, Henry II's age marks the beginning of an epoch.

In other aspects of royal administrative development, the reign of Henry II constitutes a revival and elaboration of Henry I's policies rather than a new beginning. As the functions of the household staff became gradually more specialized, separate administrative departments began to emerge. The increasing professionalization of the exchequer (now moved from Winchester to Westminster) is attested to not only by an unbroken series of annual pipe rolls but also by a treatise—*The Dialogue of the Exchequer*—which explains in detail the duties and procedures of exchequer officials. The work of the chancery was increasing both in amount and in sophistication and would continue to do so during subsequent reigns. In brief, the royal coterie of servants, advisers, scribes, and cronies was evolving gradually into a bureaucracy of professional administrators.

It was in the field of law, above all else, that Henry II made his unique contribution.[8] Indeed, he has been called, perhaps without excessive exaggeration, the father of the English Common Law. Here again he followed in the tradition of Henry I; but many policies that Henry I had merely begun his grandson carried to consummation.

In the days of Henry II the royal court significantly increased the range of its judicial activities and the complexity of its organization until, by the reign's end, a number of separate bodies were hearing cases in the king's name. The great council—the assembly of magnates and prelates that met with the king on extraordinary occasions—served as the royal tribunal in cases of the very highest importance—such as the trial of Archbishop Thomas Becket in Northampton in 1164. Pleas of lesser significance were usually heard by the ill-defined group of administrative officers and royal intimates who accompanied the king on his endless travels—a group which later historians have called the "small council."

The small council, in its judicial capacity, was presided over by the king or one of his chief judges; it evolved in later years into the separate tribunal known as the court of the King's Bench. Since the small council was occupied with a great burden of royal business—judicial and nonjudicial —and since it was constantly on the move, it had its drawbacks as a body to which subjects might conveniently turn for royal justice. Litigants might have their cases postponed repeatedly as the small council shifted its attention to urgent political matters; or they might have to chase the king and his court hundreds of miles across England and France before finally catch-

---

[8] The standard general work is F. Pollock and F. W. Maitland, *The History of English Law Before the Time of Edward I* (rev. reissue of 2nd ed., 2 vols., Cambridge, 1968). A good recent summary is R. C. Van Caenegem, *The Birth of the English Common Law* (Cambridge, 1973).

ing up with them. In order to mitigate these difficulties, the twelfth-century kings—Henry II in particular—began to establish subdivisions of the royal court. As early as Henry I's time the court of the exchequer, which met twice annually at Winchester to handle fiscal administration and accounting, was also serving as a tribunal in cases involving royal finance. Before long the exchequer court's judicial scope had widened, illogically but conveniently, to include certain cases unconnected with the royal finances. But since the king or his regent was usually present for the semiannual audits, and since the barons of the exchequer—the members of the exchequer court—tended to be the same persons who normally heard cases in the king's perambulating court, the gain in efficiency was slight.

Around 1178 Henry II took the further step of establishing a small body of royal justices to sit permanently at Westminster with the power to hear all but the most important of the royal pleas that might be brought before it. This court, consisting sometimes of five men, sometimes of more, often included the treasurer and the chief justiciar (as the English regent now came to be called). It was distinguished by having its own separate seal and, in later years, a special name—the court of Common Pleas. But under Henry II it was still experimental and inchoate. It occasionally met elsewhere than at Westminster; it was at times almost indistinguishable from the small body of exchequer officials that worked at Westminster the year round; and when the king visited Westminster, as he often did, it was fused into the main royal court.

The system of royal tribunals—the great council, the small council (the later King's Bench), the exchequer court, and the special court at Westminster (the later court of Common Pleas)—was augmented by a revival and expansion of Henry I's policy of sending out itinerant justices to hear royal pleas in the shires. Under Henry I their activities had been sporadic; by the closing years of Henry II's reign they were going out on annual circuits that covered large portions of England, bringing the king's justice into remote corners of the kingdom. Their tours were still not completely regularized, for Henry II was inclined to experiment endlessly, increasing or decreasing the number of justices, the number and geographical range of their several circuits, and the scope of their duties. Besides their judicial activities, they served as general royal agents in the countryside—helping to keep the sheriffs in check, holding inquests relating to royal revenues, and safeguarding the king's rights over his own demesne lands. Their jurisdiction was limited to certain kinds of royal pleas, but with the passing of time they acquired the power to hear every kind of case. Their general eyres or "assizes"—as their tours were called—were already becoming the vital links between the king and the counties.

Henry II was determined to expand the royal authority and uphold the royal peace throughout the English countryside. He accomplished this in part through the activities of his itinerant justices. But much of his power in the counties depended on the loyalty and effectiveness of his chief local agents, the sheriffs, who tended to be more independent and often less trust-worthy than the members of his immediate court. In 1170 he undertook a thoroughgoing inquest of his sheriff's activities, afterwards replacing most of them with more dependable nominees. The sheriff was obliged to execute royal orders that were usually transmitted through a writ from the royal chancery. As the local representatives of an increasingly literate administra-tion, an efficient sheriff had best be literate himself; and it has been aptly observed that the considerable authority over the countryside exercised by Henry II was made possible only by a significant rise in lay literacy. Govern-ment by the written word demanded local officials who could read.

Yet, even with active itinerant justices and effective sheriffs, Henry II was faced with the formidable problem of maintaining local law and order without a police force. In his Assize of Clarendon of 1166, augmented by the Assize of Northampton of 1176, he ordered that inquest juries of twelve men from each hundred and four men from each town be required to meet periodically. These juries were obliged to report the names of notorious local criminals to the king's sheriff or itinerant justice. The accused criminals were then forced to submit to the ordeal and were suitably punished if they failed to pass it. The ordeal was a crude and ancient procedure of Germanic law [9] that was passing out of favor with the twelfth-century Church; the Lateran Council of 1215 effectively brought an end to the practice by forbidding churchmen to participate in it. While Henry II employed it as a traditional method of determining guilt or innocence, he evidently did so with some hesitation, taking the precaution of providing that even if the denounced criminal should pass the ordeal he was nevertheless subject to banishment from the kingdom.

It should be clear that the juries established by the Assize of Clarendon were fundamentally different from the modern trial jury. The task of the modern jury—to decide whether the accused is guilty or innocent—was performed in Henry II's system by the ordeal. His juries were closer in spirit to our grand juries: they were indictment juries rather than trial juries, and their chief purpose was to supply information. Similar juries had been em-ployed in the Anglo-Norman period, not only to identify criminals but also to provide local data of various kinds to the royal administration. They were used during the Domesday inquest to supply the facts on which the survey was based, and their obscure genesis has been traced by contending scholars to both Anglo-Saxon England and the Carolingian Empire. Henry I used local juries on occasion to attest to facts relating to legal cases, but it was only under Henry II that they became a part of a regular legal system.

---

9 Chapter 1, p. 19. It is difficult to determine what percentage of those who submitted to the ordeal passed and what percentage failed. A record of Hungarian legal cases in the early thirteenth century provides us with an important clue: of 208 people whose guilt or innocence was established by the ordeal of the hot iron between 1208 and 1235, 130 passed and 78 failed. Van Caenegem, *Birth of the English Common Law*, p. 68.

As such, they mark a significant extension of royal jurisdiction into areas traditionally reserved for the local courts of hundred and shire.

Henry II also extended royal jurisdiction systematically into the vast and bewildering area of land disputes. We have already noted the importance and complexity of landholding in medieval England. Although the Norman kings—particularly Henry I—adjudicated disputes among their great tenants-in-chief and occasionally intervened in lesser conflicts over land, these matters were customarily handled in the private baronial courts. It was only in Henry II's time that the full authority of royal jurisdiction was brought to bear on this crucial area of law.

The procedures of the baronial feudal courts were slow, antiquated, and otherwise unsatisfactory; but the traditional machinery of the royal courts was little better. Henry II determined to provide a swift and rational method of settling land disputes which would not only improve the quality of justice but also bring an immense amount of new business into the royal courts. Thus, he instituted a series of "possessory assizes"—forms of legal action designed not to determine who had the best *right* to the land in question but whether a plaintiff had been *forcibly* dispossessed or disinherited within a relatively recent period of time. In this way he hoped to reduce the violent aspects of land rivalry by preventing a claimant, even one with a just claim, from taking possession of an estate by force. And whereas the question of title to land could be immensely complex and ambiguous, the question of whether someone had been recently driven from his land was relatively simple to determine.

The most important of Henry II's possessory assizes was the Assize of Novel Disseisin. It provided that a landholder who claimed to have been recently and violently dispossessed could purchase a royal writ ordering the local sheriff to summon a jury and inquire of it whether or not the plaintiff had been driven from his land. If its decision was affirmative, the sheriff, with the full weight of royal authority behind him, was to restore the disputed land to the plantiff.

Novel Disseisin was only one of several possessory writs established by Henry II. Of the remainder, one is of particular interest: the writ of Mort d'Ancestor. This writ required the sheriff to ask the jury whether the plaintiff's father had held the land in question when it last passed to an heir. If so, and if the plaintiff was the eldest son, he was to be given the land. The writ of Mort d'Ancestor, when understood in the context of the vague and insecure inheritance arrangements of the Anglo-Norman age, illustrates vividly Henry II's willingness to support the principle of normal inheritance.

Toward the end of his reign, Henry II instituted a legal action known as the Grand Assize, which addressed itself not to the question of violent dispossession but to the more fundamental question of who had the best title to the land. As in the case of the possessory assizes, the question was answered by a local jury consisting of men who were likely to know the situation well. Previously, questions of rights to land were commonly settled in feudal courts by the violent custom of trial by battle; the two disputants, or their representatives, simply fought it out. The new procedure was bound to commend itself to an age in which reason and logic were coming into high regard; and the ultimate effect of the royal land assizes was to make the royal courts the chief adjudicators of land quarrels of all kinds. Englishmen learned to turn to the king for quick, rational justice, and the feudal courts were outclassed in the competition.

Henry I and Henry II, between them, achieved an enormously significant extension of royal jurisdiction at the expense of feudal and local justice. The various local peculiarities in legal custom—Kentish law, Northumbrian law, Danelaw—were giving way to a uniform royal law, a *common* law shared by all Englishmen. Thus, the political unification of the Wessex kings had its counterpart and consummation in the legal unification achieved by the two Henrys and their successors.

The emergence of a national legal system under Henry II and its dependence on literate laymen are well illustrated by the appearance of England's first systematic legal treatise, attributed traditionally (and probably wrongly) to Henry II's chief justiciar, Ranulf Glanville.[10] "Glanville's" treatise is practical and utilitarian rather than philosophical—by and large it is a manual explaining the nature and uses of the judicial writs for sale at the royal chancery. Englishmen were not yet ready to speculate on the fundamental nature of their jurisprudence. But the treatise is nevertheless an intellectual landmark in the rise of a coherent body of royal law.

As the common law was evolving under Henry II, a profoundly different legal tradition was developing on the continent. Henry's law, precocious though it was in many respects, had its roots in Germanic custom; whereas continental law was gradually passing under the influence of the Roman legal tradition, which was undergoing a notable revival in the twelfth-century universities. In one sense, Roman law is popular law, resting as it does on the concept that ultimate political authority inhered in the Roman people. But it passed into the twelfth-century West in the rather autocratic form it had acquired at the hands of Justinian. For it was above all Justinian's *Corpus Juris Civilis* that was studied and expanded by the continental Roman lawyers of the twelfth century. The legal concepts of the Roman republic and early empire had been deeply colored by the absolutism of sixth-century Byzantium. When these concepts began to influence Western Europe once again in the High Middle Ages, they tended to make continental governments not only more rational but also more autocratic.

Roman law had a far greater influence on the continent than in England. This was owing in part to geography, for England was remote from Italy, where the study of Roman law centered. But much more im-

---

10 The actual author is unknown, but he was clearly someone associated with Henry II's court and intimately familiar with its methods. Historians commonly call the work, for convenience, Glanville's treatise.

portant, when the revived Roman law was first making its impact on European politics in the mid-twelfth century, France and other continental states were still relatively disunited and amorphous, whereas the English monarchy already had a powerful administrative and legal tradition behind it. To continental monarchs, Roman law seemed an ideal tool with which to build strong, centralized political structures; the Angevin kings of England would quite naturally prefer to rely more upon the Germanic traditions of the Anglo-Saxon and Norman kings that had already carried the monarchy so far. Hence, although the Roman law of the continent made a distinct mark on English legal development, its influence was not decisive. The common law remained essentially an indigenous phenomenon. It would evolve in later centuries into one of the dominating legal traditions of the world.

Henry II and the Church

For all its achievements in the realms of commerce, agriculture, administration, and thought, the twelfth century remained fundamentally an age of faith. Indeed, a great deal of the creative originality of the period was devoted, in one way or another, to the service of Christianity. The best historians of the age regarded historical development as the progressive unfolding of a divine plan. Scholars such as St. Anselm and John of Salisbury were interested primarily in God and his relationship to man. Kings, barons, and knights went on crusades to the Holy Land. Architects devoted their talents to the building of abbeys and cathedrals. By the time of Henry II the powerful Romanesque style had reached its fullest development and had spread across the length and breadth of Western Europe; and in the course of his reign a stunning new style—the light, upward-reaching Gothic—was making its appearance.

The creative surge of high medieval Europe was accompanied by a major effort to reform the Church and by a profound intensification of piety at all levels of society. The struggles over lay investiture left the twelfth-century papacy and episcopacy more powerful than ever before, and the holders of high ecclesiastical offices were often men of sanctity as well as practical wisdom. Of course, kings and noblemen retained a strong voice in ecclesiastical appointments, and the universal Church was still plagued with unworthy, time-serving bishops and abbots, and incompetent, even licentious priests. Still, there can be little question that the moral caliber of the clergy was gradually rising. And the papacy was steadily extending its control over the Church through its wide-ranging legates and its expanding administrative organization.

The medieval Church succeeded in bringing the faith to the ordinary Christian as never before. A fully elaborated system of dioceses and parishes covered the entire European countryside. Through the system of the seven sacraments—fully elaborated only in the twelfth century—the ordinary Christian believer received the grace of the Christian God, through priestly intercession, at every important juncture in his life. At birth, baptism cleansed him of the inherited taint of sin and initiated him into the community of the Church. At puberty, the sacrament of confirmation reinforced the grace received at baptism and gave him the spiritual strength with which to enter adulthood. His wedding was blessed by the sacrament of marriage. If he chose a priestly vocation, he received the sacrament of holy orders. Throughout his adult life he periodically received absolution from his sins through the sacrament of penance—confessing his transgressions to a priest fully and sincerely and with a firm intention of amendment. His relationship with God was intensified at regular intervals through the sacrament of the eucharist, in which he consumed the body of Christ in the form of bread. And at his death his spirit was strengthened and purified for the last journey through the sacrament of extreme unction. Through the sacraments, through regular attendance at Mass (at which the eucharist was celebrated), and in countless other ways, the life of the average medieval Christian was deeply influenced by the Church. Cruelty, avarice, lust, and violence continued to afflict society, as they always have, but religious awareness was never far from the center of men's minds.

The general deepening of piety throughout Western Europe had tangible effects, not only in the Crusades and the construction of churches, great and small, but also in the foundation of numberless monastic houses. The kings and barons of Norman England had been generous in building and patronizing monasteries, and the Benedictine life had become more popular than ever before. At the same time, there emerged new monastic movements dedicated to far more austere interpretations of the Benedictine rule. The greatest of these, the Cistercians, began in 1098 at Cîteaux in the Burgundian wilderness. Cîteaux was ruled in its early days by a gifted English abbot, St. Stephen Harding; it began a notable epoch of international expansion early in the twelfth century when St. Bernard of Clairvaux joined the community. A supremely eloquent, strong-willed mystic, St. Bernard was also gifted and effective in the realm of practical affairs. He was to become the most admired churchman of his age, and as his fame grew the Cistercian movement grew with it. By 1115 Cîteaux had four daughter houses; by 1200 some five hundred Cistercian monasteries were scattered across Europe.

Inevitably the movement spread to England—in the later years of Henry I—and by Stephen's death in 1154 the kingdom had some fifty Cistercian abbeys. They were stark, undecorated buildings, contrasting dramatically with the elaborate churches and conventual buildings of some of the wealthier centers of traditional Benedictinism; yet even now the beauty of Cistercian ruins such as Fountains and Rievaulx, set in wilderness areas of Yorkshire, is deeply moving. In such remote abbeys, encircled by their fields and pastures, white-clad Cistercian monks lived out their simple, ascetic lives

FOUNTAINS ABBEY, YORKSHIRE (12TH CENTURY)
The simple, graceful beauty of the Cistercian style is evident even in the
ruins. *National Monuments Record.*

Meanwhile other churchmen were working toward the very different
ideal of greater involvement in everyday life. Such had been the goal of
the Gregorian reform papacy—to go out into the world rather than withdraw
from it, to Christianize Europe and redeem it, to establish "right order" in
society. The twelfth-century Church, in England as elsewhere, was steadily
expanding its scope in such areas as law, administration, and education.
Monasteries and cathedrals became increasingly active in the education
of the young, and centers of higher education such as Oxford and Canterbury were evolving under ecclesiastical auspices. Canon law was developing
into a science and was administered by an increasingly elaborate network
of ecclesiastical courts separate from those of the king and his barons.
In the area of secular administration, too, churchmen played a decisive role.
Well equipped by the relative excellence of their education, they ran the
exchequers and chanceries, served as trusted intimate counselors at court,
wrote the histories of their times, and carried on the work of scholarship.
There might be conflicts on occasion between archbishops and kings, but
there could be no separation of church and state.

Henry II, in his effort to extend the royal jurisdiction, not only at the expense of local and feudal courts but also at the expense of ecclesiastical courts, was undertaking a policy that ran directly counter to the growth of ecclesiastical jurisdiction. But the papacy at the time was again deeply involved in a struggle with the Holy Roman Emperor; and had Henry enjoyed the full cooperation of the English episcopacy he might well have succeeded in carrying out his policies unhindered. As it was, however, his effort to limit the jurisdiction of the ecclesiastical courts encountered the violent opposition of the new archbishop of Canterbury, Thomas Becket, and resulted in a fateful struggle between the king and his primate.[11]

The public career of Thomas Becket was divided into two phases of about equal length. For eight years, from 1154 to 1162, he served as Henry II's chancellor and boon companion. In 1162 Henry appointed him archbishop of Canterbury to succeed Theobald (who died in 1161); and for the following eight years, until his dramatic murder in 1170, he was Henry's most implacable foe. Much has been written of the transformation in Becket's character from the roistering, worldly chancellor to the stern archbishop. The complexities of Becket's personality will always remain obscure. All one can say for certain is that he was an exceedingly talented man who, as chancellor, served his king faithfully and skillfully and, as archbishop, fought with equal ardor for what he conceived to be the interests of the Church. The perfect chancellor, and one of England's most famous archbishops, he has sometimes been described as an actor—a person with a flair for the dramatic who was capable of playing to the hilt each of his two roles. This viewpoint is superficial and contrived. More probably, the heavy responsibilities he assumed at his elevation to the archbishopric of Canterbury caused him to undergo a genuine religious conversion. Archbishop Thomas was no play actor but a fervent ecclesiastical reformer in the tradition of Pope Gregory VII and St. Anselm, and a late-blooming saint on the pattern of Augustine of Hippo. If sometimes the archbishop was lacking in generosity of spirit, one must nevertheless concede that his later years were infinitely more difficult by his uncompromising dedication to the Church. We must grant him the honesty of his convictions.

Henry, of course, could not have anticipated Becket's conversion. He must have assumed that in appointing Becket to the archbishopric he was installing a pliable friend at the apex of the ecclesiastical hierarchy. But almost immediately, Becket asserted his independence and began to treat Henry not as his master but as his spiritual son. Henry, quite naturally, was surprised and resentful, and hostility soon developed between the two men. Early in 1164 Henry forced Becket and the other English bishops to consent

---

[11] For a brief, sensitive, and sympathetic biography of Becket, see David Knowles, *Thomas Becket* (Stanford, 1970). For an overview of various historical judgments of the Becket controversy, see Thomas M. Jones, *The Becket Controversy* (New York, 1970). The subject is also comprehensively discussed in W. L. Warren, *Henry II*, pp. 399–555.

to a list of customs relating to church-state relations known as the Constitutions of Clarendon. These customs were, of course, strongly pro-royal. Henry II maintained that they represented common practice in the days of Henry I, and with one or two possible exceptions they did. Yet for several reasons they were difficult for reform churchmen to accept. For one thing, although Henry I had acted contrary in many ways to the new spirit of ecclesiastical reform, he had never been so bold—or so foolish—as to commit his practices to writing. He may have ignored many of the privileges that reform churchmen claimed, but he never asked his churchmen to give their formal sanction to his policies. Moreover, the English Church had achieved a fair measure of independence during Stephen's reign and had attained a position much more in harmony with the contemporary reform ideology. Certain of the provisions in the Constitutions of Clarendon must have appeared to reform churchmen as distasteful retrograde steps. This was particularly true of the provision forbidding appeals to Rome without royal permission and the provision establishing a degree of royal jurisdiction over "criminous clerics," who had traditionally been subject to Church courts alone.

The proper treatment of criminous clerics was the most bitterly disputed issue in the Henry-Becket controversy. Some clerics, particularly those in minor orders, engaged in crimes of violence, then threw themselves on the mercy of the ecclesiastical courts. They were often given light punishments; frequently they were defrocked and released without further penalty. The monarchy resented such soft treatment of criminals and sought to punish secular crimes in secular courts. The Constitutions of Clarendon stipulated that "If a cleric has confessed or been convicted, the Church shall protect him no further." In short, the defrocked cleric was to be arrested and tried for his crime in a royal court. Becket objected that no man should be tried and punished twice for the same crime.

The issue of the criminous clerics symbolized a far deeper controversy. The twelfth century witnessed a rise in the centralized power of the English royal administration and a concurrent expansion of ecclesiastical administration. In the Becket dispute we are seeing two worlds in collision: the secular world of the royal bureaucracy and the spiritual world of the English and international Church. Two different governments—royal and ecclesiastical—were in conflict. Similar disputes occurred off and on throughout high medieval Europe and were, indeed, merely particular manifestation of a single fundamental conflict inherent in the divergent ideals of the epoch. It was basically a power struggle—a struggle for precedence between the universal Church and the rising secular states. The rivalry between Henry II and Becket was one of its most dramatic episodes.

Shortly after subscribing to the Constitutions of Clarendon, Becket reversed himself and appealed to the pope for support. The papacy, having its hands full with Germany, sought to compromise, wishing neither to offend King Henry nor to repudiate its faithful servant Becket. Henry had by now lost all patience with Becket and resolved to break his spirit. Toward the end of 1164 Henry ordered him to stand trial before the king's great council in Northampton. Becket was accused of various offenses allegedly committed during his service as chancellor. Claiming clerical immunity from royal jurisdiction, Becket fled the country to appeal his case to the pope. In so doing he was challenging one of the basic articles of Henry's Constitution of Clarendon—the prohibition of unlicensed appeals to Rome.

There followed a protracted struggle between the fiery king and the exiled archbishop. The papacy managed for nearly six years to placate the archbishop while restraining him sufficiently to avoid a complete break between England and Rome. The crisis reached its climax in June 1170. Henry II, anxious to protect the hereditary principle of royal succession, wished to have his eldest son crowned. Since the archbishop of Canterbury was unavailable, Henry turned to Canterbury's ancient rival, the archbishop of York. When Becket heard that the archbishop of York had presided over a royal coronation, he was furious at the affront to the dignity of Canterbury. With papal backing, he threatened to lay England under the ban of interdict. Deeply alarmed at this threat, which would have had the result of closing all of England's churches, Henry II worked out a temporary reconciliation with Becket that left all major issues unresolved but allowed the archbishop to return to England.

A truce that failed to resolve any of the conflicts was perhaps worse than no truce at all. Just before returning to England, in the late autumn of 1170, Becket shocked Henry by excommunicating all the bishops who had participated in the coronation. Henry, livid with rage, is reported to have cried out to his court, "Will no one rid me of this turbulent priest?" And four of his knights, responding to their king's fury, journeyed to Canterbury with vengeance in their hearts. On the evening of December 29, 1170, they hacked Becket to pieces in Canterbury Cathedral, in the presence of numerous onlookers. Becket murmured, "I accept death for the name of Jesus and his Church." And he fell to the stone floor with his arms outstretched as though in prayer.

The deed had a powerful impact on public opinion in England and the continent. Becket was immediately hailed as a martyr, and his tomb at Canterbury became an immensely popular pilgrimage center. He was quickly canonized, and his bones were reputed to be a source of miraculous cures. To Henry, Becket's murder was a source of profound embarrassment. The king denied that the four knights had acted under his orders, and we can well believe that Henry would not have been so foolish as to deliberately undertake such a violent and self-defeating policy. Nevertheless, Henry was not absolved of all responsibility. He had been Becket's archenemy, and if the four knights were not acting on his command they were at least responding to his anger. The king was obliged to do penance by walking

THE MURDER OF THOMAS BECKET AT CANTERBURY CATHEDRAL, 1170
In the upper panel, the archbishop, at dinner, is warned of the
arrival of four knights. In the lower panel he is murdered in
the cathedral, while his monks hide in terror. *British Museum.*

barefoot through the Canterbury streets and undergoing a flogging by the
Canterbury monks. He was also compelled to repudiate the Constitutions
of Clarendon, to permit appeals to Rome without specific royal license, and
to refrain from subjecting criminous clerics to capital punishment. On the
surface of things, the martyred archbishop would seem to have won the
victory.

In reality, the expansion of royal justice at ecclesiastical expense suffered only a partial and temporary interruption. Although the Constitutions
of Clarendon were withdrawn, most of their provisions remained effective
in fact if not in law. Henry continued to place trustworthy royal servants
in high ecclesiastical offices; and in the later years of his reign he succeeded
in keeping tight control over the Church without any dramatic violations
of canon law or harsh conflicts with the papacy. His earlier policy of
flamboyant aggression, symbolized by the Constitutions of Clarendon, gave
way to a more effective policy of subtle and silent maneuvering. The Becket
affair notwithstanding, Henry II succeeded in ecclesiastical affairs, as elsewhere, in advancing his realm toward administrative and legal centralization.

The Angevin Empire

In discussing the development of England under Henry II we must never overlook the fact that Henry's authority extended far beyond the island kingdom. He was the first of England's kings to have greater wealth and power outside the kingdom than within it. Many of his legal and administrative policies in England were applied to some of his continental domains as well—Normandy in particular. The Norman ducal court and the Norman exchequer paralleled those of England. Henry issued a military ordinance for his French land that was quite similar to the English Assize of Arms and undertook a feudal survey of Normandy in 1172 quite similar to the *Cartae Baronum* in 1166. Nevertheless, one can separate England from the remainder of the Angevin Empire without excessive violence to historical reality, for Henry's constellation of territories was in reality no empire at all. Each territorial unit he controlled had its own separate government and distinct customs; the heterogeneous lands were held together solely by their allegiance to a single individual. There was no central "imperial" government, no unified body of imperial law, but rather a myriad of separate administrations of varying efficiency, held together by the intelligence and tremendous energy of Henry II. Still, from the military and diplomatic standpoint—if not from the standpoint of law and administration— the Angevin Empire must be regarded as a single entity. England was its most tightly administered district and a major source of wealth, whereas the continental territories required the bulk of Henry's military efforts to subdue their rebellious nobles and guard them against the growing pressure of the French monarchy.

Having inherited a huge conglomeration of territories, Henry aspired to still more. He campaigned—with only partial success—to extend his authority into the province of Toulouse in southern France. And he won a degree of control over eastern and central Ireland through the invasion and settlement of a few of his ambitious vassals and, later, through his own direct intervention. In 1185 he went so far as to install his son John as lord of Ireland, recalling him later when he suffered a military disaster at Irish hands. But for Henry II, the Irish campaigns, so significant to later English history, were of mere secondary importance—little more than an afterthought. From the beginning of his reign to the end, his military and political interests were focused primarily on France.

In the years of Henry II the French monarchy was coming of age. Since 987 the crown had been in the hands of the Capetian family. This dynasty had managed to secure its hold on the French throne by producing male heirs at the proper time; but until the twelfth century its actual power had remained severely limited. Its direct authority was restricted to a small area of north-central France embracing Paris and Orleans and known as the Ile de France; and even here it was plagued by a host of recalcitrant minor barons. To be sure, the great dukes and counts of France

ATLANTIC OCEAN

SCOTLAND

NORTH SEA

IRELAND

NATIVE IRISH

ANGLO-NORMAN FEUDAL COLONIES

Irish Sea

Dublin

NORTH WALES

Newburgh

LORDS MARCHERS

ENGLAND

London

English Channel

THE ANGEVIN EMPIRE

DOMINIONS OF HENRY II

Held from Henry II by vassals.

Ruled by Henry II directly as king.

Royal Domain of the King of France.

Held by Henry II as vassal of the King of France.

Held by vassals of the King of France

NORMANDY

FLANDERS

Rhine R.

HOLY ROMAN EMPIRE

BRITTANY

PERCHE

MAINE

ANJOU

BLOIS

Paris

ISLE OF FRANCE

CHAMPAGNE

BURGUNDY

TOURAINE

LOIRE

BOURBON

FRANCE

POITOU

AQUITAINE

Rhône

Bordeaux

Garonne R.

GASCONY

TOULOUSE

SPAIN

—even the duke of Normandy himself—were crown vassals, but on the whole they ignored their obligations to their feeble lord unless it was in their interest to ally with him.

In the twelfth century, however, the power of the Capetian monarchy was growing. King Louis VI (1108–1137) succeeded in taming the barons of the Ile de France, thereby providing the monarchy with a secure, if limited, territorial base. His successor, Louis VII (1137–1180), was a genial, pious man who extended the prestige of the monarchy by serving as a rallying point for the French nobility against the immense power of the Angevin Empire. More and more, the French nobles outside Henry II's dominions looked to Louis VII for leadership and submitted their disagreements to the court of this self-effacing, honest king.

To Louis VII, the growth of the Angevin Empire was an ominous development. From his diminutive territorial base in the Ile de France, he faced a vast configuration of territories controlled by his nominal vassal, Henry II. England, Normandy, Maine, Anjou, Brittany, Touraine, and Aquitaine had all been joined together in an empire that dwarfed the French royal domain. On the other hand, the Capetian monarchy had the advantage of a nominal overlordship over Henry II's French territories, and the further advantage that these territories were heterogeneous—too extensive to defend easily and in some cases quite loosely governed. Aquitaine in particular had a long tradition of baronial independence, and outside the northern Aquitainian province of Poitou the ducal authority tended to be nominal.

Thus, the Angevin Empire had serious weaknesses that the French monarchy might exploit. Under Louis VII the exploitation was only half-hearted, consisting largely in a policy of fomenting rebellion among Henry II's sons and his much-abused wife, Eleanor of Aquitaine (Louis's own ex-wife). Henry left himself open to such tactics. He alienated his wife by his infidelities and annoyed his sons by giving them titular authority over various districts of his empire, while reserving actual political authority for himself. Urged on by the French king, and resentful of their father's authoritarian policy, Henry II's three eldest sons, Henry, Richard, and Geoffrey, rebelled against the king in 1173–74. They were supported by their mother and by a portion of the continental nobility, but were able to win the backing of only a few English barons. In the end the rebellion collapsed, and Henry II sought to prevent future ones by keeping his wife in comfortable imprisonment and placating his sons with greater responsibility and authority. All this did little good. Young Henry and Geoffrey both died in the midst of plots or insurrections—Henry in 1183 and Geoffrey three years later. At Louis VII's death in 1180 the French crown passed to his shrewd and ruthless son, Philip II, "Augustus" (1180–1223), who adopted a far more aggressive anti-Angevin policy than his father had pursued.

Consequently, Henry II's final years were deeply troubled. The great king could keep the peace everywhere except within his own family, and Philip Augustus was able to exploit to the fullest the rebelliousness of

Henry's offspring. In the late 1180s both of Henry's surviving sons, Richard and John, were in league with Philip Augustus and in rebellion against their aging father. On the eve of his death in 1189 Henry was forced to make a humiliating submission to this hostile coalition, and tradition has it that his dying sentence was one of bitter self-reproach: "Shame, shame on a conquered king."

But Henry II's defeat in 1189, although a personal tragedy, had little effect on French or English history. For despite the involvement of King Philip Augustus, the rebellion was fundamentally a family affair, and on Henry II's death the Angevin Empire passed intact to his eldest surviving son, Richard the Lion-Hearted. Philip Augustus' machinations had done him little good. The French monarch, however, was both patient and persevering. He was intent on the destruction of the Angevin Empire and was prepared to devote his whole life to the task if necessary. Henry II had held grimly to his continental lands. It remained to be seen whether his sons could do as well.

THE VISION OF THE HOLY GRAIL. From *Le Roi Arthur et les Chevaliers de la Table Ronde. Giraudon.*

III

THE COMMUNITY OF THE REALM
1189 to 1307

The Loss of Normandy and the Signing of Magna Carta

Richard the Lion-Hearted (1189–99) was above all else a warrior. He was much admired by the military nobility for his skill at arms, his mastery of siegecraft, and his passion for battle. While crusading in the Holy Land, he conducted the siege of Acre with such enthusiasm that even when he was ill he had his men carry him to the city walls on a litter so that he might fire his crossbow at the enemy.

Richard was also in tune with the new aristocratic style of courtly manners, witty talk, and chivalrous display that was just then becoming fashionable among the Anglo-French nobility. A troubadour at the court of Henry II had complained about its lack of style: "There was no banter, no laughter, no giving of presents." At Richard's court the mood was different, for Richard had spent his youth in Aquitaine—the homeland of the troubadours—and he wrote troubadour poetry himself. Yet there were those who criticized him severely for his outbursts of temper and his acts of cruelty; the contemporary writer Gerald of Wales described him as a person who "cared for no success unless it was reached by a path cut by his own sword and stained with his enemies' blood." But on the whole, Richard was respected in his time as a masterful warrior and crusader; and in subsequent generations his reputation rose to heroic heights.

He has fared less well at the hands of modern historians. He made no personal contribution to English constitutional and legal development and, indeed, spent less than six months of his ten-year reign in England. (This statistic is enshrined in every textbook, and we have no intention of neglecting it here!) [1] The nineteenth-century historian Sismondi described

---

[1] John T. Appleby entitled his history of the reign *England Without Richard* (1966).

him as "a bad son, a bad brother, a bad husband, and a bad king." But historians who condemn Richard in such uncompromising terms are perhaps judging him by anachronistic standards. Because we now know that the Angevin Empire was ephemeral and that the crusading movement was ultimately a failure, we are prone to discount Richard's activities in defending his French territories and in winning glory on the Third Crusade. Yet these are the very activities that won him respect among his contemporaries and thereby insured the success of his reign. His remarkable military prowess and chivalric reputation retained for him the loyalty of his vassals and subjects, even when he himself was far away. Hence he preserved the integrity of the Angevin Empire and was never seriously threatened by internal rebellion.

The Reign of Richard I

Immediately after his coronation in 1189, Richard began preparing for a crusade. Jerusalem, which had fallen to the Christian warriors of the First Crusade in 1099, had been retaken by the talented Muslim leader Saladin in 1187. Beginning in 1190 a multitude of European warriors set off on the Third Crusade, with the goal of recapturing the Holy City. This crusade was led by three distinguished monarchs: Emperor Frederick Barbarossa of Germany, King Philip Augustus of France, and King Richard of England. Considering the magnitude of the effort and the distinction of its leaders, the Third Crusade must be regarded as a failure—but it was a romantic failure that added much to the fame of Richard the Lion-Hearted. Richard became the real leader of the movement. Frederick Barbarossa

RICHARD COEUR DE LION
The tomb effigy of the Crusader king lies near those of his father, Henry II,
and his mother, Eleanor of Aquitaine, in the chapel of Fontevrault Abbey,
Anjou, France. *Giraudon.*

drowned while crossing a river on his way to the Holy Land; and Philip Augustus—who was psychologically unsuited for crusading—abandoned the venture after joining with Richard in the capture of the important port of Acre. The longstanding French-Angevin conflict made the two monarchs natural rivals, and, having quarreled with Richard, Philip left for France to plot against him. Richard was left in command of the campaign against Saladin.

In this great Muslim chieftain Richard found an adversary as valiant as himself. While fighting one another the two warriors developed a strong mutual admiration; and when, after months of campaigning, Richard found it impossible to take Jerusalem, he entered into a treaty with Saladin which guaranteed the rights of Christian pilgrims in the Holy City. He then set out for home to take his revenge on Philip Augustus. On his return journey he had the misfortune of being captured by the duke of Austria and handed over to his enemy, Emperor Henry VI of Germany, son and heir of Frederick Barbarossa.

Europe was outraged that a crusading hero should receive such treatment, but Henry VI refused to give up his valuable hostage until his terms were met. In the end England submitted to ruthless taxation in order to raise the immense sum of one hundred thousand pounds—literally a king's ransom—and Richard was obliged to grant Henry VI the overlordship of England, to hold his kingdom as a fief of the Holy Roman Empire. Only then was Richard set free.

On his return in 1194 Richard had several scores to settle. Philip Augustus had been doing what he could to subvert the Angevin Empire, which was held together only by the loyalty of its barons to their chivalric, ill-treated lord. Philip had even sought to persuade Emperor Henry VI to keep Richard in perpetual custody. Accordingly, the last half of Richard's reign was marked by endemic warfare against France; and it soon become clear that on the battlefield Philip Augustus was no match for his illustrious adversary. Richard more than held his own, and at his untimely death from a battle wound in 1199 he was threatening the French throne itself.

In England, during Richard's absence, the bitter Angevin tradition of family discord had asserted itself in the person of Richard's younger brother, John. When Richard departed from England for the crusade he left the kingdom in the control of his chancellor, William Longchamp, Bishop of Ely. Longchamp was an able but heavy-handed administrator whose low birth and imperious airs soon made him widely unpopular. John attempted to place himself at the head of the movement against Longchamp with the ultimate goal of wresting England from Richard's control. He succeeded in having Longchamp removed from office but failed to win control of the Angevin Empire for himself. Thereupon he began to plot with the ever-willing Philip Augustus against his absent brother. The plotting was ineffectual, however, and on Richard's return John was obliged to beg his mercy and forgiveness. Richard is recorded as replying in a generous but patronizing tone: "Think no more of it, John; you are only a child who has had evil counselors."

In the years after Longchamp's fall, the administration of England passed into the hands of a brilliant and trustworthy royal official, Hubert Walter, who was raised in 1193 to the archbishop of Canterbury. More an administrator than a pastor, Hubert Walter did not distinguish himself as a man of God. But he provided Richard with something that Henry II had sought in vain: a trusted supporter at the head of the English Church. More than that, Hubert Walter, who dominated the English administration during the last half of Richard's reign and the first third of John's, presided over an era of immense significance in English administrative history. In addition to his exalted position as archbishop of Canterbury he served as Richard's justiciar and as John's chancellor. In his time the royal administration functioned with unprecedented efficiency (the hundred-thousand-pound ransom is merely one illustration of this), and royal records were maintained far more extensively than ever before.

Hubert Walter and his able administrative colleagues provided a degree of continuity between the reigns of Richard and John. The two brothers were so contrary in personality, however, that their reigns form two distinct epochs. Royal administration had made great progress in the twelfth century, but the quality of royal leadership remained of fundamental importance. And even more than the chivalrous Richard, John was to make his own impression on the development of the English state.

King John: An Evaluation

John's reign (1199–1216) is marked by three great conflicts: with the French monarchy, with the papacy, and with the English barons. Each of these struggles ended in failure for John, and his failures were of momentous consequence in the making of England. They resulted in the disintegration of the Angevin Empire, the establishment of papal lordship over England, and the issuing of Magna Carta.[2]

John himself is an elusive figure. In many respects he was Richard's opposite—unchivalrous, moody, suspicious, a mediocre general, but highly intelligent and deeply interested in the royal administration. He is at once unattractive and fascinating. Historians of the nineteenth century tended to regard him as a brilliant, unscrupulous villain. J. R. Green described him in these words:

"Foul as it is, hell itself is defiled by the fouler presence of John." This terrible view of his contemporaries has passed into the sober judgment of

---

[2] King John has received much attention. Two scholarly accounts are highly recommended: Sidney Painter, *The Reign of King John* (Baltimore, 1949), and W. L. Warren, *King John* (London, 1961). The latter is somewhat more popular in approach and more readable.

The Angevin Kings of the Twelfth and Thirteenth Centuries

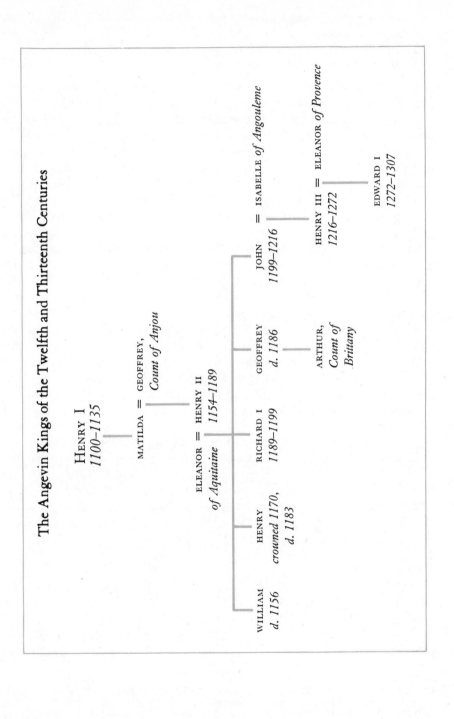

history . . . in his inner soul John was the worst outcome of the Angevins. He united into one mass of wickedness their insolence, their selfishness, their unbridled lust, their cruelty and tyranny, their shamelessness, their superstition, their cynical indifference to honor or truth.[3]

Since these words were written, historians have tended to modify their appraisal of John. Some have ascribed his difficulties to mental illness: "It is our opinion that John Lackland was subject to a mental disease well known to-day and described by modern psychiatrists as the periodical psychosis. . . . Among his Angevin ancestors were fools and madmen." [4] Modern psychology shares with medieval penance the happy quality of forgiving all sins, and by portraying John as a psychotic it is possible to absolve him.

Other historians have sought to rehabilitate John in different ways. The mind of the twentieth century is skeptical of such concepts as the foulness of hell, corrupt inner souls, or masses of wickedness, and there has been a serious attempt to demonstrate that John was considerably maligned by his contemporaries. Many of the most infamous atrocity stories relating to his reign, for example, come from the writings of two thirteenth-century historians from St. Albans—Roger Wendover and Matthew Paris—who have been shown to be biased and inaccurate on the subject. Roger Wendover was bitterly hostile to John, and Matthew Paris copied from Wendover and elaborated his tales. From the works of these men comes the story that John ordered his soldiers to seize Archdeacon Geoffrey of Norwich, bind him with chains, cast him into prison, and torture him to death by crushing him beneath a leaden cope. This unedifying event is said to have occurred in 1209; yet sixteen years later, in 1225, this same Archdeacon Geoffrey became bishop of Ely. It is known that there were several Geoffreys connected with Norwich and that Roger Wendover may have got them confused; but, if so, we can accept the remainder of the anecdote only with grave reservations. Again, Matthew Paris reports that at the death of Archbishop Hubert Walter in 1205 John made the disrespectful statement, "Now for the first time I am king of England." The same historian relates that when John's talented justiciar, Geoffrey Fitz Peter, died in 1213, the monarch exclaimed, "By the feet of God now for the first time am I king and lord of England." Unless we wish to add redundancy to John's numerous sins, we must view both tales with skepticism.

Still, even though such stories may be exaggerated or even false, John was the sort of person about whom they could be believed. He was a repellent, unlovable man who probably murdered his nephew (Arthur of Brittany) in a drunken rage, who killed hostages, starved prisoners, and broke his word with exurberant abandon. Such behavior fell far short of

---

[3] J. R. Green, *History of the English People* (special ed., Nations of the World Series), I, 237. Green's *History* was first published in London in the years 1877–1880.

[4] C. Petit-Dutaillis, *The Feudal Monarchy in France and England* (London, 1936), p. 215.

the standards that twelfth- and thirteenth-century England demanded of its kings; and John's behavior cost him the respect of his subjects and ruined his effectiveness as a political and military leader. The story is told of how St. Hugh, Bishop of Lincoln, once tried to frighten John into changing his ways by showing him a carving of tormented souls in hell, at the Angevin abbey of Fontevrault. But John turned aside to gaze at some carvings of proud kings, telling Bishop Hugh that he intended to pattern himself after them.

Richard had been successful in preserving his patrimony because his barons and lesser subjects trusted and respected him. John, although his authority was not compromised by long absences, failed because he lost his barons' confidence. They did not demand a living saint as their monarch—many of John's predecessors had been ruthless and cruel men—but they did demand consistency of policy and military prowess. And John was, above all, inconstant. He was capable of almost senseless lethargy, excessive caution, even panic. The barons, who were willing to forgive much in an able warrior-king, gave John the humiliating nickname "Softsword," and right or wrong the image had a fatal effect on John's leadership. His barons,

HEAD OF KING JOHN
John's effigy, on his tomb at Worcester Cathedral, was carved at about the time of his death in 1216. *Copyright A. F. Kersting.*

regarding him as suspicious and untrustworthy, often refused to join his military expeditions or fight his battles. The more they did so, the more suspicious and untrustworthy John became. In the generations since the Norman Conquest, monarchy and nobility had often been at odds, but never before was the cleavage so sharp.

Nonetheless, John's reign was not without its triumphs. Military and diplomatic policies toward Wales and Scotland succeeded as seldom before. His vassals extended their authority over two-thirds of Ireland, and the native Irish kings of the remaining third recognized him as their overlord. He undertook to give England a strong, well-organized navy: by 1205 it numbered fifty-one oared galleys and could be expanded to several times that figure by commandeering merchant ships. He devoted much intelligent attention to the royal administration. He enforced the law strongly and—unless it was against his interest—justly. Indeed, his accession marks the beginning of a great new epoch in the administrative history of the realm. Three of medieval England's most notable administrators worked under him and evidently received his full support: the chancellor-archbishop, Hubert Walter; the justiciar, Geoffrey Fitz Peter; and the treasurer, William of Ely. Royal records became more abundant and more exact. Now for the first time, royal charters and other correspondence issuing from the chancery began to be copied and preserved.

Like his predecessors, John was keenly acquisitive, and the tightening of royal law and administration was accompanied by a distinct increase in taxation. Many of the unpopular practices of John's Norman and Angevin predecessors were carried to extremes—arbitrarily high reliefs, abuses of the king's authority over wardships and marriages—and to these were added new fiscal expedients, such as higher and more frequent scutage levies and a greater incidence of taxes on rents and chattels. England was prosperous and could doubtless afford such exploitation; and John, who had inherited an empty treasury from Richard, was in desperate need of funds. Nevertheless, the overall effect of John's financial policies was to increase still further his unpopularity and to heighten his reputation as an arbitrary tyrant.

The Collapse of the Angevin Empire

When John acceded to the throne of England and assumed the leadership of the Angevin Empire in 1199, he faced a multitude of difficulties.[5] His reputation was already damaged, not so much by the nature of his earlier machinations against his crusading brother (filial and fraternal disloyalty were by no means unprecedented) as by their utter futility. He inherited from Richard an effective but expensive and demanding military policy in France and an exhausted treasury. Moreover, he was confronted from the

---

[5] The collapse of the Angevin Empire under John is treated masterfully and in great detail by Sir Maurice Powicke, *The Loss of Normandy* (2nd ed., Manchester, 1961).

first with a dangerous rival to the throne in his nephew, Arthur of Brittany—son of his late brother Geoffrey and grandson of Henry II. Since John managed to win England and most of the continental territories, Arthur, quite naturally, received the full support of the persistently troublesome Philip Augustus of France.

Philip and Richard the Lion-Hearted had been at war when Richard died, and the hostilities continued into the early months of John's reign. In 1200 a truce was arranged, but Philip continued to await his opportunity to shatter the Angevin inheritance. The opportunity came a mere three months later when John, on a tour of Aquitaine, suddenly and unexpectedly entered into marriage. The bride was a young girl in her early teens, Isabel, the heiress of the important Aquitainian county of Angoulême.

John's motives in selecting his young wife seem to have been based on both passion and politics. Isabel was a beautiful girl, and Angoulême was one of the more troublesome feudal principalities in turbulent Aquitaine. By establishing firm control over Angoulême, John could extend his authority in southern France considerably. But Isabel's hand was already promised to the neighboring lord of another important Aquitainian principality—Hugh the Brown of Lusignan. In making Isabel his wife, John had forestalled a dangerous feudal alliance between Lusignan and Angoulême; he had also gravely offended the Lusignan family. According to the custom of the day, he might have assuaged the Lusignan hostility by granting Hugh the Brown certain territorial compensations, but the headstrong king chose to scorn the Lusignans and thereby earned their fierce enmity. In the months that followed, John alienated a number of other Aquitainian barons by seizing their lands and accusing them of treason. He was creating a dangerous legacy of hatred in his continental dominions.

In the spring of 1202 King Philip Augustus made his move. Taking advantage of an appeal by the Lusignans to his feudal court, Philip summoned John to Paris to answer their complaints. As king of England John was subject to no one; but as duke of Aquitaine and Normandy, count of Anjou, and lord of numerous other continental principalities, he was the vassal of the king of France. As such he was bound by feudal custom to answer the summons to his lord's court, and when he refused to do so Philip formally deprived him of his French fiefs. Philip had contrived to place himself in the position of the good lord whose vassal had wronged and defied him; he sent his armies against Normandy with the full force of feudal law behind him.

The campaign went well for John at first. In a bold military stroke he succeeded in capturing Hugh the Brown and several of Hugh's Lusignan kinsmen together with Arthur of Brittany. But John nullified the victory by his subsequent foolishness. He released the Lusignans in return for a ransom and promises of loyalty that they did not keep; and he apparently murdered his nephew Arthur. Conclusive proof of the murder has never been found, but rumors of it spread quickly and John's reputation was darkened still further. Meanwhile, the king was abusing his barons, friend and foe alike, and increasing his unpopularity among his continental vassals.

Ultimately John had to depend on the loyalty of these vassals for the defense of his continental inheritance, and his mistreatment of them was a fatal error. In the course of the year 1203 one castle after another fell to Philip Augustus, while John moved aimlessly and lethargically around Normandy watching his patrimony crumble. In December 1203, with much of Normandy still under his control, he left for England, apparently in panic. By the middle of 1204 all Normandy was in King Philip's hands. Meanwhile Maine, Anjou, and all of John's former continental territories north of Aquitaine had fallen to the French monarchy. All that remained were portions of distant Aquitaine, whose turbulent barons preferred a remote and ineffective lord like John to a powerful monarch near at hand. The Angevin Empire was now defunct. John had sustained a monstrous military and political disaster.

England's French territories were not severed completely and would not be until the mid-sixteenth century. But from 1204 onward England was far more autonomous than before, and its kings tended to devote most of their attention to the island kingdom itself. Modern Englishmen, looking at events in retrospect, are inclined to regard this development as a fortunate one. To John, however, it was a profound humiliation that had to be avenged. For the next decade he devoted his considerable political and diplomatic talents to the creation of an alliance system designed to crush Philip Augustus and permit the reconquest of Normandy and Anjou.

The Struggle with the Papacy

In the meantime, John had become involved in a violent conflict with the papacy over the selection of a new archbishop of Canterbury to replace Hubert Walter (d. 1205). The archbishopric of Canterbury had been a storm center in the reigns of William Rufus, Henry I, and Henry II. Under John, as on these previous occasions, the basic issue was ecclesiastical independence versus royal sovereignty over the English Church. It was, as before, a trial of strength between the claims of the universal Church and the English state. But far more than before, the church-state struggle in John's reign was a direct confrontation between the English monarchy and the Roman papacy.

The Investiture Controversy had been settled long before in compromise; but the question of lay control over the appointments of bishops and abbots remained unresolved. The kings of England subscribed overtly to the policy of free canonical election but in fact controlled appointments to important offices in the English Church through subtle—or sometimes not so subtle—maneuvering. As long as royal influence was applied quietly and without serious opposition all was well. But if the king acted clumsily and created an issue, the papacy could be expected to intervene in behalf of proper canonical practices. This was particularly true in the opening years of the thirteenth century, when the papacy was occupied by Innocent III—a man of outstanding intelligence, energy, and self-confidence. Innocent III was history's most powerful pope, and it was John's misfortune to come to grips with such a man.

Hubert Walter had been a masterful royal administrator but a less than inspiring archbishop. The monks of Canterbury, who enjoyed the traditional canonical privilege of electing the archbishop, were anxious not to have another royal tool on the Canterbury throne. John was just as anxious to place one of his own loyal subordinates in the exalted position. Working quickly to forestall the king, the Canterbury monks elected one of their own number and sent a delegation to Rome to have him confirmed. Infuriated at this display of independence, John forced the monks to retract their choice, elect his own man, and send another delegation to Rome to obtain confirmation of the new candidate. Thus the issue had been raised, and Innocent III was in a position to adjudicate the dispute. He made good use of his opportunity by repudiating both nominees and persuading the Canterbury monks in Rome—now a goodly number—to elect a churchman of his own choice. The new archbishop was a noted English scholar, Stephen Langton, who had been out of the country some years teaching on the continent.

John refused to accept an "outsider" and rebelled against Innocent's interference. Every archbishop of Canterbury in memory—even troublesome ones like Thomas Becket—had been royal nominees; and John refused to give up the privileges of his royal forebears and abandon control of the Canterbury succession. Accordingly, Stephen Langton was barred from entering England. Innocent III, for his part, regarded Langton's election as strictly canonical and gave him full support. As a result of the impasse, Innocent laid England under interdict, suspending all church services and all sacraments except baptism and confession for the dying.

The interdict lasted seven years. John survived this awesome ecclesiastical penalty remarkably well, and even turned it to his financial advantage by confiscating ecclesiastical revenues. But in the end he was obliged to submit. Innocent III was threatening to depose John and was encouraging Philip Augustus to undertake an invasion of England. And John himself, whose grand design for the reconquest of Normandy and Anjou were reaching its climax, needed all the support he could obtain. Hence he made peace with the papacy in 1213; in the following year the interdict was lifted. Stephen Langton was admitted to England and installed in his archbishopric, and John agreed to restore at least a portion of the confiscated revenues.

Having surrendered, John determined to salvage as much as possible from the situation by winning the full support of the previously hostile pope. Of his own accord, so it seems, he gave to Innocent III what William the Conqueror had long ago refused to Gregory VII: he made England a papal fief, undertook to become Innocent's vassal, and promised an annual tribute payment to the papacy.[6] He took the further step of vowing to lead a crusade to the Holy Land. The projected crusade never materialized, for John always claimed more urgent business at home. But by his submission to papal vassalage and his crusading vow he succeeded in capturing the friendship of Rome. Consequently, historians have credited John with snatching victory from defeat. This interpretation seems doubtful; for Innocent's future support was of no great use to John, and Archbishop Stephen Langton turned out to be a man of independent spirit who tended to favor the barons in their forthcoming struggle with the crown. Nevertheless, in 1214 John still had hopes of recouping his previous losses. With the papal struggle at an end, he was ready at last to move decisively against Philip Augustus.

During the years of the interdict, John had been building a coalition of French and German princes against the French monarchy. In 1214 the chief parties in the coalition were Otto of Brunswick, John's nephew and a serious contestant for the disputed throne of the Holy Roman Empire; the counts of Flanders and certain neighboring principalities; and John himself. After several false starts John set forth for the county of Poitou in northern Aquitaine with as many English knights as he could persuade to accompany him. His expedition was intended as part of a grand design: he was to attack Philip Augustus through Poitou while his German and Flemish allies invaded France from the northeast. The strategy was well conceived, but it ended disastrously. John subdued Poitou and incorporated a large number of Poitevan knights into his army, but when these knights encountered an army led by Philip Augustus' son they refused to fight, claiming that they could not engage in armed conflict against their overlord. John was obliged to retire, in rage and frustration.

Philip Augustus himself led an army against John's German and Flemish allies and won an overwhelming victory over them near the Flemish village of Bouvines. Philip's victory extinguished John's last hope of recovering the lost continental fiefs. It also marked a significant advance in the authority of the French monarchy, which surged ahead of Germany as the great power on the continent. Thus the disintegration of the Angevin Empire in 1204 was confirmed by the decisive French triumph at Bouvines in 1214. John's careful plans were ruined by a battle at which he was not present.

Magna Carta

John's alliance system had been cemented with subsidies and bribes, which had obliged the king to tax England ruthlessly. In the wake of

---

6 The English monarchy continued to pay papal tribute off and on until the fourteenth century; it was officially repudiated only in 1366. At the time of John's submission, a number of other kingdoms—Poland, Sicily, Denmark, Sweden, and Aragon—were also papal vassal states.

Bouvines the calamitous failure of John's foreign policy was manifest to all. His prestige had never been lower, and many of his tax-ridden English barons were ready for rebellion. Early in 1215 the insurrection began, and by early summer it was obvious that the king could not contain it. His enemies were demanding a written guarantee of good law and just governance based on the coronation charter of Henry I, which had been reissued in 1154 by Henry II. In June 1215, after protracted negotiations, John came to terms on the meadow of Runnymede and affixed his seal to Magna Carta.[7]

The Great Charter is a much broader statement of rights and privileges than the charter of Henry I. It was the product of long bargaining among John, Archbishop Stephen Langton, barons who remained loyal to John, and barons of various degrees of hostility toward him. Its sixty-three clauses embraced the full spectrum of baronial grievances. Despite the specific and practical nature of many of the provisions, collectively they reflect—at least by implication—the rudiments of a coherent political philosophy.

Historians have not always agreed on the implications of Magna Carta. Until fairly recently it was widely regarded as the fountainhead of English liberty and the bulwark of constitutional monarchy. Some historians, reacting against this naive view, have described Magna Carta as a reactionary document—an assertion of feudal particularism at the expense of the enlightened Angevin monarchy. In reality, the Great Charter was both feudal and constitutional. It looked backward and also pointed forward. It was a step in the transition from the ancient Germanic notion of sacred custom and the feudal idea of mutual contractual rights and obligations to the modern concept of limited monarchy and government under the law. Earlier efforts to limit the expanding royal authority—the revolts of Stephen's reign, for example—were parochial in spirit and anarchic in consequence. In 1215, rebellious barons were once again seeking to curb an autocratic king, but they were also protesting the entire autocratic tradition of the Angevin dynasty. In doing so they were moving, haltingly, unconsciously, toward what would later be called constitutional monarchy.

Their demand of a written confirmation of privileges had precedents not only in earlier English coronation charters but also in documents drafted elsewhere in Europe—by Emperor Frederick Barbarossa to the towns of the Lombard League in 1183, by King Alphonso VIII of Leon to his barons in 1188. And similar charters were being forced out of European rulers all through the thirteenth century in Germany, Hungary, southern Italy, Sicily, and elsewhere. They were products of many of the same forces that underlay Magna Carta: military misfortune; the rising expenses of government; more effective administration, producing more inventive and ruthless means of collecting taxes; and a growing conception on the part of powerful sub-

---

[7] On the Great Charter see J. C. Holt, *Magna Carta* (Cambridge, 1965).

jects of their specific legal rights. But in one vital respect, Magna Carta was unique. Other charters were aimed at achieving autonomy for baronies or other local districts, whereas Magna Carta was national in scope and viewpoint. King John's barons, perhaps because their ancestral holdings had been scattered here and there across the land ever since the Conquest, sought not to exclude the royal government but to influence it—to make it act in their interest and respect their customary rights.

Baronial rights and privileges are the chief items of business in Magna Carta; yet the barons were not incapable of a wider social vision. Incorporated into the charter is the concept that the king is limited by tradition and custom in his relations with free Englishmen of every class—burghers and peasants as well as knights and barons: "To no one will we sell, deny or delay rights of justice." "No free man may be arrested or imprisoned or deprived of his land or outlawed or exiled or in any way brought to ruin, nor shall we go against him or send others in pursuit of him, except by the legal judgment of his peers or by the law of the land." The exact nature of "the law of the land" remained vague, but the barons felt it important to assert that there was such a law, to be discovered in custom and traditional usages, and that the king was bound by it. The concept was expressed more precisely a generation later by the great legist, Henry Bracton: "The king should be under God and the law." Political philosophers of the twelfth and thirteenth centuries were drawing sharp distinctions between the king who abided by the law and the tyrant who abused and ignored it. In Magna Carta these notions receive practical expression.

John had said, "The law is in my mouth." Such a doctrine was not only offensive to the feudal spirit but subversive to baronial interests. The king whose will was law could charge reliefs, levy scutages, and confiscate property as he pleased. Magna Carta forbade such practices in specific clauses: "Scutage and aid shall be levied in our kingdom only by the common counsel of our kingdom." "No widow shall be forced to marry so long as she wishes to live without a husband." "No one shall be distrained to render greater service from a knight's fee or from any other free holding than is thence owed." It was with practical building blocks such as these that the structure of the English limited monarchy was built. For implied in the numerous specific and highly pragmatic provisions of Magna Carta is the concept of an overarching body of law that circumscribes the power of the king.

There remained the problem of creating some kind of machinery to force the king to honor his concessions. Henry I had promised many things to his subjects in his coronation oath, but he ignored these promises once the crisis of his accession was passed. Clearly, mere royal promises were not enough to restrain an unscrupulous king with the full power of the royal administration behind him. The search for some institutional means of limiting royal authority, in fact as well as in theory, was to occupy England for centuries to come. The later Middle Ages found a tentative solution in parliament. The barons of 1215 employed a far cruder sanction: a watchdog committee of twenty-five barons who were to act against the king, if he violated the charter, by summoning the English people "to distrain and distress him in every way possible." In effect, the barons had no better reply to a royal repudiation of Magna Carta than the desperate sanction of popular and baronial rebellion. And they were soon called upon to exercise that sanction.

"In 1215," writes J. C. Holt, "Magna Carta was a failure. It was intended as a peace and it provoked war. It pretended to state customary law and it promoted disagreement and contention. It was legally valid for only three months, and even within that period its terms were never properly executed." Yet it survived the turbulence of John's final months, was reissued repeatedly in the thirteenth century, and became a part of the common law. Largely ignored in the days of the Tudors, it was revived, reinterpreted, and passionately asserted by the opponents of the seventeenth-century Stuart kings. It has never been entirely forgotten. In later centuries it came to be regarded as a document fundamental to the protection of individual liberty. This was far from the intention of its original drafters, but it is a tribute to the quality of their work. "It was adaptable. This was its greatest and most important characteristic." [8]

In John's view, however, Magna Carta was merely an expedient to escape a temporary difficulty. He had no intention of honoring his promises; he quickly secured from his sympathetic papel overlord absolution from his oath to the barons, which was, he argued, obtained under duress. Consequently, John ended his reign in the midst of a full-scale insurrection. The rebelling barons appealed for aid to King Philip Augustus; the French king sent an army to England led by his son Prince Louis. John died in 1216 with the French in London and the country wracked by war.

In one sense, the dissident barons were fighting to reverse a tradition of royal absolutism that had begun with the Norman kings and been carried still further by their Angevin successors. In another sense, they were fighting against a single man—a monarch who had earned their opprobrium by his duplicity and ruthlessness. This fact is dramatically demonstrated by the speed with which the baronial insurrection dissolved in the wake of John's passing. In the words of an earlier historian, "John's death virtually ended the war." The French invasion "was doomed to fail when the kingdom ceased to be divided against itself; and the one insuperable obstacle to the healing of its divisions was removed in the person of John." [9]

---

[8] Holt, *Magna Carta*, pp. 1, 2.
[9] Kate Norgate, *John Lackland* (London, 1902), p. 286.

Monarchy and Community:
The Troubles of Henry III

When King John died in 1216 he left as heir his nine-year-old son Henry III, who governed and misgoverned England for the next fifty-six years.[1] During the first decade of his long reign Henry was merely a nominal king, for the royal government was in the hands of regents. Fortunately for the realm, the young king's regents included men of singular ability and generous purpose. One was the legate Cardinal Guala, who exercised the right of guardianship in behalf of England's papal overlord. Another was William Marshall, England's most illustrious baron, a doughty and aged warrior who had risen from a common tournament jouster to become earl of Pembroke and who had remained faithful to King John through all his various moods and fortunes. A third was the talented justiciar, Hubert de Burgh, who had ascended from a minor landed family to the highest post in the royal administration and had won for himself the earldom of Kent. These three men, together with several others, comprised a select group of leading barons and high ecclesiastics who ruled England in the name of the child-king. Together they worked to heal England's old wounds and restore unity. Louis of France was forced to abandon his campaign, Magna Carta was reissued, and England was freed of strife and permitted to enjoy unimpeded the prosperity of the age.

---

[1] The two most thorough and penetrating works on the period are both by Maurice Powicke: *The Thirteenth Century*, Oxford History of England, Vol. IV (2nd ed., Oxford, 1962), and *King Henry III and the Lord Edward* (2 vols., Oxford, 1947). On constitutional history see Bertie Wilkinson, *Constitutional History of England, 1216–1399* (3 vols., New York, 1948–1958), and F. Thompson, *The First Century of Magna Carta* (Minneapolis, 1925).

As the years passed, the personnel of the governing group changed. Cardinal Guala left the country in 1218, and William Marshall died the following year. In the meantime Archbishop Stephen Langton, having returned from a visit to Rome, assumed an important position in the regency. In the early 1220s Langton and Hubert de Burgh were the chief instigators of royal policy; and although Hubert was the object of a certain amount of baronial jealousy, the regency government continued, by and large, to prosper.

At length, in 1227, the young king declared himself of age. At nineteen, he felt ready to assume the responsibilities of government; and in retrospect it can perhaps be said that he was as ready at nineteen as he would ever be. Stephen Langton died the following year, but the young king remained more or less under the influence of Hubert de Burgh until Hubert's fall from power in 1232.

One of the chief reasons for Hubert's downfall was his opposition to an ill-considered military campaign that Henry was determined to undertake. Disinclined to let practical advice temper his impulses, Henry was a man who longed for the unhampered exercise of the royal prerogative but did not know how to use it wisely. Although possessed of many talents, he was an uninspiring leader and an ineffective king. He was intelligent, even learned, but not in matters of statecraft. He was pious, but his piety was narrow rather than deep. As the contemporary historian Matthew Paris observed, "In proportion as the king was thought deficient in prudence in worldly affairs, so was he the more distinguished for his devotion to the Lord—for it was his custom each day to hear three masses . . . and when the priest elevated the body of our Lord, Henry usually held the priest's hand and kissed it." Henry was a man of discrimination, but only in judging art, not men. Generous with his friends, loyal to his papal overlord, faithful to his wife, he was suspicious of nearly everybody else. His moody disposition, mercurial temperament, and acid tongue lost him the respect of his barons. At times he could seem firm, but his firmness was actually mere obstinacy. His reign was long but inglorious.

Matthew Paris describes Henry as "of medium stature and compact in body. One of his eyelids drooped, hiding some of the dark part of the eyeball. He had robust strength but was careless in his acts." A court jester is reported to have remarked that Henry III was like Jesus Christ; when asked why, he replied that, like Jesus, Henry was as wise at his birth as he would ever become.

The Civilization of the Thirteenth Century

Despite the incapacity of its king, England in the reign of Henry III participated fully in the achievements of high medieval civilization. Although centered on France, the culture of the High Middle Ages made its impact on England as well. On both sides of the Channel the expansion of

HENRY III
The gilt-bronze effigy circa 1294, was one of two life-sized figures commissioned by Edward I for a memorial chapel in Westminster Abbey. *Copyright A. F. Kersting.*

arable lands proceeded. The towns continued to grow in size, wealth, and privileges. Commerce increased in scale and intensity, and the economy was kept lively by a process of gradual inflation. The great trade of English wool for Flemish cloth grew ever larger, and in time a flourishing cloth industry began to develop in England itself. Tin mining rose to the level of an important industry. With the rising productivity of English fields, more and more surplus grain was produced to serve not only as a significant export commodity but also as a cushion against famine years. The peasantry itself profited only modestly from this prosperity; but the lesser knights (the later gentry) and the townsmen became increasingly affluent and important; and the great barons lived on a scale previously undreamed of. The grim, cramped castles of the eleventh century gave way to elaborate stone fortifications and ample and relatively well-furnished manor houses.

Throughout the twelfth and thirteenth centuries the birthrate of all classes seems to have been rising while, as a result of increased food production and greater internal security, the death rate was diminishing. Consequently, the population of England appears to have at least doubled and perhaps tripled between the late eleventh century and the late thirteenth. The England of Domesday Book probably had a population of between one and two million; whereas late thirteenth-century England contained between three and six million inhabitants. These statistics, although exceedingly approximate, testify unmistakably to England's economic progress in the post-Conquest centuries.

The economic vigor of the thirteenth century was accompanied by a cultural creativity that saw the significant artistic and literary traditions of twelfth-century Europe develop into rich maturity. In the field of architecture, for example, the reign of Henry III, and that of his illustrious French contemporary, Louis IX (St. Louis), marked the apogee of the Gothic style. Originating in the twelfth-century Ile de France, Gothic architecture—with its radically new principles of design and canons of beauty—reached its culmination in such French cathedrals of the thirteenth century as Chartres, Reims, and Amiens. It was less massive than the Romanesque style it superseded and far more graceful. The thick walls necessary to the structural stability of Romanesque churches were made superfluous by such Gothic innovations as the flying buttress, the pointed arch, and the ribbed vault. The new churches were skeletal frameworks of stone in which walls served only as screens and were replaced more and more by huge, lustrous windows of colored glass. These structural ideas quickly spread to England where, in one instance, they resulted in a nearly perfect imitation: King Henry III, a devotee of French culture, personally directed the rebuilding of Westminster Abbey in the French High Gothic style, much as Edward the Confessor had supervised the building of its Norman Romanesque predecessor. But elsewhere the new French architecture was modified in accordance with English tastes into a distinctive variation known as Early English Gothic. Its vaults did not rise to such great heights, nor were its clerestory windows quite so large. Its interiors were often painted and sometimes enlivened by the use of dark marble columns that contrasted with wall surfaces and arches of light-colored stone. The east ends of these churches, behind their high altars, were squared rather than rounded as in France. The upward thrust of the columns and pointed arches was held firmly in check by strong horizontal lines, creating a sense of harmonious balance. Withal, Early English Gothic was less audacious, less tautly dramatic than French High Gothic, but just as well proportioned and in its own way equally successful. It inspired the building of great cathedrals such as Salisbury, Wells, and Lincoln, as well as numerous village and abbey churches, a great many of which, like the cathedrals, still stand essentially unchanged.[2]

---

[2] Two excellent works that relate Gothic architecture to the cultural background of the High Middle Ages are Erwin Panofsky, *Gothic Architecture and Scholasticism* (reprint, Cleveland, 1957), and Otto von Simson, *The Gothic Cathedral* (2nd ed., New York, 1962). On a more popular level see Jean Gimpel, *The Cathedral Builders* (new ed., New York, 1961). For the English styles see the richly illustrated *English Cathedrals* by Geoffrey Grigson, Martin Hürlimann, and Peter Meyer (new ed., London, 1961).

WESTMINSTER ABBEY AND
SALISBURY CATHEDRAL,
CONTRASTING STYLES OF GOTHIC

Westminster, built by Henry III in
the style of the French High Gothic,
emphasizes vertical movement and
light. By contrast Salisbury, in the
modified Early English Gothic,
conveys a greater sense of solidity
through the use of counterbalancing
horizontal structures. *National
Monuments Record.*

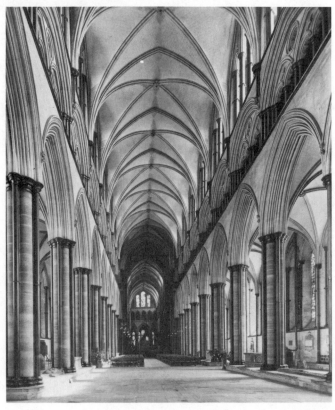

The cathedrals were not, as is sometimes thought, mere monuments to ecclesiastical vainglory, built through the toil and impoverishment of unwilling masses. Our evidence suggests that they were products of a great common faith—of a powerful religious folk culture embodying a Christian world view that was shared by all orders of society. They were the highest artistic achievements of an age of belief in which architects, sculptors, glassmakers, and ordinary builders worked toward the achievements of a shared aspiration to adorn their towns and manifest their faith. The fullest exercise of their creative powers was achieved not in spite of the prevailing ecclesiastical culture but through it. Their finest works, the high-medieval cathedrals, illustrate even today that romantic individualism is not the only path to artistic excellence—that in certain periods of cultural vitality great works of art can arise from a self-abnegating commitment to the ideals of the wider community. In the High Middle Ages these ideals included civic pride, devotion to the Church and her saints, and love of God. It appears, from incomplete evidence, that high-medieval cathedral builders, though no less human than modern artists, tended to be less alienated from society. They did not believe in art for art's sake, and judging from the noble serenity of their sculpture they were generally happier for it. No medieval artist, so far as we know, cut off his ear.

The literature of the thirteenth century, although perhaps less significant than its architecture, is nevertheless impressive. The growing lay literacy of the twelfth century had by now reached the point where written records were being kept at many baronial courts and manors. Secular vernacular literature flourished in a variety of forms: the political song, the round (England's first known round, "Sumer is icumen in," dates from this period), and most notably the romance. English was becoming gradually more important as a literary vehicle, but French retained its dominance among the English aristocracy until the next century, and in the romance it found a congenial form of expression.

The romance is a synthesis of two earlier literary forms: the *chanson de geste* (song of great deeds) and the lyric poem. The chanson de geste was popular in northern France and England during the Anglo-Norman era. It was a rough and bellicose narrative poem that stressed the heroic virtues of loyalty and warlike prowess typical of the earlier feudal aristocracy. Its characteristics are splendidly exemplified in the "Song of Roland," an exciting, bloodthirsty tale of an actual battle between a powerful Moslem army and a small knightly band led by Charlemagne's nephew. The "Song of Roland" is said to have been a favorite of William the Conqueror himself.[3]

---

[3] William of Malmesbury alleges that at the onset of the battle of Hastings, the Normans advanced against the English singing "the song of Roland." If so, it was probably in an earlier form than the earliest version known to us today (transcribed by an anonymous author sometime between *c.* 1100 and 1130).

The lyric poem, a product of the very different cultural milieu of southern France was short, sometimes witty, and often romantic. In the course of the later twelfth century, the southern lyric, with its emphasis on idealized love and refined behavior, was transmitted by aristocratic southerners such as Eleanor of Aquitaine and her daughter Marie, Countess of Champagne, into the courts of northern Europe. There, it contributed to the romanticizing of the knightly ideal and to a significant transformation in poetic expression from the rough and intensely masculine epic style of the chanson de geste to the thirteenth-century romance. This new literary style was narrative in form like the chanson de geste, but romantic in mood like the lyric poem. The thirteenth-century romances drew heavily for their subject matter on a series of tales relating to the court of the half-legendary British monarch, King Arthur—tales that originated in Wales and were given international publicity by Geoffrey of Monmouth, a churchman active in England and Wales in the time of Henry I and Stephen, and whose fanciful *History of the Kings of Britain* was read widely on both sides of the Channel. In the later twelfth and thirteenth centuries the Arthurian legends, along with other ancient Welsh tales such as the adventures of Parsifal and Tristan, were beautifully and imaginatively developed by poets in France and Germany. The sensitivity of the twelfth and thirteenth century romance, contrasting sharply with the crude power of the chanson de geste, attests to the growing sophistication of medieval European civilization.

Secular culture achieved much in the thirteenth century, but it continued to be deeply influenced by the ideals of Christianity. The Church remained a powerful force not only in the daily lives of its members but also in the arenas of regional and international politics. The papacy reached the height of its power and controlled the universal Church as never before —through its legates, its authority over bishops and abbots, and its superbly developed central administrative machinery. But success and affluence are always likely to present dangers to a spiritual institution (as to others), and there can be no question but that the thirteenth-century Church had lost its lean and hungry look. Its prelates were becoming increasingly absorbed in the problems of political power at the expense of their spiritual and pastoral responsibilities, and pious reformers could point occasionally to shocking instances of corruption. An archiepiscopal visitation to a small thirteenth-century Norman nunnery yielded these data:

> Johanna de Alto Villari kept going out alone with a man named Gayllard, and within a year she had a child by him. The subprioress is suspected with Thomas the carter, her sister Idonia with Crispinatus, and the prior of Gisorcium is always coming to the convent for Idonia. Philippa of Rouen is suspected with a priest of Suentre, of the diocese of Chartres; Margurita, the treasuress, with Richard de Genville, a cleric; Agnes de Fontenei, with a priest of Guerreville, of the diocese of Chartres. . . . All wear their hair improperly and perfume their veils. Jacqueline came back pregnant from visiting a certain chaplain who was expelled from his house as a result of

this. Agnes de Monsec was suspected with the same chaplain. Emengard and Johanna de Alto Vilari beat each other. The prioress is drunk almost every night.

Such instances are far from typical, however. Widespread ecclesiastical corruption was the product of subsequent centuries. The great weakness of the Church in the thirteenth century was not vice but complacency. If there were licentious nuns in Normandy, there was also a stern and pious archbishop to discipline them. The Church retained a powerful impulse toward piety and reform which manifested itself in the spiritual dedication of countless lay and clerical believers, in the exemplary lives of many great prelates, and above all in the dynamic activities of the new mendicant orders.[4]

Arising in the early thirteenth century, these orders—the Franciscan and the Dominican—brought new dynamism to the spiritual life of Western Christendom. The Franciscan and Dominican friars lived by a rule, as monks did; but unlike their monastic predecessors they shunned the walls of the monastery and traveled far and wide to preach among the people—especially the people of the rising towns, who were exhibiting a spiritual thirst that the traditional ecclesiastical organization could not quench. The Franciscans directed their energies primarily toward the poor, while the Dominicans preached to the wealthy and powerful—and to heretics. Both orders dedicated themselves to chastity, obedience to their superior, and individual and corporate poverty. In the beginning the Franciscan and Dominican orders had no property at all, and even though their immense success and popularity soon forced them, in the interest of organizational coherence, to accept jurisdiction over houses, churches, and small parcels of land, they never remotely approached the vast landed wealth of the earlier Benedictines or Cistercians. The Dominicans came to England in 1221, the Franciscans in 1224. Before long their activities spread to every major town. In England, as on the continent, the mendicant orders brought vigorous new life to the Church by their fervent, compassionate preaching, their unpretentious holiness, and their boundless enthusiasm. To these virtues the Franciscans added still another: the gay and artless simplicity inherited from their remarkable founder, St. Francis of Assisi (d. 1226).

Despite their original simplicity, however, the Franciscans were quick to join the Dominicans in enriching the intellectual life of the European universities, which were now rising to great prominence. Several important universities—most notably, Paris, Bologna, and Oxford—had risen in the vibrant intellectual environment of the twelfth century; but they became organized and established educational institutions only in the thirteenth. Bologna was Europe's greatest center for the study of civil and canon law.

---

4 On English monasticism in general see the works of Dom David Knowles: *The Monastic Order in England, 940–1216* (2nd ed., Cambridge, 1966), and *The Religious Orders in England*, I, *1216–c. 1340* (Cambridge, 1948).

Paris excelled in philosophy and theology, which were regarded as the supreme intellectual disciplines of the day and which the scholars of the thirteenth century developed and elaborated in brilliant fashion. Franciscan and Dominican theologians of remarkable ability graced the Paris faculty, which included, at one time or another, the three finest philosophical minds of the age: the Dominicans St. Albertus Magnus and St. Thomas Aquinas and the Franciscan minister-general, St. Bonaventure. In his tightly-organized *Summa Theologica* and *Summa Contra Gentiles*, Aquinas created an exhaustive, compelling fusion of reason and Christian revelation that brought medieval theology to mature synthesis and culmination. His intellectual system stimulated vigorous controversy in its own time and has done so ever since; but it has also proven remarkably durable and retains, to this day, its power to win intellectual converts. It is an impressive illustration of the profundity of thirteenth-century culture and, indeed, one of the great achievements in the history of thought.

England shared in the intense intellectual life of the thirteenth century, particularly through its two universities—Oxford and Cambridge. There, as at Paris and Bologna, distinguished faculties offered courses in law, medicine, theology, and the liberal arts.[5] Among the various subdivisions of philosophy was one known as "natural philosophy," roughly equivalent to what we know as science. And it was in science, above all else, that England made its distinctive contribution to medieval learning. Indeed, it has been argued that the most significant progenitor of modern European science was the great English scholar-churchman Robert Grosseteste (d. 1253), bishop of Lincoln and first chancellor of Oxford University.[6] A master of Greek, a theologian, an ecclesiastical statesman active in the political affairs of his day, and a keen student of both Platonic and Aristotelian philosophy, Grosseteste did his great pioneering work in the field of scientific methodology. His attempts to explain such phenomena as comets, rainbows, and color seem crude by later standards; but his emphasis on mathematics and, above all, his articulation of a logical experimental method, prepared the way for the impressive scientific advances of subsequent centuries. Grosseteste wrote extensively on methodology, outlining a procedure that contained most of the crucial ingredients of the modern scientific approach: careful observation, the framing of a hypothesis, and the checking of the hypothesis against the actual behavior of natural phenomena—a process akin to what we would now term experimental verification. Sound methodology is basic to science, and in Grosseteste's work it was set forth in detailed rational form for the first time, though in a terminology strange to modern

---

5 The liberal arts in medieval curricula were seven in number: arithmetic, geometry, astronomy, music, grammar, rhetoric, and dialectic (logical philosophy).

6 A. C. Crombie, *Robert Grosseteste and the Origins of Experimental Science* (Oxford, 1953), has succeeded in convincing some historians, though by no means all, that Grosseteste's ideas were crucial to the development of modern scientific methodology.

scientists. Grosseteste cannot be regarded as the father of science, for he drew heavily from his Greek and Islamic predecessors; but from the Western European standpoint, there is reason to regard him as its foster father.

Robert Grosseteste exerted a deep influence on his successors, particularly among English scholars of the Franciscan order. Although not a Franciscan himself, he was instrumental in establishing the order at Oxford, and Franciscan friars were among his most devoted students. The scientific orientation of English Franciscanism derived from Grosseteste's inspiration and perhaps also from the deep love of nature exhibited by St. Francis himself. It expressed itself during the later thirteenth century in the works of Roger Bacon. Roger was a Franciscan friar whose extensive writings contain, alongside a good deal of superstitious fancy, a passion for experimentation and for the application of mathematics to scientific investigation: "Reasoning does not disclose these matters; on the contrary, experiments are required, performed on a large scale with instruments and by other necessary means." At times, Roger Bacon assumes the role of scientific prophet: "Experimental science controls the conclusions of all other sciences. It discloses truths which reasoning from general principles [the favored method of the Paris theologians] would never have discovered. Finally, it sets us on the way to marvelous inventions which will change the face of the world."

An age that achieved so much in the realms of art, literature, and thought might well be expected to demonstrate its creativity in politics as well. And such was the case. The thirteenth century witnessed a momentous growth in the power of the French monarchy that began with King Philip Augustus' conquest of much of the old Angevin Empire and his stunning victory at Bouvines, continued with the distinguished reign of the saint-king, Louis IX (1226–1270), and concluded with the powerful, ruthless Philip IV ("the Fair": 1285–1314), whose royal administration achieved an unprecedented degree of efficiency and centralization. Drawing from the great heritage of Roman law and also from the precocious administrative institutions that the Angevin monarchs left behind them in Normandy, the Capetian kings of France made their kingdom the richest and most illustrious in Europe.

Yet France, with its size and its legacy of local particularism, remained less centralized, less subordinated to its royal government, than England. For England, too, made impressive progress during the thirteenth century in law and administration. The achievements of the twelfth century were continued and developed. The rising affluence of the lesser knights and the burghers was accompanied by a growing sense of political responsibility and an increasing participation in local administration. The shire courts, which were coming to play an ever greater role in the royal judicial system, were operated by members of the knightly gentry. The town governments and town courts fell more and more under the control of the burghers themselves—in particular, the wealthy merchants and master craftsmen.

Accordingly, political responsibility was slowly filtering down from the great magnates to the prosperous middle group of shire gentry and well-to-do townsmen. The great majority of the population remained relatively impotent and inarticulate, but the political base was nevertheless broadening. Even the semifree serfs became slightly more involved in the affairs of the kingdom. For, prior to the thirteenth century, only freemen were allowed the privilege of bearing arms—the possession of arms had traditionally been a mark of free status. In the thirteenth century, however, arms were permitted to serfs, who thereby assumed some small share of the responsibility for defending the land and maintaining internal order. It would be hazardous to make too much of this new privilege, which was also a new obligation, but it cannot be ignored.

Out of this diffusion and responsibility there arose a concept vital to the politics of the age and to the future development of English constitutional government: the notion of a "community of the realm." The concept of community by no means embraced all Englishmen. At first it was restricted to the king and his barons, but gradually it came to include prosperous members of the lesser knightly class and the burghers. These groups contributed much to the operation and enrichment of the kingdom, and it was reasonable that they should have some voice in its governance. There was much disagreement as to precisely what their political role ought to be, but as the century progressed, the notion became firmly rooted that a ruler who ignored the interests of the "community of the realm" was no king but a tyrant.

This notion was by no means subversive of the continued growth of a centralized government. Even more than at the time of Magna Carta, the issue was not whether a strong royal administration should exist, but how it should be controlled. In the course of the thirteenth century the struggle for control of the central administration machinery was at times violent, but the machinery itself became steadily more elaborate and efficient.

The chief agency of government, under the king, was the small council with its varied responsibilities—administrative, fiscal, and judicial. It advised the king, dealt with financial matters too great or too complex for the exchequer to handle, served as the essential nucleus of all meetings of the great council, and functioned as the high tribunal of the realm. It was a court of common law—the King's Bench—with jurisdiction over great civil and criminal cases. It could function, too, as a feudal court, adjudicating disputes between royal vassals. And it had also become a court of equity, handling cases that could not be properly or fairly settled in the feudal, shire, or common-law courts. As time went on, more and more of the judicial business brought before the council was delegated to a body of specialized royal justices. Not infrequently these justices sat with the king and his small council, and occasionally they merged into a still larger tribunal of king, small council, and great council. But much of the time they functioned primarily as a separate court with something of the same independence as the exchequer court and the court of Common Pleas. It was they who would in time, as an independent body, assume the functions and title of the court of King's Bench. Their chief business was the trial of criminal cases in the king's name.

The small council maintained close relations not only with the common-law courts but also with the major administrative offices of exchequer and chancery, whose chief officers, the treasurer and chancellor, were normally council members themselves. The exchequer, permanently at Westminster, shared financial responsibility with the wardrobe—the financial office that accompanied the king on his travels and handled day-by-day expenses. Exchequer recordkeeping became more rigorous, and exchequer procedures achieved an unparalleled level of efficiency. The chancery, an increasingly active branch of the royal household, maintained custody of the Great Seal. Chancery officials were responsible for drawing up a growing variety and number of royal documents—charters, royal letters, administrative and judicial writs—and authenticating them by use of the Great Seal. Since the time of King John, the chancery had been regularly preserving copies of these documents—"enrolling" them—in records such as the charter rolls, patent rolls, and close rolls. Under Henry III a new type of seal, the Privy Seal, was kept in the king's traveling court; it thus became possible for the chancery, with its Great Seal, to "go out of court" and function as a separate department of state. This process of differentiation was not completed, however, until the fourteenth century.

Royal administration and royal law grew side by side. The reign of Henry III produced an impressive, systematic legal treatise—Henry de Bracton's *On the Laws and Customs of England*—a thoughtful and humane study that far transcended Glanville's work of the previous century and illustrated clearly that English law had come of age. Bracton, both a widely experienced royal judge and a serious student of the principles of Roman law, devoted his treatise chiefly to an analysis of the vast accumulation of precedents on which the English Common Law was based; but he was able to look beyond the precedents themselves to what he regarded as the fundamental principles behind them. One such principle was the notion that the king, although subject to the law himself, was the ultimate source of justice in the realm. Henry I and Henry II had been moving toward this goal, and in Bracton's time it was coming ever closer to realization.

The thirteenth century saw the establishment of a coherent and comprehensive legal system. The royal courts of King's Bench, Common Pleas, exchequer, and justices in eyre [7] were staffed for the first time by what can be described as professional judges and were given a sturdy juridical and philosophical foundation by Bracton's great treatise. With the evolution of a strong royal bureaucracy, a structured and professional judiciary, and

---

[7] See above, pp. 138–39.

the vital concept of community, feudal monarchy was being left far behind. Yet it was the contractual assumption of feudalism itself—the notion of subject's rights before the lord-king—that gave the English monarchy of the thirteenth century its tone and its direction.

Henry III: The Limitation of the Royal Prerogative

The age of Henry III was a crucial epoch in the history of English constitutional development. The historian G. O. Sayles has aptly described the reign as "a commentary upon the Great Charter." More than that, it was a commentary on one of the central problems inherent in Magna Carta and in medieval political theory as a whole: Given that the king's authority is bound by customary limitations—that "the king should be under God and the law," as Bracton put it—how could such a principle be translated into workable political institutions? The answer was found in the concept that the king should govern in the interests and with the cooperation of the "community of the realm."

English government had always been, at least to some extent, the product of a dialogue between monarchy and community. The Anglo-Saxon kings acted on important occasions in consultation with their Witan; the Norman and Angevin kings usually summoned their great councils to advise them on important decisions and drew continually on the advice and administrative support of their small council. But well into the thirteenth century the great and small councils had neither a power of veto nor a fixed membership; if the king chose to abuse his rights over the baronage, ignore their counsel, and overtax his subjects, there was little recourse short of rebellion. The search for a more effective means for the barons to share in governance was the major concern of English politics under Henry III. And through most of his reign, dissident barons worked toward this end by struggling to gain control of the king's small council. In this way they hoped to assure the rights set forth in Magna Carta and to reverse the long trend toward royal absolutism that had been so evident under the Norman and Angevin kings.

As his reign progressed, Henry III tended more and more to forgo his barons' advice and to exclude them from participation in the central government. Particularly after about 1232, the king packed his small council with his own professional administrators and with favorites whom the barons described contemptuously as "foreigners"—relatives and associates of his wife, Eleanor of Provence, who were only too anxious to enrich themselves through royal favor in this rich island kingdom. Matthew Paris remarks that day by day the king was losing the affection of his natural subjects:

> He enticed to his side all the foreigners he could, enriched them, and, despising and despoiling his English subjects, intruded aliens into their place.... Men from Poitou busied themselves in oppressing the nobles of the country, and especially religious men, in a thousand ways.

The situation was aggravated by Henry's obvious dislike and distrust of his English nobles. Matthew Paris tells how Henry flew into a rage against the important earl, Robert de Ros, and called him a traitor. "You lie," the earl replied: "I have never been a traitor and never will be. If you are just, how can you harm me?" "I can seize your grain and thrash and sell it," the king responded. "Do so," answered the earl, "and I will send back your threshers minus their heads." Friends interceded to quiet the quarrel, but Matthew Paris observes that the windy words bred anger and hatred. As one historian has aptly said, the king had the tongue of an asp.

Henry III was by no means the first king to govern without serious regard for the advice of his magnates. The English political tradition was still sufficiently amorphous to allow a king to rule arbitrarily, as long as his policies were reasonably successful and palatable to the barons and as long as he maintained fairly good personal relations with them and did not squeeze them too hard. King John had failed and squeezed, and Magna Carta was the result. Similarly, Henry III's nonbaronial government engendered a vigorous reaction for two reasons. First, his policies—which involved huge, chimerical foreign schemes and lavish spending—seemed ill conceived and subversive to baronial interests; he was obliged to appeal frequently for baronial aids, and the barons granted them with increasing reluctance. Second, the barons were mindful of the recent example— during the regency—of a successful government based on baronial advice and council. This memory sharpened in the barons' minds the traditional notion that they were the king's "natural counselors."

The Struggle with the Dissident Barons

In the decades following 1232 baronial opposition increased. A growing number of magnates, feeling more and more excluded from the process of royal governance, endeavored repeatedly to replace Henry's French and household favorites in the small council with their own representatives. In 1234 they presented a list of grievances to the king in his great council; and, with the support of the new archbishop of Canterbury, Edmund Rich— who threatened Henry with excommunication—they forced him to dismiss his former counselors and accept in their place nine men approved by the barons. By now membership in the small council was becoming more clearly defined than in earlier times, and the custom arose of requiring counselors to swear an oath of loyalty and good council to the king.

Henry III soon resumed his earlier policies, ignoring the barons and recalling his former advisers. In 1236 a baronial demonstration against foreign participation forced him to take refuge for a time in the Tower of London, but it effected no change in the makeup of his small council. At a great council meeting in 1237 the barons refused him requested aid unless he purged the small council and brought in "natural counselors"—namely, barons. Henry again submitted, again momentarily, to the appointment and swearing in of twelve men acceptable to the barons, including several of themselves. Once the great council disbanded, the king brought back his favorites.

The comedy was repeated with variations in the great council of 1244, and baronial dissatisfaction steadily intensified. But the king managed to muddle through from crisis to crisis and to keep his small council virtually free of baronial influence until 1258. At that time a crisis occurred that proved too much for Henry; as a consequence, the royal government was forced to undergo a profound reorientation.

Henry's successive crises with his barons came about because of his incessant need to appeal to them for money beyond the customary royal revenues. Basically, the financial position of the mid-thirteenth century monarchy was sound; the difficulty was that medieval monarchies had nothing to correspond to the national debts of modern governments. There were no normal means of raising funds to meet extraordinary expenses, except to borrow at short term and high interest from individuals or groups (merchants, churchmen, Jewish bankers), or to beg the barons' permission to levy a special tax. Matthew Paris mentions various undignified money-raising methods Henry was forced to employ. He pawned his jewels, and even sold them. He trumped up charges against Jewish bankers and threatened them with imprisonment unless they paid thousands of pounds into the royal treasury. To the abbot of Ramsey he wrote, "My friend, I earnestly beg you to assist me by giving, or at least lending me one hundred pounds, for I am in need and must have that sum without delay." On one occasion he approached each of his barons in turn, saying "I am a poor man and entirely destitute of money . . . and whoever will do me this favor, to him I will return it when an opportunity occurs; but whoever denies me the favor, to him will I also deny any."

Henry's financial difficulties were largely of his own making, for the virtue of thrift was unknown to him. In Maurice Powicke's words,

> He maintained a great household, swollen by foreign kinsmen and their protégés, by a company of knights and by a crowd of officials. He was hospitable and liked big ceremonial feasts. He was a lavish patron of the arts and had a passion for building, for the decoration of his castles and houses, for jewels and precious stones and fine clothes. Tenacious of his rights, he was involved in frequent lawsuits at Rome, where he had to maintain expensive guardians of his interests not only as his proctors but as pensioners among the cardinals and officials of the Curia. The sums he spent annually on gifts of wood, venison, robes, pensions would have been the despair of a modern committee of ways and means.[8]

Added to all these expenses were the high costs of Henry's grandiose ambitions in foreign affairs. Repeatedly and fruitlessly he tried to recover

---

[8] Powicke, *Henry III and the Lord Edward,* I, 303.

Normandy and Anjou—paying soldiers, bribing allies, and financing rebellious French barons. When these efforts failed, he turned his attention to more distant parts. The crisis of 1258 between Henry and his barons was a direct result of Henry's attempt to place a son on the throne of the kingdom of Sicily.

For a century the papacy had been engaged in a power struggle with the Hohenstaufen dynasty of the Holy Roman Empire. Following the death of the brilliant and dangerous Emperor Frederick II in 1250, the pope sought Henry III's cooperation in dividing the vast territories the Hohenstaufens had ruled. In the 1190s this dynasty had added the rich Norman kingdom of Sicily and southern Italy to its extensive dominions. Now the papacy was determined to sever these southern districts from the remainder of the Holy Roman Empire and place them under a new dynasty. So it was that in 1254 the pope offered the Sicilian crown to Edmund, second son of King Henry III.

The offer was less generous than it might seem. The pope had been trying for several years to dispose of the Sicilian crown, and two important princes had already rejected it. They were probably wise to do so. Henry III accepted the crown for his son but was also obliged to assume the enormous debt the papacy had incurred in connection with its campaigns against the Hohenstaufens in Sicily. It was a sum in excess of ninety thousand pounds—almost as great as King Richard the Lion-Hearted's ransom. To make matters worse, the years following 1254 saw the actual control of the Sicilian kingdom fall into the hands of an able bastard Hohenstaufen named Manfred. Edmund's hopes of winning a kingdom to go with his new crown seemed dim indeed.

But once committed to paying the huge papal debt, Henry III could not renege without great difficulty and embarrassment. He found himself committed to a ruinously expensive and fruitless venture. When he fell behind in his payments the Vicar of Christ threatened to excommunicate him. Henry was obliged to turn to his barons for financial aid; they agreed to help him, but only in return for radical political concessions. In 1258 he surrendered to the demands of his magnates and allowed them a significant degree of control over the royal administration.

Henry's Sicilian dream emptied his treasury and obliged him to sacrifice his royal independence. Moreover, it forced him to come to terms at last with the French monarchy. In the Treaty of Paris (1259) he formally recognized the Capetian dominion over the former territories of the Angevin Empire in northern France and did homage to Louis IX for Gascony and other southern French lands that had remained more or less under English control since the catastrophes of John's reign. And in the end Henry lost Sicily, too. The papacy eventually found a more stalwart champion against Manfred in the person of Charles of Anjou, Louis IX's younger brother. It was Charles rather than Edmund who finally won Sicily from the Hohenstaufens.

In 1258, however, the fate of Sicily was still uncertain, and Henry III was obliged to make terms with his magnates. His submission took the form of a letter in which he granted

> that by twelve faithful men of our council already elected, and by twelve other faithful men elected by the nobles, who are to convene at Oxford one month after the coming feast of Pentecost, the condition of our kingdom shall be ordered, rectified, and reformed in keeping with what they shall think it best to enact for the honor of God, for our faith, and for the good of our kingdom.... And whatever is ordained in this manner by the twenty-four elected by both sides and sworn to the undertaking—or by the majority of them—we will observe inviolably.... Moreover, the aforesaid earls and barons have promised that on the completion of the business stated above they will in good faith endeavor to arrange that a common aid is rendered us by the community of our realm.

The deliberations of the twenty-four men resulted in an agreement known as the Provisions of Oxford (1258), which sought at one blow to make the community of the realm a political reality. First of all, there were to be at least three formal meetings of the great council each year; they were to include in their membership not only the chosen counselors of the king but also twelve men "elected" by the "community"—i.e., selected by the magnates. It was further stipulated that "the community shall regard as binding whatever these twelve shall do." Moreover, the small council passed under the control of a baronial executive committee—the Council of Fifteen—with the power of "advising the king in good faith regarding the government of the kingdom and all matters pertaining to the king or the kingdom, and of amending and reforming everything that they shall consider in need of amendment or reform." The Council of Fifteen was given a powerful voice in the royal administration through its power to appoint three of the great officers of state: the chancellor, the treasurer, and the justiciar. It had authority over the exchequer and worked with the king to supervise the activities of sheriffs and other local officials.

The Provisions of Oxford also included a number of administrative reforms, designed particularly to correct abuses in property laws; additional reforms of a similar nature were established in a corollary document, the Provisions of Westminster (1259). In general, the magnates accepted the strengthening of the central administration that had occurred over the past several generations. They merely wished to share in the control of the administrative machinery until a new and more trustworthy king should accede to the throne. They sought what they conceived to be good government—government in the baronial interest. They had despaired of enjoying such government as long as Henry III ruled unimpeded. Their methods of limiting royal authority—frequent great council meetings and the Council of Fifteen—represent a far more enlightened and mature approach than that of John's barons in 1215.

Still, their solution was too extreme to be lasting. Under the provisions, the central administrative machinery remained as powerful as ever, but the king himself was reduced to virtual parity with the greater magnates. Many barons, deeply troubled over the emasculation of kingship the Provisions of Oxford implied, gradually became disenchanted with their more radical leaders. In time the experiment in limited monarchy became racked by baronial dissension, and by 1262 Henry III found himself in a position to abolish the provisions altogether. Absolved of his oaths by the pope, he undertook once again to rule by his own authority.

Some of Henry's barons had evidently hoped that the king might learn from his misfortunes. They were badly disappointed, for Henry's renewed personal rule was just as willful, just as cavalier as ever. Consequently, in 1263 baronial opposition asserted itself once again.

The leader of the insurgents in 1263 was Simon de Monfort, Earl of Leicester and brother-in-law of the king. Earl Simon was a remarkable character—passionate, adventurous, and fearlessly self-confident—capable of inspiring some with intense loyalty and high hopes, others with terror and hatred. A younger son of a great baronial family of central France, Simon had come to England seeking his fortune and had become earl of Leicester. He had once been a favored friend of Henry III, but in time, like so many other barons, he had a falling out with the king. Simon was one of the powers behind the Provisions of Oxford and had served on the Council of Fifteen. When Henry rescinded the provisions in 1262, Simon had been forced into exile, but he returned in 1263 to lead the disaffected barons.

Toward the close of 1263 king and magnates agreed to submit their dispute to the arbitration of the universally respected Louis IX of France. St. Louis' impartiality was famous, but he had an uncompromising respect for the prerogatives of royalty; the baronial notions of cooperative government and community of the realm were beyond his experience. His verdict, known as the "Mise of Amiens" (1264), constituted a ringing denunciation of the baronial cause:

> We suppress and annul all the aforesaid provisions, ordinances, statutes, and obligations, by whatever name, and all that has followed from them. . . . We also decree and ordain that the said king, of his own will, may freely appoint, dismiss, and remove the justiciar, chancellor, treasurer, counselors, lesser justices, sheriffs, and any other officers and ministers of his kingdom and household, as he was used and able to do prior to the time of the aforesaid provisions.

Left without a scrap of their hard-fought program, Henry's baronial opponents felt that they had no recourse but to take up arms.

The rebellion of 1264–65 was not simply a struggle between king and baronage. As has been suggested, the barons were by no means of one mind. Few of them approved of Henry III, but many had a keen respect for the royal office and distrusted the radical goals of the opposition leaders.

Nobody, of course, wished to abolish the monarchy—the day of Oliver Cromwell was four centuries away—but insurgents such as Simon de Montfort would not hesitate to govern the realm in the name of a captive king.

Thus there were barons on both sides, and not a few magnates switched teams in the midst of the struggle. The opposition was led by Simon de Montfort, the royalist force by Henry III's eldest son, the Lord Edward, now growing into manhood. There were many who looked hopefully toward this intelligent, chivalrous young warrior, wishing that he, not his father, were their king.

The first phase of the rebellion culminated in a pitched battle at Lewes in May 1264. The Lord Edward fought well, but the insurgents won the field. Henry III had to submit to the rebellious magnates, and Edward was held hostage to insure the king's cooperation. For the next fifteen months Simon de Montfort was the *de facto* ruler of England, governing in Henry's name. The king had no voice whatever in the affairs of the realm.

Simon attempted to govern in the spirit of the Provisions of Oxford. He summoned the great council frequently and strove to broaden its representative structure. He shared his authority with two colleagues, the earl of Gloucester and the bishop of Chichester, and the three were assisted by a permanent executive council akin to the former Council of Fifteen but now reduced to nine members. Nobody could justly accuse Simon of harboring dictatorial ambitions, but many remained deeply suspicious of his casual attitude toward the royal dignity. All in all, his government represented too sharp a break from the traditions of his age. As the months went by, he saw his party eroded by disaffection and his widespread support dissolve. His colleague, the earl of Gloucester, joined the royal cause, and in May 1265 the Lord Edward escaped from imprisonment and began to raise an army. At the battle of Evesham, in August 1265, Simon de Montfort's army was routed and Simon himself was slain. The experiment in baronial government was at an end, and Henry III resumed his authority.

King Henry was to live another seven years, but during this final phase of his troubled reign authority passed more and more into the hands of his able son and heir. The issues of the long crisis of 1258–1265 were settled in the royal favor in the Dictum of Kenilworth (1266) and the Statute of Marlborough (1267); but the Lord Edward had the good sense to be a gracious victor and to respect the interests and opinions of the "community." He rejected the severe limitations on royal power imposed by the Provisions of Oxford but accepted the enlightened legal reforms that the barons at Oxford had urged. Hence England was at peace with itself once again, and by the time Edward succeeded to the throne on his aged father's death in 1272 he had already won the confidence of his subjects.

The Rise of Parliament and the
Reign of Edward I

The struggles of Henry III's reign and the far-flung wars of Edward I's both contributed significantly to the evolution of parliament—the supreme political achievement of thirteenth-century England.[1] Throughout the High Middle Ages the word *parliament* was used in a variety of contexts. It is derived from the French verb *parler*, "to speak," and originally applied to a meeting of any kind at which views were exchanged—a parley. It was used in the early twelfth-century "Song of Roland" to describe a mere dialogue. But by the later twelfth century it was acquiring the more specialized meaning of a large deliberative meeting. It was used, for example, in connection with Henry II's great dispute with Becket at the Council of Northampton and John's confrontation with his barons on the occasion of Magna Carta. During the thirteenth century its meaning gradually narrowed to meetings of the king with his great council or his small council—particularly when it functioned as a high tribunal.

It was only in the late thirteenth century that "parliament" came to apply specifically to an important meeting of the great council; and not until the fourteenth century did the term acquire any strict institutional significance. Until then there was no conception of an *institution* known as parliament. Instead there was the curia regis—the king's court meeting either in small council or great council. "Parliament" was used to describe *the meeting it self*

---

[1] A good survey of parliamentary origins in England is G. L. Haskins, *The Growth of English Representative Government* (Philadelphia, 1948). For the larger context see Bertie Wilkinson, *The Creation of Medieval Parliaments* (New York, 1972), a stimulating essay illustrated by excerpts from contemporary and modern writers. Important scholarly articles on the subject are collected in E. B. Fryde and Edward Miller, eds., *Historical Studies of the English Parliament*, I, *Origins to 1399* (Cambridge, 1970).

the meetings themselves. The thirteenth-century parliament was not an institution but an occasion. Only later was "parliament" used to describe the
great council itself; and by then it met with growing regularity, exercised
increasingly specific powers, and governed jointly with the king.

The Evolution of Parliament

Much scholarly controversy has surrounded the question of precisely
what constituted a thirteenth-century parliament. What were its functions?
What groups participated in it? What classes were represented in it?
Scholars have learned that no specific answers can be supplied to these
questions—that, indeed, the questions themselves are misleading. For even
at the century's end, "parliament" was still an amorphous concept, and the
composition and functions of such assemblies remained ill-defined.

Of some things we are certain. The small council, with its increasingly
professional expertise, served as the vital core of every parliament and was
responsible for initiating and transacting most of its business. Barons and
prelates were also usually present; the greatest of them were summoned
individually by special royal writ, although there remained for a time some
doubt as to precisely which landholders were entitled to a summons. Late-
thirteenth-century parliaments sometimes also included representatives of
the towns, the shires, and the lower clergy. The growing tendency to add
these representative elements to the great council constitutes one of the
most significant constitutional developments of the thirteenth century. It
must not be imagined, however, that members of the lowest social orders—
peasants or landless workers or urban journeymen—were included. Rather it
was the prosperous middling group of landholding shire knights and established merchants or master craftsmen who were represented.

The functions of these assemblies varied no less than their composition.
They entertained petitions from subjects and local groups for the redress of
grievances. They sat as the high court of England, hearing pleas of unusual
significance. They advised the king on great matters of state, such as the
undertaking of a war or the conclusion of a peace. And they were empowered to grant him special aids.

Ultimately, parliament's financial role was destined to be the key to its
power; but in the thirteenth century that role was limited to the custom of
approving extraordinary taxes. "Scutage and aid shall be levied in our kingdom only by the common counsel of our kingdom." Such had been one of
John's promises to his barons in Magna Carta. And as the thirteenth century
progressed, the concept of consent became increasingly important. In 1297
the monarchy made the explicit concession that no extraordinary taxes would
be levied by the king without the assent of the whole community of the
realm. A particularly convenient means for the community to express its
assent to uncustomary taxes was through meetings of the great council—
that is, through parliaments. And as the king's customary revenues became

increasingly inadequate to meet the rising costs of administration and war, parliamentary grants became ever more essential and frequent.

It should not be concluded, however, that the nonfiscal functions of parliaments were of secondary importance. Far from it. But under an anti-baronial monarch such as Henry III, parliaments tended to be valued above all for their financial support of the crown. Their advice was not wanted. This tendency is illustrated patently in the parliament that Henry III summoned in 1237. He put no business whatever before his barons on that occasion but merely asked them to approve an aid. It was the deep resentment engendered by this sort of royal treatment of the great magnates—the natural counselors of the king—that had underlain the Provisions of Oxford and the crisis of 1258–1265.

Royal financial need seems to have been a particularly important motive in the inclusion of representatives from the towns and shires. Shire knights were summoned by John to a meeting of the great council in 1213, and again by Henry III in 1254. On both occasions their chief function seems to have been to speak for their shires in approving an aid to the king. In 1261 Henry III summoned them once again to give him moral and financial support in his struggle with his baronial opponents. The shire knights joined the barons in a parliament summoned by Simon de Montfort in 1264; and in 1265 Simon summoned a famous parliament that included, in addition to the magnates and prelates, two knights from every shire and two burghers from every town or city. Simon's chief purpose seems to have been to broaden the base of his revolution and to make manifest the notion of a community of the realm that embraced great landholders, townsmen, and shire gentry.

The burghers and shire knights appear again in some of the parliaments of Edward I. King Edward experimented constantly and creatively in the composition of his parliaments. The two lesser orders were present at only four of the thirty parliaments held during the first quarter century of his reign; but during its final decade they were called frequently to serve alongside the great lords. Townsmen and shire knights were summoned to Edward's first parliament in 1275, "to discuss together with the magnates the affairs of our kingdom." A grant was made, but the new king was probably as anxious for their moral support as for their financial help.

Edward I's most famous parliament—the so-called Model Parliament of 1295—was summoned at a crucial moment in his reign: a Scottish war, a Welsh rebellion, and a French invasion of Gascony combined to threaten the security of the realm. The three groups represented in the parliament of 1275 were summoned once again in 1295, and to them were added representatives of the lower clergy. Despite its name, the Model Parliament did not serve as a model for the future. The knights and barons met together in one group, the clergy met in a second group, and the townsmen in a third —on the pattern of the later French Estates General. In the fourteenth century the lesser clergy resolved to exclude itself from parliaments altogether, preferring to meet separately and deal with the king in ecclesiastical convocations. And the burghers and shire knights began to meet in a separate group that became the nucleus of the House of Commons. The magnates and highest prelates, left to themselves, evolved into the House of Lords.

The increasing participation of burghers and shire knights in the thirteenth-century parliaments signified that the power of the English monarchy was to be shared not only with the magnates but with the lesser classes

EDWARD I PRESIDES OVER PARLIAMENT
To the left are churchmen; to the right, barons. Judges are seated on wool sacks between the two groups, while Edward is flanked by the King of Scots and the Prince of Wales and, beyond them, the archbishops of York and Canterbury. *Society of Antiquaries, London.*

as well. The community of the realm was significantly broadened and was becoming a political reality. Still, one must be cautious when speaking of parliament and limited monarchy in thirteenth-century England. These concepts are apt to convey to the modern mind a degree of constitutionalism undreamed of in the High Middle Ages. As the century closed, the power of parliaments was still exceedingly vague. Its members served the king as judges and counselors no less than as grantors of royal subsidies. They occasionally bargained modestly and discreetly for government favorable to the interests of the community in return for the granting of extraordinary fiscal support. But if any bargaining was done, either explicitly or implicitly, it was the magnates who took the lead. Lesser orders might sometimes be represented in parliaments, but they were for the most part inarticulate.

Why was it that these lesser orders came to be represented at this particular historical moment? The reason is not difficult to discover. In the thirteenth century they were growing in affluence, and their political and social importance was increasing. They were forces to be reckoned with, and their allegiance and support were becoming more and more important to the central government—whether controlled by Henry III, Edward I, or Simon de Montfort. Moreover, shire knights and burghers in the thirteenth-century parliaments represented a considerable degree of wealth, and the monarchy needed the financial support of these orders to meet its soaring expenses. Originally it obtained such support by sending its officials out into town and countryside to meet with them separately, but it could deal with them more conveniently in a parliament. It is doubtless a gross oversimplification to say that the king summoned representatives of shire and town merely to get his hands on their money; but this was unquestionably one of his motives, and an important one.

The political events of thirteenth-century England were not alone responsible for the evolution of parliament. In the course of the High Middle Ages, parallel institutions were emerging throughout Western Christendom: the French Estates General, the Spanish Cortes, and similar representative bodies in Italy, Germany, and the Low Countries. Parliament, in short, was merely one of a considerable number of representative institutions that arose in thirteenth- and fourteenth-century Europe. Underlying them all was an old and widely shared tradition that the king was not absolute but was bound by custom and law. This view owed something, perhaps, to primitive Germanic custom and something also to feudalism. It was reflected in the opinions of contemporary philosophers such as St. Thomas Aquinas, who insisted that a king must rule in accordance with good law and in the interest of his people; otherwise he need not be obeyed. This was in no sense a democratic idea—St. Thomas was a dedicated monarchist—but it was, potentially, constitutional.

Other medieval representative assemblies succumbed to the rising royal absolutism of the early modern era, but parliament lasted. It derived its strength from the unique character of the medieval English political experience. More than any other such assembly it was a national body—not a fusion of regional groups, not a potential rival to the royal government but an integral part of it. The English parliament was built on the solid foundation of vigorous local government. Representatives of shire and town came to parliaments with valuable political experience gained from their local administrative activities. Shire knights had been employed ever since Henry II's time to handle judicial, financial, and administrative affairs in the counties. Through the procedure of the sworn inquest they served on juries to provide information for the royal justices—identifying suspected criminals, reporting on local conditions, and performing a variety of other duties in behalf of the king's government. Town representatives were equally rich in political experience, having served in their borough courts or as inquest jurors charged with indicting criminous townsmen before the king's itinerant justices at the shire courts. Parliament, therefore, evolved naturally out of a political system in which the middle ranks of the social order shared administrative responsibility with king and magnates and were accustomed to participating in royal governance.

There is obviously nothing democratic about the thirteenth-century parliaments; nor can it really be said that they were instrumental in limiting royal power. The king's authority in thirteenth-century England was limited by the opinion of the community and the custom of the realm; and most of the parliaments of the age were summoned on *royal* initiative for the purpose of doing the king's judicial business or winning support for some policy or tax. Rather than limiting the monarchy, they served it. Simon de Montfort notwithstanding, the parliamentary idea developed in thirteenth-century England because the monarchy—particularly under Edward I—regarded parliaments as useful instruments of royal policy. On the other hand, we know that many centuries later parliament did become a deeply significant democratic institution, and in the broadest sense we can regard it as a bridge between medieval feudalism and modern democracy. But the kings and magnates of the thirteenth century, who would have despised democracy had they known about it, had not the slightest notion of engaging in institutional bridge building. They had problems enough of their own.

Edward I (1272–1307): *Law and Administration*

The reign of King Edward I, a crucial epoch in the development of parliamentary custom, was creative in other respects as well.[2] The new king had demonstrated his vigor and ability long before his father's death by his victory over Simon de Montfort at Evesham, and by his intelligent exercise

---

[2] In addition to the works cited in note 1 of Chapter 8 see, on the reign of Edward I, George Holmes, *The Later Middle Ages, 1272–1485* (New York, 1962). On Edward's legal achievements, see T. F. T. Plucknett, *The Legislation of Edward I* (Oxford, 1949). L. F. Salzman, *Edward I* (London, 1968) is a short and not entirely satisfactory biography.

of power during Henry III's final years. When Henry died in 1272 Edward was away on a crusade. As the illustrious eldest son of the late king, he had no worries about his succession; he returned to England in a leisurely fashion, settling affairs in Gascony on his way and reaching home only in 1274.

A mature and self-confident man of thirty-five, Edward began ruling England in a style radically different from that of his father. For Edward was a man whom the nobles could trust and admire. He was a courageous and skillful warrior, a man of chivalrous instincts, a nobleman among noblemen. His presence was almost awesome: he was so tall that he stood head and shoulders above an ordinary crowd. His hair was dark but turned snowy white as he grew old. His handsome features were only slightly marred by a drooping left eyelid, perhaps inherited from his father. And his long, powerful arms and legs enabled him to excel at swordsmanship, riding, and jousting. One contemporary called him "the best lance in the world." Despite a tendency to lisp, he was a fluent, persuasive talker. At times he could terrify his adversaries with his explosive temper: when an ecclesiastical synod objected to his levying a tax against the Church, he flew into such a rage that the dean of London Cathedral dropped dead on the spot.

Although Edward's great passions were fighting and hunting, he could when necessary devote himself with singleminded intelligence to the less robust pursuits of law and administration. He possessed a profound respect for law, characteristic of the best of an age that produced Bracton and Thomas Aquinas. Like them, he had an intense desire for system and definition, which led him to bring to completion the great legal achievements of Henry II, Hubert Walter, and the administrators of Henry III. Edward I has been called "the English Justinian," and like that great emperor of sixth-century Byzantium he created a powerful and durable synthesis of the legal traditions of past centuries.

In the words of a seventeenth-century chief justice, "The very scheme, mould and model of the common law was set in order by the king [Edward I], and so, in a very great measure, has continued the same in all succeeding ages to this day." Edward I gave structure and system to the Common Law, but in doing so he rendered it less flexible than before. No longer could monarchs extend their jurisdiction merely by deciding to create new writs—new forms of action; no longer could the law develop freely from precedent to precedent. Through the extensive series of statutes under Edward I, the latitude and individual interpretation previously exercised by royal judges were severely limited. By and large, judge-made law gave way to enacted law; thereafter only by issuing new statutes could significant changes be introduced into the legal structure.

It was under Edward I that *statute* became a meaningful concept. The ancient notion that law was traditional and unchanging had long been inconsistent with the realities of legal development. As far back as Alfred the Great, the promulgation of law depended on the judgment of the king.

The imposition of the danegeld under Ethelred the Unready constituted new law; and the possessory assizes of Henry II unquestionably bore the mark of original legislation. Nevertheless, contemporaries were apt to regard the Anglo-Saxon dooms as mere clarifications or interpretations of existing custom, the danegeld as a desperate expedient (later, as an old tradition), and the Angevin assizes simply as new administrative procedures. By Edward I's time it was coming to be understood more clearly than before that the king, with baronial consent, might indeed change old laws and create new ones. But original legislation was regarded as an act of unusual significance and solemnity that could only be introduced in the form of a statute.

The issuing of statutes long antedated Edward I's reign. Later medieval jurists came to regard Magna Carta as the first statute; and the term is used to describe several acts of Henry III. Even under Edward I, a great deal of the statutory law continued to do no more than summarize earlier practice. But in Edward I's reign, and not before, it becomes possible to distinguish statutes from the more routine royal ordinances. In the fourteenth century the distinction becomes progressively sharper: an ordinance might be issued by the king in his small council; a statute could only be enacted by the king in parliament. This necessary association between parliaments and statutory law was of enormous importance, for it led eventually to parliament's power to legislate. In Edward's time, however, the parliaments were relatively subservient, and the king took the initiative in issuing statutes.

Bracton had insisted that the king was the fountainhead of all justice—that magnates and prelates who operated courts of their own did so only by royal leave. It was Edward I's goal to translate this theory into reality. The royal administration insisted that private franchises [3] would be recognized only if they could be shown to date from before the reign of Richard I (1189–1199) or if they had been granted since then by royal charter. As early as Henry III's reign, efforts were made to enforce this principle through writs of *quo warranto* ("by what warrant?") which initiated investigations of the legal foundations of private franchises. When Edward returned from his crusade in 1274 he began to initiate *quo warranto* proceedings on a large scale, with the result that a great many illegal franchises were eliminated and legal ones were subjected to tighter royal control. The Statute of Gloucester (1278) carried this royal policy considerably further:

> All those who claim rights of jurisdiction by charters of the king's predecessors as kings of England, or by any other title, shall come before the king or the itinerant justices on a certain day and at a certain place to show what sorts of franchises they claim to have, and by what warrant.... And if those who claim to have such franchises fail to come on the aforesaid day, those franchises shall be taken into the king's hand by the local sheriff.

---

[3] Private franchises were geographical areas in which the legal machinery was operated by some great private landholder.

The Statute of Gloucester was followed by a period of complex disputes in which the monarchy asserted its jurisdictional rights firmly but with sufficient restraint to avoid widespread hostility. In 1290 Edward's policy culminated in the Statute of *Quo Warranto*, which provided that rights of jurisdiction unsupported by explicit royal grant must be confirmed by the king's charter regardless of how long the rights had been exercised. Again, Edward was often willing to confirm previously unchartered franchises; but in the process of doing so the principle was firmly established that a baron might exercise private justice only by royal delegation. The absolute primacy of royal jurisdiction, toward which the monarchy had so long been moving, was achieved at last.

Edward's statutes also made significant contributions to property law, clarifying and simplifying some of the bewildering issues arising from the labyrinth of feudal tenures. Feudalism, as we have seen, was never a simple affair; and by the later thirteenth century William the Conqueror's original land distributions had become hopelessly tangled by many generations of disputes over rights, inheritances, marriage settlements, "temporary" grants, forfeitures, and subinfeudations. Great chains of lord-vassal relationships, running down through many degrees of subordination, created considerable confusion regarding rights to land and often resulted in endless buck-passing when it came to performing feudal obligations. A certain Roger of St. German, for example, held an estate in Huntingdonshire in fief from Robert of Bedford, who held it of Richard of Ilchester, who held it of Alan of Chartres, who held it of William le Boteler, who held it of Gilbert Neville, who held it of Devorguil Balliol, who held it of the king of Scotland, who held it of King Edward I. Such a situation could hardly have commended itself to Edward's orderly mind.

Consequently, Edward strove to bring some degree of order to the anachronistic feudalism of his day. The Statute of Westminster of 1285 undertook (1) to specify conditions under which a lord might confiscate the land of a tenant who failed to perform his required services and (2) to establish clear rules governing conditional and temporary land grants. The Statute of Mortmain (1279) prohibited land grants to the Church without the license of the grantor's lord; for once an estate was granted to the Church —which never "died"—the land was permanently alienated from lay control. Most significant of all was the Statute of *Quia Emptores* (1290), which established an absolute prohibition against further subinfeudation. Thereafter, if a tenant sold a part of his land he no longer retained any claim of lordship over the buyer. The buyer then held the land directly of the seller's lord, and the seller himself dropped out of the feudal chain altogether. *Quia Emptores* by no means made feudalism illegal; but it did have the effect, as time went on, of diminishing the importance of lord-vassal relationships below the level of the king and his tenants-in-chief. It was an important, although partial step from the feudal concept of dependent landholding to the modern practice of outright ownership of land.

The same passion for system that infused Edward's statutes prompted him to undertake creative reforms of the machinery of administration. The assertion of royal legislative supremacy in the statutes of Gloucester and *Quo Warranto* was paralleled by the growth and systemization of the king's own legal machinery. The highest tribunal in the land consisted of the king himself sitting in parliament or passing judgment with the advice of his small council. But unless a legal case involved particularly important persons or raised some unusually difficult legal subtlety, it was handled by one of the three royal courts sitting at Westminster or by itinerant judges working in the countryside. At Westminster were the common-law courts of exchequer, Common Pleas, and King's Bench (now separated from the small council). All three were staffed with professionals—trained lawyers in the case of the King's Bench and Common Pleas, and expert accountants at the exchequer. The King's Bench handled cases of special royal concern, the exchequer dealt with cases involving royal revenues, and the remaining cases went to Common Pleas.

The exchequer was of course not only a court but also, and pre-eminently, the key institution in the royal fiscal system. Exchequer, chancery, council, and household were the four chief organs of governmental administration under Edward I. The exchequer, usually supervised by the treasurer, continued to serve as the central accounting office for royal revenues. By Edward's time it was responsible not only for the accounts of the sheriffs but also for those of numerous other local officials who collected money for the king.

By the end of Edward I's reign, the chancery was becoming increasingly independent of the royal household. As the fourteenth century progressed it evolved from a mere royal record-keeping office into a separate department of state that, like the exchequer, became permanently stationed at Westminster. There it carried on and expanded its traditional work of issuing royal documents and judicial writs under the Great Seal and preserving copies of them in ever-increasing numbers and types of chancery records. The chancellor and his clerks were by now professional, salaried administrators.

Heretofore we have distinguished between great council and small council; but now, more and more, the great council was developing into the institution of parliament, and the term "council" therefore came to apply exclusively to the smaller group of royal advisers—judges, administrators, and baronial intimates—that we have previously termed the small council. This group remained flexible and ill-defined in membership and continued to accompany the king as he traveled through his lands. In 1258 the magnates had attempted to assert control over the council, and they would make further attempts in the course of the fourteenth century; but in Edward I's reign it was a thoroughly controlled and increasingly professional instrument of the royal will.

The household, too, accompanied the royal person. It had evolved considerably since late-Saxon and Norman times, but it retained its essential character as a body of royal servants whose tasks ranged from menial duties to important administrative responsibilities. Since chancery and exchequer had become separate departments, it was necessary for the king to maintain smaller parallel institutions in his own household so that he could transact business quickly no matter where he was. The Great Seal was kept at Westminster, but the traveling household included its own staff of writing clerks and a keeper of the Privy Seal. In the late thirteenth and early fourteenth centuries the Privy Seal was being used by the household with increasing frequency as a means of authorizing the chancery to issue documents under the Great Seal. In this way, chancery authentication of household documents became a more or less automatic procedure.

Similarly, some of the financial duties formerly performed by the exchequer had now been taken over by the clerks of the royal wardrobe. They supervised receipts and disbursements in the king's household and sometimes assumed responsibility for paying the wages of troops and other military expenses when the king was engaged in foreign campaigns. Considerable tax revenues went directly into the wardrobe without being received or recorded by the exchequer. In later times, when baronial supervision of the exchequer was threatening royal independence, the king could extricate himself by depending more fully on the wardrobe which, as a part of the royal household, was subject to less baronial interference.

In the twelfth century, the sheriffs and itinerant justices had been the chief connecting links between crown and countryside. Both institutions continued to function in Edward I's reign, but in the meantime many new royal officials had emerged at the local level. Local justice was sometimes handled by royal judges on special commission to hear a particular case or series of cases. At other times a group of royal judges and important men of the district was empowered to hear, in the king's name, all the cases in a particular shire. As always, the efficient execution of royal justice at the local level resulted in high royal revenues; and it was now becoming increasingly apparent that the king's judges were, in effect, draining money from the countryside. Hence the general county eyre came to be regarded as unduly oppressive; as the fourteenth century progressed, popular opposition forced the monarchy to limit the activities of its traveling justices.

Royal administration in the counties involved a delicate balance between central authority and local initiative. This balance was a matter of immense importance in the evolution of English government, for it meant that the royal administration could function effectively at the local level without suppressing the political vigor of the counties themselves. Rather than fighting blindly against the royal administration or being crushed by it, local notables could participate in it, protecting their own interests and gaining political experience in the bargain. Accordingly, magnates and gentry became involved not only in their own regional affairs but in the affairs of the realm. Their sense of community and local responsibility was significantly enhanced.

The remarkable nature of this phenomenon can best be appreciated by contrasting Edward I's England with contemporary France. In general, the French royal government ruled the countryside through officials sent from the royal household—men without local roots, who were transferred regularly from one jurisdiction to another. This fact contributed both to the royal autocracy and to the local particularism that afflicted France in the early modern centuries. In England, however, important local men participated vigorously in the royal administration of the countryside. They accompanied the royal judges on eyres of the counties, often served as the king's sheriffs, and occupied numerous local offices charged with maintaining peace and collecting royal revenues. The coroners, who investigated murders and other felonies, were normally drawn from the local gentry, as were the keepers of the peace who saw to the maintenance of order and apprehended criminals. Local men also were strongly represented among the host of assessors, customs officials, and tax collectors who served the king in shire and town.

A man who functioned as a royal official might hope thereby to rise, through a royal favor, to a higher social and economic position. Royal service was by no means an unobstructed road to riches, but the patronage system pioneered by Henry I continued to flourish and expand; more than a few spectacular careers were built on royal rewards for faithful service. By skillful use of the vast patronage at his disposal, an able king such as Edward I could usually count on the devoted service of his acquisitive subordinates. At a time when the once-powerful feudal concepts of homage and fealty were dissolving, greed and ambition remained as powerful incentives for loyalty between a lord and his men.

Even in the early days of Anglo-Norman feudalism, money had been used to buy loyalty and hire troops; now feudalism was becoming hopelessly anachronistic and money was more than ever a dominant force in society. Feudal personal ties persisted after a fashion, but their gradual decay was hastened by Edward I's prohibition of subinfeudation. The feudal aristocracy remained, by and large, in its former dominant position in society; and many feudal ideas endured—even intensified—as magnates came to revel increasingly in elaborate tournaments, heavy armor, heraldic devices, and self-conscious chivalry. But the fundamental concept of service in return for land tenure was dead, and the armies of Edward I fought for wages.

Edward I's reign witnessed the development of the long bow and the progressive decline in the importance of cavalry. Mounted knights then merely formed the small cores of armies that abounded in mounted archers and infantrymen. Edward's Statute of Winchester of 1285 defined the military responsibilities of the English population along the lines of Henry II's Assize of Arms (1181),[4] which had already been amended and expanded more than once under Henry III. It became customary for the king to grant "commissions of array" to local notables, licensing them to raise forces in

------

4 See above, pp. 136–37.

their shires from among the local inhabitants whose military obligations were set forth in the Statute of Winchester. The knights who were owed to the king by his tenants-in-chief could still be summoned, but they now demanded wages for their services. More important was the use of mercenaries under contract. Edward I employed the policy—which was developed much more fully in the fourteenth century—of entering into contracts for life with important lords, binding the lords to supply mercenary contingents for the army in return for regular retaining fees. This arrangement—known as the indenture system—was extended to contracts between the lord and his own military followers. Just as the lord undertook to supply troops to the king in return for regular payments, so the lord's own men undertook to follow him into battle in return for similar payments. Since the contracts were normally for life, the relationships created by the indenture system tended to be stable and permanent, and the subordination of man to lord which the system entailed gradually took the place of the older feudal relationships. The vastly expanded indenture system of the fourteenth century has been called "bastard feudalism"; it created, in effect, a social hierarchy bound together by money.

Under Edward I the indenture system was still in its infancy, but it was already becoming a burden on the royal treasury. Indeed, by medieval standards, the numerous wars of Edward I were immensely expensive. Edward was a vigorous warrior-king whose ambitions far outran the normal resources of the monarchy, and he was obliged to exploit every conceivable source of revenue. His desperate need for money was a very important motive for his summoning of numerous parliaments; he frequently wrung from them the authority to collect a substantial percentage of his subjects' chattels or annual rents—a fifteenth in 1290, a tenth in 1294, a twelfth in 1296, and a ninth in 1297. He taxed the clergy with similar severity and thereby aroused vigorous opposition from Robert Winchelsey, Archbishop of Canterbury (1294–1313), and from the pope. He collected heavy customs dues, particularly from Italian merchants who were monopolizing the export of English wool; and he turned to these same Italian merchants for large loans when his tax revenues failed to meet his expenses. In return, he took the Italian merchants under his special protection. Previous kings had depended for loans on the English Jewry, but in 1290, Edward expelled the Jews from England in order to get his hands on their wealth. Yet for all his skillful and sometimes inhumanly cruel ingenuity, Edward failed to balance his books; his heirs were left with a debt-ridden government.

The Wars of Edward I

The reign of Edward I splits into two distinct periods. Between his return from the crusade in 1274 and the beginning of his war with France in 1294, his foreign policy was highly successful, and he pursued his domestic policies of administrative and legal centralization without significant op-

1294-
1307

position from his subjects. But from 1294 until his death in 1307 his wars were inconclusive, and his relations with his subjects were stormy.

Edward reigned in an age when older concepts of feudal monarchy were gradually giving way to a new concept of national sovereignty. We should not regard Edward I's England as a national state in anything like the modern sense. Yet in England, France, and other European states of the time, the political authority of kings was steadily superseding that of feudal magnates. There was still a good deal of feudalism in Edward's outlook; but it usually took the form of exploiting his rights of feudal lordship to the fullest in order to increase his own power and prestige at the expense of his vassals. This was particularly true in his relations with Wales and Scotland—over which English kings had long claimed a rather vague suzerainty. Edward's troubles with France arose from the fact that his French contemporary, King Philip the Fair (1285–1314), shared his policy of exploiting rights of lordship over vassal states. Edward, as duke of Aquitaine, was Philip's vassal for his lands in Gascony, and he resented Philip's behaving toward Gascony as he himself behaved toward Wales and Scotland.

Edward's greatest military triumph was his conquest of Wales. The Anglo-Welsh controversy had been going on ever since the Anglo-Saxon invasions, and the steady aggressions of the Anglo-Norman frontier lords had resulted in a significant westward extension of English authority at Welsh expense. Still, despite innumerable royal expeditions into Wales, the independence of that mountainous Celtic land endured.

Edward's Welsh campaign began in 1277 as a result of Prince Llywelyn's refusal to do homage. Edward invaded Wales and succeeded in winning Llywelyn's homage and restricting his authority; but in 1282 Llywelyn and other Welsh lords rose in rebellion once again. Edward raised a large army and invaded for a second time. In the course of the struggle Llywelyn was killed (December 1282). By the spring of 1283 all Wales was in Edward's hands, and its independence was permanently lost. Thereafter, it was regarded as an integral part of the English realm; the term "Prince of Wales" no longer referred to an independent Welsh ruler but became the customary title for the king of England's eldest son. So it has remained ever since.

Considering the antiquity of the Anglo-Welsh conflict, Edward's conquest was remarkably rapid and easy. The Welsh rebelled in 1287 and again in 1294–95; but although the latter rebellion succeeded in embarrassing Edward and delaying a projected expedition against France, neither uprising threatened seriously to undo the conquest of 1282–83.

The struggle with Scotland promised for a time to bring Edward an even more notable victory, but in the end Scotland eluded Edward's grasp. Again the issue turned on Edward's claims to suzerainty. As overlord of Scotland, Edward was called upon by the Scottish nobility in 1290 to adjudicate a disputed royal succession. He began his task by demanding and

HARLECH CASTLE, WALES
Built by Edward I between 1285 and 1291 to secure his hold on Wales,
castles such as Harlech were a heavy drain on the treasury. Harlech alone
cost the equivalent of almost $3 million in modern currency. *Aerofilms Ltd.*

receiving the allegiance of the Scottish magnates, and thereupon took
temporary possession of Scotland while pondering the relative merits of the
two royal claimants—Robert Bruce and John Balliol. At length, late in 1292,
he decided in Balliol's favor. For the next three years he engaged in a
heavy-handed assertion of his overlordship—violating custom by hearing
judicial claims of Balliol's Scottish subjects at Westminster, and even summoning Balliol himself to answer a complaint of one of his own countrymen.
Some Scottish magnates evidently preferred Edward to Balliol; but the
English king's imperious behavior was creating a dangerous legacy of resentment. In 1295, at a time when Edward was deeply involved in French
matters, Balliol and the Scots rebelled.

Abandoning for the moment his plans to invade France, Edward
turned his attention northward and in 1296 led a brilliantly successful expedition against the Scots. Balliol was forced to abdicate and Edward
assumed direct control over Scotland. He dramatized his impressive achievement by bringing back to England as a souvenir of his campaign the Stone
of Scone on which, by ancient custom, the Scottish kings were crowned. But
the unification of England and Scotland under one monarch was quickly
challenged by the fierce independence of the Scots. In 1297 a new rebellion
broke out, led by a member of the lesser nobility named William Wallace.
The rebellion alternately flared and simmered as repeated English in-

vasions failed to re-establish Edward's power in its former fullness. Finally, in 1304, most of the Scottish nobles submitted to Edward and the uprising was brought to an end with the capture of Wallace in 1305.

In the following year still another insurrection broke out, led this time by Robert Bruce, grandson of the former claimant to the Scottish throne. Bruce, as it turned out, was the real hero of this Scottish war of independence. Crowned king of Scotland by his rebellious followers in 1306, he was defeated in battle by Edward but retained his poise and carried on the struggle. Edward I died in 1307 on the road to Scotland, still seeking the tantalizing prize that had often seemed within his grasp and yet always escaped him. His son, Edward II, proved no match for Robert Bruce, and consequently Scotland was able to consolidate its independence. Not until the seventeenth century were the two crowns joined at last—in the person of James I. And even then it was a Scottish king who became king of England.

Scottish independence was won by the fierce tenacity of the Scots themselves; but their cause was aided immeasurably by the fact that at crucial moments in the conflict Edward I was preoccupied with his struggle against Philip of France. The Anglo-French controversy had begun long before, with the Norman Conquest, when the English monarchy first became involved in the preservation and extension of French territories. The rivalry persisted, off and on, into the nineteenth century. Over this vast span of time, relations between the two kingdoms were characterized by repeated wars separated by peaceful intermissions, sometimes of considerable duration. When Edward I ascended the throne, England and France had not engaged in serious hostilities for a generation; the outstanding issues between the two monarchies had been resolved by the Peace of Paris of 1259. This agreement, as we have seen, provided that the English king should hold Gascony as a vassal of the king of France.

In the course of the thirteenth century England and Gascony had developed a considerable degree of economic interdependence. Gascon wine was exchanged for English cloth, grain, and other products; the trade between the two lands gradually assumed such importance that the prosperity of Gascony came to depend heavily upon its English connection. Edward himself valued Gascony highly; he spent a number of months establishing order there in 1273–74, on his return journey to England from the crusade; and in the later 1280s he spent the better part of three years there strengthening his authority. Edward was highly sensitive about his rights in Gascony and could not be expected to relinquish them without a vigorous struggle.

There were several reasons for the renewal of the Anglo-French conflict, but the basic one was Philip the Fair's insistence on exercising to the fullest degree his rights of overlordship over Gascony. For the first two decades of Edward's reign, England and France were at peace, and Edward was able to concentrate without serious interruption on his efforts to subdue

Wales and Scotland and systematize the English administration. In 1293, however, Philip the Fair, on the pretext of a dispute between English and Gascon pirates, summoned Edward to his court. Like John nearly a century before, Edward refused the summons. Philip replied in 1294 by undertaking to conquer Gascony.

It has been said that after 1294 Edward I's ambitions became too great for his resources. This is not altogether true. Broadly speaking, the three fundamental goals of his diplomacy—the conquest of Wales, the establishment of hegemony over Scotland, and the retention of Gascony—had all been vigorously asserted long before 1294. Edward was by no means the master of events in the 1290s; his difficulties arose chiefly from the aggressive new policy of Philip the Fair. As far as the Gascon situation was concerned, Edward was on the defensive.

Philip's hostile actions prompted Edward to take vigorous and expensive countermeasures. He wove a network of alliances against France—much as John had done earlier—and prepared for a large-scale invasion. But in committing himself to the enormously difficult task of reasserting his authority in distant Gascony in the teeth of the powerful French monarchy, he presented a tempting opportunity to his previous victims. A dangerous Welsh rebellion in 1294–95 caused him to delay his French expedition; and the Scottish uprising of 1295–96 necessitated still another postponement. By 1297, when the French expedition was ready at last, Edward's alliance system had broken down, his prestige was badly damaged, and his heavily-taxed subjects were sullen and rebellious.

Edward launched his French expedition in the summer of 1297 in an atmosphere of unrest and disaffection; he returned in the early fall after an inconclusive campaign. After several years of complex negotiations, peace between England and France was finally established in 1303 on the basis of the *status quo ante bellum*. Nothing was gained and, from the territorial standpoint, nothing was lost. The pact was sealed by marriages between Edward I and Philip the Fair's sister and between Edward's son (the future Edward II) and Philip's daughter Isabella. The latter marriage would provide future English kings with a claim to the French throne, thereby contributing to the outbreak of the Hundred Years War in the fourteenth century.

Edward I succeeded in retaining Gascony; but the struggle with France, together with concurrent campaigns in Scotland and Wales, undermined the king's relations with his English subjects. The great difficulty was money. The normal royal revenues were grossly inadequate to meet the costs of these widespread military enterprises. Between 1294 and 1298 Edward's military expenses alone ran to something like 730,000 pounds. Over these same years the crown's ordinary income—from demesne lands, the profits of justice, the forests, customs revenues and so on—came to roughly 150,000 pounds. Consequently Edward had to borrow from everyone in sight and to request special aids from his subjects. He collected such aids each year from 1294 to 1297—a tenth of the income of all his lay land-holders in 1294, an eleventh in 1295, a twelfth in 1296, and a ninth in 1297. He won similar substantial grants from his burghers and clergy, as well as special taxes on exports over and above the normal customs dues. But each of these special taxes required the acquiescence of the groups being taxed, and they acquiesced with increasing reluctance. In short, the year 1294 marked the end of a long political honeymoon. Edward's reign was marked thereafter by protracted domestic conflict. Only once, however, did the conflict reach the threshold of open rebellion, and even then the insurrection was averted by timely royal concessions.

The great domestic crisis of Edward I's reign occurred in 1297. By then Edward's foreign policy was straining English resources almost to the breaking point; and the Gascon expedition, together with the concurrent uprising of Robert Bruce in Scotland, constituted a military and diplomatic crisis of major proportions. Moreover, the savagely taxed nobles, gentry, and burghers resisted additional exactions for a foreign policy of question-able outcome. The gentry violently opposed Edward's effort to make every-one with an annual landed income of twenty pounds or more take up the burdensome responsibilities of knighthood; and some of the magnates re-fused to serve in distant Gascony. Finally, the Church, led by the archbishop of Canterbury, Robert Winchelsey, refused to pay additional taxes without express papal approval. In taking this stand, English churchmen were following the policy of the pope himself. In 1296, Pope Boniface VIII—the last of the great medieval popes and perhaps the most overbearing of them —issued the bull *Clericis Laicos* which specified that every occasion of royal taxation of the clergy required specific papal permission. Whatever the canonical grounds for this bull, it was contrary to the custom of recent years and aroused violent royal opposition in both England and France. The struggle between Philip the Fair and Boniface VIII over royal taxation of the clergy is a dramatic and well-known episode in European history; but the controversy raged in England as well.

Edward managed to weather the crisis of 1297. Never again was he able to assert full control over Scotland, although he continued to try; never again were his relations with his subjects as untroubled as they had been, although after the French settlement of 1303 he was once again in full con-trol of the domestic situation. The conflict with the Church subsided toward the end of 1297, when Pope Boniface modified his bull. In the same year the laity was assuaged by a royal confirmation of Magna Carta, accom-panied by new concessions granting, among other things, that extraordinary taxes should thereafter be levied only by consent of the community of the realm assembled in a parliament.

Despite these and other concessions, Edward was as jealous of his prerogatives in England as in Wales, Scotland, and Gascony, and in his final years he began once again to tighten his hold on the English realm. On the election of a docile pope in 1305 he secured papal backing for the repudiation of some of his earlier concessions and succeeded in arranging the suspension of his old antagonist, Archbishop Winchelsey, who was forced into exile. Edward was a determined man, and events seemed once again to be going in his favor. It is possible that he might have won Scotland, too, for at his death in 1307 he was on his way northward with a powerful military expedition. But in his closing years the obedience of his subjects was based more on force from above than on affection from below. It was abundantly clear that his realm had been severely overstrained by his remorseless insistence on his selfstyled "rights" at home and abroad.

Despite Edward's severity, and despite the inconclusive outcome of his Scottish wars, his reign remains one of the most impressive in the annals of England. It was a period of immense accomplishment and crucial constitutional development—an age in which the common law reached maturity and parliaments became a normal part of the machinery of government. As medieval England's greatest lawgiver, Edward fully merits the laudatory title, "the English Justinian," which later historians gave him. But his similarity to Justinian was not limited to the field of law. As Helen Cam has pointed out, it extended also to war and finance: "Like Justinian, Edward had overtaxed the resources of his realm, and his successors, like Justinian's, had to pay the penalty." [5]

---

[5] H. M. Cam, *England Before Elizabeth* (New York, 1960), p. 113.

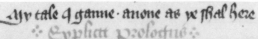

THE CANTERBURY PILGRIMS BEGIN THEIR JOURNEY. *British Museum.*

IV

MONARCHY IN CRISIS

1307 to 1399

The Early Fourteenth Century

10 The adjective "transitional" can be applied with some justice to any historical epoch, but it is particularly appropriate to the fourteenth century.[1] In this era many of the characteristic institutions of the Middle Ages were decaying; yet their modern counterparts had not yet appeared in recognizable form. The fourteenth century was not an age of feudalism but of "bastard feudalism." Devotion to the medieval Church was giving way to rebellious anticlericalism, but patriotic devotion to the state still lay in the future. The medieval intellectual synthesis was breaking up, but nothing comparable had arisen to take its place. The century closed in a mood of deep dissatisfaction with the traditional political, social, economic, and religious structures, but there was little consensus as to what new forms should replace them.

The Change in Mood

On the continent no less than in England, the prosperity and the relative social cohesion of the thirteenth century were giving way to a new mood of violence and unrest. In the eleventh, twelfth, and thirteenth centuries the population had been rising rapidly on the wings of a vigorous economy, and the frontiers of Christendom had undergone a significant expansion. Within Europe vast quantities of new farmland had been created out of forests and swamps, and Western civilization had been pushed far outward beyond its earlier boundaries into Spain, Sicily, Syria, and the

---

[1] The standard work on fourteenth-century England is May McKisack, *The Fourteenth Century*, Oxford History of England (Oxford, 1959). Another excellent survey, covering the period from 1290 to 1485, is M. H. Keen, *England in the Later Middle Ages* (London, 1973). The period is approached from a constitutional perspective in Bertie Wilkinson, *The Later Middle Ages in England* (London, 1969).

Baltic lands. But as the fourteenth century opened, these external and internal frontiers had ceased to expand, and after a time they began to recede. The Christian reconquest of Spain came to a halt; Granada—the remaining Muslim foothold on the Iberian Peninsula—continued under Islamic control until 1492. The Teutonic Knights, who had pushed German-Christian power far eastward and northward along the Baltic shore, were gradually being driven back. In 1291 Acre, the last important bridgehead of the Crusaders in the Holy Land, was lost; and by the mid-fourteenth century a dangerous new Muslim power, the Ottoman Turks, was beginning to move into the Balkans.

The fourteenth century also saw the onset of a widespread agrarian and commercial depression, although its impact varied from year to year and from place to place. While the clearing of forests and marshes continued in certain parts of England, the process of opening new fields to cultivation was generally complete by the later thirteenth century. Virtually all the potentially fertile lands in England were by then being tilled. The medieval system of strip fields and heavy plow had been expanded to its limits; what new lands were cleared tended to be only marginally productive. As the population continued to expand, it either spilled onto these marginal lands or made do with smaller holdings. In either case, the result was a decline in the peasants' standard of living and a precarious situation in which one or two bad crop years could cause widespread starvation. These conditions of agricultural saturation brought about a gradual leveling off of prosperity and population: by the late thirteenth century England's population had ceased to grow at its former rate, and by the early fourteenth century it had reached a plateau of something between three-and-a-half and six million persons. Thereafter population began to decline—slowly at first, but cataclysmically at the onset of the Black Death in the mid-fourteenth century. Land revenues fell in the wake of the plague, and fields and villages were abandoned on a large scale. To aggravate the situation, the climate of the entire northern hemisphere seems to have been changing for the worse. The prosperous civilization of the twelfth and thirteenth centuries was accompanied by a cycle of unusually warm, dry weather—a blessing for a land such as England. But in the late Middle Ages it turned cold and damp. As a result, harvests were often skimpier than before, and people tended to huddle together in the unsanitary, rat-infested houses of England's towns.

Famine and plague caused unimaginable suffering among the English peasantry of the fourteenth century. But by decimating the peasant population they created a labor shortage that worked ultimately to the peasantry's advantage and tended to subvert the economic position of the great lords. Previously unchallenged in the social structure, the nobility now suffered not only from reduced land revenues but also from a progressive decline in their military importance as a knightly cavalry force. Common infantry, which had always played an important role in English warfare, became more significant than ever with the advent of the longbow under Edward I. In the battles of the fourteenth century, a body of trained archers was often the key to victory. With the coming of gunpowder and the development of artillery later in the century, the armored knight was becoming an anachronism. The decline of the nobility relative to other classes in society is illustrated by the marked increase in the power of townsmen and gentry in fourteenth-century parliaments. Still, the decline must not be exaggerated. At the end of the century, and for many generations to come, the landed nobility remained powerful. It had to share its power more and more with other classes; it was forced to undergo a severe economic squeeze; but despite all, it managed to retain its position at the top of the social order.

While land income was dropping, the commercial structure of England was experiencing major changes. During the first half of the century, Italian merchants continued by and large to serve as the chief royal bankers and to take a vigorous part in the English wool trade. But increasingly, English merchants themselves were striving to control this trade and to enjoy its considerable profits. Under Edward I, foreign merchants—Italians, Flemings, and Germans from the cities of the Hanseatic League—controlled about two-thirds of the wool trade; but already English merchants were undertaking a serious struggle to get more of the trade into their own hands. They sought to concentrate the selling of English wool in one foreign trading center under English control—in a single town that would be given a royal monopoly on wool exportation. Such a center was called a "staple."

The first staples were created in the 1290s at Dordrecht and Antwerp in the Low Countries by Edward I. Anxious to build up his war chest, Edward found it advantageous to concentrate the wool trade so that it could be easily supervised and efficiently taxed. Edward II established the first compulsory staple at St. Omer in 1314; and Edward III, responding to the financial squeeze of the Hundred Years War, established staples at one time or another at Antwerp and Bruges. Foreign merchants still played an important role in the trade, but now, unless specially privileged, they were obliged to buy their wool at the staple from English traders.

The monarchy began to favor English merchants more wholeheartedly after the collapse, midway through the century, of the Bardi and the Peruzzi—the two Italian merchant firms on which Edward III had particularly depended for loans and whose fall resulted in part from his refusal to repay them. In 1363 the king established a staple at Calais—in northeastern France but under English occupation—and gave control of it to a group of English merchants known as the Company of the Staple. This company was granted an absolute monopoly of the wool trade; the one exception being that wool could still be shipped by sea to Italy. The wool monopoly was lucrative indeed to the Company of the Staple, enabling it to dominate the trade for many years thereafter. But during these years the wool trade as a whole was declining as a result of the steady rise of the English cloth

industry. English wool was being consumed more and more in the manu-
facture of English cloth, so that the amount remaining for export decreased
steadily. English weavers were exempt from the high royal duties on wool
and, as relative newcomers on the economic scene, were less bound by
anachronistic guild regulations. They were therefore able to undersell their
continental rivals and, in time, to win large markets not only in England
but across the length and breadth of Europe. As the fourteenth century
closed, English merchants themselves were beginning to penetrate deep
into the continent, competing successfully in areas that had long been
dominated by the merchants of Flanders and the Hanseatic League. No
longer merely a source of raw materials, exploited by foreign traders,
England was now a great textile producer. Its merchants were beginning
to demonstrate the sort of initiative that would, in later centuries, make
their kingdom the commercial nexus of the world.

English towns also underwent fundamental changes. The economic
forces of the fourteenth century brought about the decline of many towns—
Oxford and Lincoln, for example—that were centers of agriculture or of the
faltering wool trade. But at the same time, the rise of cloth manufacturing
transformed towns such as Norwich, York, and Coventry into thriving textile
centers. The intensification of the cloth trade made the great city of London
more prosperous than ever; and the port of Bristol, on England's western
shore, was becoming London's chief rival. In general, the labor shortage
brought about by the population decline had the effect of presenting tempting new opportunities to the lesser urban classes—the journeymen and minor
craftsmen—whose services were much in demand. But these opportunities,
opened momentarily by social and economic change, were closed by political
force. The wealthy and privileged merchant guilds, and the important
craft guilds—such as those connected with cloth manufacturing—guarded
jealously their traditional control of urban economic life and town government. Ruling as narrow oligarchies over English towns, they clung to their
valuable monopolies, repressed the rising organizations of journeymen and
the guilds of the lesser crafts, and did everything in their power to keep
wages down. Consequently, the later fourteenth century witnessed a series
of severe class struggles in the English towns. The ruling merchants were
dangerously threatened from time to time, but in the end they succeeded in
maintaining their power. Even though the lesser classes had the economic
trends of the age on their side, they advanced only very slowly. And the
towns themselves, although winning ever-wider privileges and increasingly
generous charters from the king, remained under royal control. Independent
city-states of the sort that abounded in contemporary Italy and northern
Germany were quite unknown in England.

In town and countryside alike, the labor shortage worked to the advantage of the lower classes of employees; the dominant groups reacted by
bending every effort to the forceable preservation of the economic status
quo, suppressing dangerous lower-class organizations and passing in parlia-

EXETER CATHEDRAL, THE NAVE, AND CARVED CAPITALS
AT SOUTHWELL MINSTER

Characteristic of the fourteenth-century Decorated Gothic style in England
were elaborate exploitation of surfaces and highly naturalistic sculptures.
The Southwell capitals are accurate depictions of oak, buttercup, and hop
leaves. *National Monuments Record*

ment statutes that aimed to fix wages at artificially low levels. The rebellious unrest that arose from these repressive policies culminated in the savage Peasants' Revolt of 1381, which will be discussed in the final chapter. Similar revolts were occurring throughout the fourteenth century on the continent as well; a particularly ferocious one broke out in France in the later 1350s. Fourteenth-century Europe suffered from a surge of violence, rebellion, and murder, a sharpening of class conflict, and increased factionalism among the nobility. Added to this were the twin horrors of plague and war. France was devastated by contending armies and rampaging bands of ill-disciplined mercenary soldiers. England suffered scarcely at all from military violence; but its inhabitants were taxed severely to support English armies and allies on the continent, and its kings were driven to the edge of bankruptcy.

Changing social and economic conditions were accompanied by a changing architecture. The Early English Gothic style of the thirteenth century—balanced, graceful, and restrained—gave way in the late thirteenth and early fourteenth centuries to a new English variation known as Decorated Gothic. Buildings in the new style—Exeter Cathedral, for example, and the exuberantly sculpted chapter house at Southwell Minster—were rich in naturalistic carving and elaborate vault ribbing. Stone tracery in windows and on walls became increasingly complex, as simple arcs and circles evolved around 1290 into twisting serpentine curves. Capitals and choir screens were adorned with marvelously lifelike stone foliage, attesting to the artist's keen perception of the natural world and his skill with the chisel.

In the 1330s there emerged the last great style of English medieval architecture—Perpendicular Gothic—which spread gradually across the kingdom and remained in vogue for the next two centuries. It is a distinctively English achievement; the contemporary French "flamboyant Gothic" was closer in spirit to the English decorated style than to the perpendicular. Exemplified by the cloister and remodeled choir of Gloucester Cathedral, Perpendicular Gothic architecture was noted for its intricately patterned vaulting and sculpted walls, in uninterrupted upward lines, and the vertical bar tracery in its windows and choir screens. A progressive thinning of columns and arches resulted in a new feeling of plasticity—a flowing unity of overall design. Spacious interiors were flooded with light from immense windows: the Gothic dream of window walls set in a slender framework of stone has seldom been so completely realized. The stately harmony of earlier Gothic architecture, based on the principle of horizontal-vertical equilibrium, gave way to the aspiring upward thrust—the passionate verticality—of Perpendicular Gothic.

In the realm of intellect, the fourteenth century witnessed a series of powerful attacks against the fusion of reason and revelation that had been achieved by the thirteenth-century scholastic philosophers. Thomas Aquinas in particular. The work of demolition was begun by the English Franciscan, John Duns Scotus (d. 1308), and was carried to its climax by another English

GLOUCESTER CATHEDRAL (AFTER 1330)
Early Perpendicular Gothic stressed sweeping upward movement, complex
vaulting, and the great east window. *National Monuments Record.*

Franciscan, William of Ockham (d. 1349). Duns Scotus was far from a mere destroyer; he constructed an elaborate philosophical system of his own, of such complexity as to captivate some later scholars, repel others, and bewilder the rest. His system of thought tended to place narrow limits on man's ability to approach God and religious truth through reason. Following somewhat in the tradition of the Franciscan scientists, he taught that the most appropriate object of human reason was the natural world rather than the supernatural; and he maintained that a number of Christian dogmas which Aquinas had regarded as rationally verifiable could be accepted only on faith.

William of Ockham went much farther, insisting on a radical distinction between empirical facts and Christian doctrines. He believed in both, but concluded that the dogmas of the Catholic religion transcend reason. The existence of God should be taken on faith. It cannot be proven, and all efforts to create a rational theology are doomed to failure. The scope of human reason was limited to the visible world of phenomena. Its separation from the world of faith severed the age-long bond between theology and natural science, freeing science to follow its own independent course.

The supreme intellectual achievement of the thirteenth century had been the welding of logic and faith into a single coherent system, and the fourteenth-century philosophers worked tirelessly to destroy that system. In so doing, they were accomplishing on an intellectual level what was being achieved concurrently on the social, economic, and cultural levels: the erosion of an old ethos and a tentative, uncertain approach toward a new one.

The Reign of Edward II (1307–1327)

Three kings ruled England in the fourteenth century: Edward II (1307–1327), Edward III (1327–1377), and Richard II (1377–1399), and of these three, two had their reigns cut short by rebellion and deposition. Edward II was the weakest and least successful of them. His inadequacies stand out in sharp relief against the iron strength of his father, Edward I, and the success and popularity of his son, Edward III.[2] He inherited from his father an over-ambitious foreign policy, a debt-ridden treasury, and a restive nobility; but Edward I failed to pass onto him the intelligence and fortitude necessary to cope with these problems. Even as a youthful Prince of Wales, Edward II had demonstrated his willfulness and incapacity, and before accepting him as their king the barons forced him to take a coronation oath of unusual scope. The oath took the form of a series of questions posed to the prospective king by Archbishop Winchelsey of Canterbury (who had returned from exile upon Edward I's death):

---

[2] On Edward II's reign see T. F. Tout, *The Place of the Reign of Edward II in English History* (2nd ed., Manchester, 1936), and J. R. Maddicott, *Thomas of Lancaster, 1307–22* (London, 1970). An interesting contemporary history of the reign is N. Denholm-Young, tr., *Vita Edwardi Secundi* (London, 1957).

"Sire, will you grant and keep and confirm to the people of England by your oath the laws and customs given them by the previous just and God-fearing kings, your ancestors, and particularly the laws, customs, and liberties granted the clergy and people by the glorious king, the sainted Edward,[3] your predecessor?" "I grant and promise them."

"Sire, will you in all your judgments, to the best of your ability, preserve to God and the Holy Church and to the clergy and people full peace and concord before God?" "I will preserve them."

"Sire, will you, to the best of your ability, have justice rendered rightly, fairly, and wisely, in compassion and truth?" "I will so do."

"Sire, do you grant to be held and kept the laws and just customs which the community of your realm shall choose, and, to the best of your ability, defend and enforce them to the honor of God?" "I grant and promise them."

The last of these four promises was the most novel and doubtless the most important, embodying as it did the concept of community that had been the source of such fierce struggles in the thirteenth century. By now it was coming to be understood that parliament was the instrument through which the community expressed its will, and of necessity Edward II summoned parliaments frequently. The new king was as willing to make promises as most of his predecessors had been, and just as ready to break them. The coronation oath is useful in disclosing to us in very general terms what the community expected of its king, but more than an oath would be required to tame the obstinate Edward II.

At the time of his coronation, Edward was twenty-four years old. He was described by a contemporary as "fair of body and great of strength." But in character he was mercurial and unknightly. His many-faceted personality is admirably described by Bishop Stubbs: "He was a trifler, an amateur farmer, a breeder of horses, a patron of playwrights, a contriver of masques, a smatterer in mechanical arts; he was, it may be, an adept in rowing and a practiced whip; he could dig a pit or thatch a barn; somewhat varied and inconsistent accomplishments, but all testifying to the skillful hand rather than the thoughtful head." In short, Edward was an eccentric. He was "a weakling and a fool," who was lacking "not only in military capacity, but also in imagination, energy, and common sense." [4] Since he was deficient in all the chivalric and military virtues of the knight, he was incapable of winning the respect of his barons, who were still sufficiently medieval to prefer their kings to be warriors and heroes, not dilettantes. His coronation ushered in a generation of bitter civil strife.

Throughout his career Edward II demonstrated a dangerous and self-defeating tendency to form powerful emotional relationships with ambitious young men and to fall hopelessly under their influence. The first such man,

---

[3] Edward the Confessor, not Edward I.
[4] McKisack, *The Fourteenth Century,* p. 95.

EDWARD II
The head of the tomb effigy at Gloucester Cathedral. *Copyright*
A. F. Kersting.

and one of the most important, was Piers Gaveston—a Gascon knight of
modest birth whose courage and ability were tainted by arrogance. Gaveston
had been exiled prior to Edward I's death because of his influence on the
Prince of Wales; but when the prince acceded to the throne he brought
Gaveston back to England and made him earl of Cornwall.

The friendship with Gaveston caused Edward II endless difficulties.
As one contemporary expressed it:

> [baronial antagonism] mounted day by day, for Piers was very proud and
> haughty in bearing. All those whom the custom of the realm made equal
> to him, he regarded as lowly and abject, nor could anyone, he thought, equal
> him in valor. On the other hand the earls and barons of England looked
> down upon Piers because, as a foreigner and formerly a mere man-at-arms
> raised to such distinction and eminence, he was unmindful of his former
> rank. Thus he was an object of mockery to almost everyone in the kingdom.
> But the king had an unswerving affection for him.[5]

It must have seemed to the barons that the bad old days of Henry III
had returned, for Edward II ignored the will of the community, scorned the

---

[5] *Vita Edwardi Secundi*, p. 3.

advice of his nobles, and listened only to the vainglorious upstart Gaveston. The magnates, for their part, were driven to form a coalition against the king, which shortly fell under the leadership of Thomas, Earl of Lancaster, Edward II's first cousin and one of the wealthiest and most powerful magnates that England had ever known. A magnate of Thomas's resources would have been unthinkable under the Norman and early Angevin kings, whose wealth far exceeded that of their greatest vassals. But over the generations the disparity between king and magnates had been reduced by royal grants of demesne lands and the consolidation of baronial estates through intermarriage. The wealth of the crown was much less overshadowing in the fourteenth century than in the twelfth: a handful of super-magnates could present a far more formidable threat to the king than in earlier times. And no magnate was more formidable than Thomas of Lancaster. At his height, Thomas held five earldoms concurrently—Lancaster, Leicester, Derby, Salisbury, and Lincoln—together with vast estates in northern and central England. He defended his lands and his interests with a large private army. His impact on English history would have been greater still had not his policies been shortsighted, capricious, and limited by and large to the satisfaction of his personal ambition. Recent attempts to present his career in a more favorable light fail to dispel the impression that he was a grasping blunderer.

Nevertheless, Earl Thomas' royal opponent was at least as blundering as he. Edward II's fruitless attempts to carry on his father's aggressive Scottish policies put the monarchy in desperate need of money. With Gaveston, he exploited every possible source of tax revenue and borrowed heavily from Italian bankers, particularly the Frescobaldi of Florence. Ultimately, however, the king was obliged to seek extraordinary financial support from his barons in parliament.

Edward's financial dependence enabled the magnates to establish a degree of control over the unwilling king. In 1310 they forced him to accept a committee of notables empowered to draw up a series of ordinances for the governing of the realm. The fruits of their work, the Ordinances of 1311, were somewhat similar to the Provisions of Oxford of half a century earlier, but were much more elaborate and thoroughgoing. They provided that both Gaveston and Edward's chief banker, Amerigo dei Frescobaldi, be exiled from England. Parliaments were to be summoned at least twice a year and were given the power of consent to the appointment of high administrative officers such as the chancellor and treasurer. More than that, the parliaments were given a veto over the appointment of important officials in the king's household itself—the master of the wardrobe and the keeper of the Privy Seal. As a further check on the financial independence of the household, the wardrobe was forbidden to receive tax revenues directly but could draw funds only through the exchequer. Finally, and perhaps most humiliating of all, the king could declare war only with parliamentary approval.

In 1311, as in 1215 and 1258, the magnates forced the monarchy to accept a comprehensive series of limitations on royal power. And as before, the royal submission was merely temporary and was followed by a period of civil turbulence. The irrepressible Gaveston returned to England from exile late in 1311, and by Christmas he was again at Edward's side. The furious magnates responded by taking up arms, seizing the royal favorite, and having him hanged. With Gaveston's execution Edward II's reign entered a new phase, unhappier than the last.

، The murder of Gaveston cost the insurgents some support. Several magnates, restive under Thomas of Lancaster's inept leadership, felt that opposition to the king had become too extreme. The land was on the verge of civil war when, in 1313, a reconciliation was arranged between king and magnates. For the moment the Ordinances of 1311 were forgotten. Open war was avoided, but the condition of the kingdom remained far from peaceful. For now the many complex and bitter rivalries among the nobility, which had troubled Edward II's reign from the beginning, reached their climax. The second and third decades of the fourteenth century are marked not only by a continual struggle between monarchy and nobility but also by savage conflicts between magnate and magnate which sometimes reached the point of private war. In 1317 the personal armies of the earls of Lancaster and Surrey clashed openly. And throughout this period, the English spirit was darkened by military disasters in the conflict with Scotland.

Edward II had great difficulty with the Scots from the beginning, and in 1314 the entire northern policy of the first two Edwards was shattered by an overwhelming Scottish victory over a large English army at Bannockburn. The Scottish triumph was so complete as to doom all further efforts to subdue the northern kingdom. In the years that followed, the Scots took the offensive against England—often with the support of dissident English earls—until Edward II arranged a peace with them in 1323. Scotland had won her independence, and Robert Bruce ruled his kingdom unchallenged. And Edward II's prestige, none too high to begin with, was tarnished still further by his humiliating military failure.

Meanwhile the king continued to have trouble with his magnates and his parliaments. Thomas of Lancaster, who had held aloof from the disastrous Scottish campaign of 1314, was now more powerful than ever; and in a parliament held in the autumn of that year he succeeded in re-establishing the Ordinances. In 1316 and 1317 he was the king's chief counselor and the supreme figure in the royal administration. He never succeeded, however, in winning Edward's confidence, nor indeed did he even try. Not only Edward II but many of his magnates were becoming alarmed at Lancaster's immense authority; and in 1318 a more accommodating group of barons rose to power in the court. Lancaster remained a potent force in the English government, but he was no longer supreme. The new men were suspicious of Lancaster and less interested than he in forcing royal government under the rigid control of the Ordinances. This moderate group included a youthful nobleman of intelligence and ruthless ambition—Robert Despenser the younger—who rose quickly to a position of inordinate power by managing to win from Edward II the affection the susceptible king had once lavished on Gaveston.

Despenser was the son and namesake of a royal official who had rendered good service to both Edward I and Edward II. Hence the younger Despenser could not be denounced as an upstart foreigner like Gaveston. He was a much abler man than Gaveston had been, and by 1321 he had risen, through the affection of the king, to a position of almost total authority in the royal court. It was Despenser rather than Edward II or his nobles who now ran the government of England.

Once again the magnates formed a coalition against the king and his favorite, led by great notables such as Thomas of Lancaster and the Mortimers—a family of Marcher lords who deeply resented Despenser's brazen policy of collecting lordships for himself in the Welsh Marches. Now, at last, the struggle between king and insurgents broke into open warfare, and at the crucial battle of Boroughbridge in 1322 Lancaster was routed by a royal army. The earl was summarily executed, and the king—or rather Despenser—won unchallenged dominion over the kingdom.

During the four years following the battle of Boroughbridge, Despenser ruled imperiously over king and kingdom, amassing estates and enemies. But his power made him overconfident, and he carelessly allowed a new coalition to develop that would ultimately prove fatal to his ambitions. Lord Roger Mortimer, imprisoned after the battle of Boroughbridge, escaped from the Tower of London in 1323 and took refuge in France. Two years later Queen Isabella, whose place in the royal affections had been usurped by Despenser, was sent across the Channel to negotiate with her brother, King Charles IV, on the long-standing Anglo-French dispute over Gascony. Once in France Isabella broke with her husband and became the mistress of Roger Mortimer; and in 1326 Mortimer and Isabella returned to England with an army. With them was the young Prince Edward, son of Edward II and Isabella, and heir to the throne.

Mortimer and Isabella at once become the center of a general uprising of English magnates against the despised Despenser and his crowned puppet. The royalist force speedily collapsed; late in 1326 the king was captured and imprisoned, and Despenser was executed. And in January 1327, a parliament formally deposed King Edward II in favor of his fourteen-year-old heir, Edward III. The act was sealed by Edward II's enforced abdication and by his murder later in the same year. Edward III inherited the kingdom, but he was still too young to rule. Actual power passed to Mortimer and Isabella, who dominated the regency government.

The deposition of a king, unprecedented in English history, was an awesome occurrence. Although a parliament was the immediate instrument of the deposition, the real agents of Edward II's downfall were Mortimer and Isabella, aided by English magnates hostile to the king. Edward II was defeated and imprisoned by means of armed rebellion; the parliament of

The Fourteenth-Century Kings

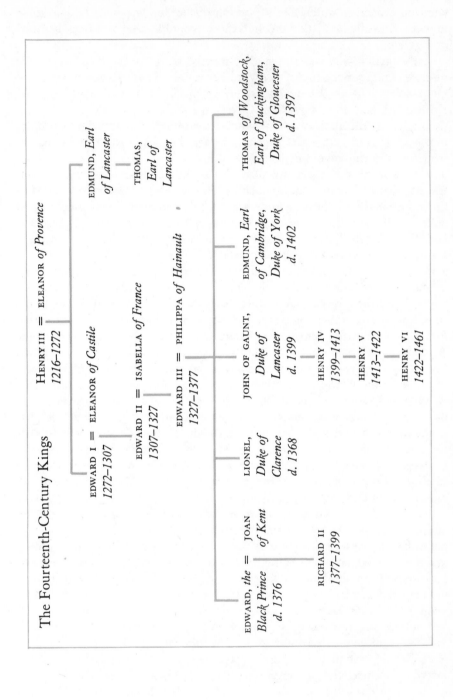

HENRY III = ELEANOR of Provence
1216–1272

EDMUND, Earl of Lancaster

THOMAS, Earl of Lancaster

EDWARD I = ELEANOR of Castile
1272–1307

EDWARD II = ISABELLA of France
1307–1327

EDWARD III = PHILIPPA of Hainault
1327–1377

THOMAS of Woodstock, Earl of Buckingham, Duke of Gloucester
d. 1397

EDMUND, Earl of Cambridge, Duke of York
d. 1402

JOHN OF GAUNT, Duke of Lancaster
d. 1399

HENRY IV
1399–1413

HENRY V
1413–1422

HENRY VI
1422–1461

LIONEL, Duke of Clarence
d. 1368

EDWARD, the Black Prince
d. 1376
= JOAN of Kent

RICHARD II
1377–1399

1327 was under the control of the insurgents and merely ratified their wishes. Nevertheless, the fact that the formalities of the royal deposition were carried out in a parliament is in itself deeply significant from the constitutional standpoint. It was through parliaments that the community of the realm spoke; and in 1327 the community gave its legal sanction to what otherwise would have been an act of high treason. Edward's deposition by parliament amounted to a major shift in the balance of political power between crown and community. Never before had it been demonstrated so vividly that royal authority was based on the assent of the community. A constitutional means had at last been found of dealing with a king who refused to abide by customary laws and the community's will: the representatives of the English people, acting in parliament, could cast him from the throne. No subsequent medieval king could safely ignore this lesson. And accordingly, from Edward II's time onward, major changes in the English political structure tended to derive not from the royal initiative but from the demands of the community.

In Edward II's time the royal element in English government reached its nadir. The monarchy was still the fulcrum of English politics, and for this very reason the reign of an incompetent such as Edward II robbed the kingdom of its political balance and brought on a state of general turbulence. Despite the ever-growing importance of English political and administrative institutions, the strength and wisdom of the monarch was the fundamental factor in the well-being of the community. Edward III was a far abler king than his father, and when he came to power the whole political orientation of England changed dramatically.

The immediate effect of the revolution of 1327, however, was a renewal of the bitterness and disaffection from which England had so long suffered. Mortimer proceeded to enrich himself from the lands of Edward II's defeated supporters; and the baronial faction that had supported the revolution soon turned to internal bickering. Moreover, the sexual relationship between Mortimer and Queen Isabella was becoming a national scandal. The two were well on their way to making as many enemies as Despenser when, in 1330, they were unexpectedly brought to ruin. Seemingly secure in their control of England, they fell victim to a court conspiracy led by the young king himself. Mortimer was seized in his room in Nottingham Castle by followers of the young king, tried by a parliament, and hanged. Isabella was permitted a generous allowance but was deprived of power. And young King Edward, having proclaimed his coming of age in this exuberant fashion, proceeded to the essential work of healing England's divisions by restoring vigorous royal leadership to his troubled kingdom.

Edward III and the Hundred Years War

11

Like Richard the Lion-Hearted, Edward III was a warrior-king.[1] Chivalrous and magnanimous, he was immensely popular—except during a brief constitutional crisis in 1341 and in his final years of senility. Historians have accused him of being a vain and grandiose fool, addicted to extravagance, dissipation, ostentatious display, and spectacular but ultimately fruitless military campaigning. Yet he succeeded to a remarkable degree in maintaining the loyalty of his magnates and his six sons. Earlier kings of England—William I and Henry II in particular—had been tormented by the revolts of ambitious offspring; but the sons of Edward III respected and supported him, and at no time in his entire fifty-year reign did his barons raise the standard of rebellion.

One key to Edward's success was his cheerful, amiable disposition. He was, as one contemporary observes, "not accustomed to be sad," and he never pushed his royal prerogatives to the point of openly challenging the laws and customs of the realm. More important was his taste for chivalry and his triumphant military campaigns—which historians have often and too quickly condemned. Pageantry and military victories were esteemed above all else by the magnates, and Edward III's theatrical behavior and soldierly exploits won him the admiring loyalty of his barons and the obedience of his subjects. To contemporaries he was "our comely king," "the famous and fortunate warrior," under whom "the realm of England has been

---

[1] There is no adequate modern biography of Edward III. On political institutions in the early part of his reign, see J. F. Willard et al., eds., *The English Government at Work, 1326–1337* (3 vols., Cambridge, Mass., 1940–1950). An excellent survey of the Hundred Years War is E. Perroy, *The Hundred Years War,* W. B. Wells, tr. (London, 1951).

nobly improved, honored, and enriched to a degree never seen in the time of any other king." His victories abroad kindled a warm glow of national pride by creating an international reputation for English military prowess: "When the noble Edward first gained England in his youth," a French writer observes, "nobody thought much of the English, nobody spoke of their prowess or courage.... Now, in the time of the noble Edward, who has often put them to the test, they are the finest and most daring warriors known to man." [2]

The Reign of Edward III (1327–1377)

Peace at home and war abroad characterized the age of Edward III. Between 1333 and 1336 he led a series of successful if inconclusive expeditions into Scotland, and later on, in 1346, the English won a decisive victory over the Scots at the battle of Neville's Cross, taking King David II of Scotland into captivity. Edward III's chief military efforts, however, were directed against France, and it was there that he won his greatest glory.

Edward's French campaigns mark the opening phase of a protracted military struggle known as the Hundred Years War. The name is inappropriate for several reasons. For one thing, the "war" lasted not for 100 years but for 115 years—from 1338 to 1453. For another, the campaigns of this period were separated by prolonged truces, often lasting a number of years. One might, in fact, reasonably regard the Hundred Years War as a series of much shorter wars. And it should be obvious by now that the conflict between the medieval kingdoms of England and France began not in 1338 but in 1066. Almost every king since the Norman Conquest had campaigned against the French at one time or another, and the Hundred Years War was in many respects merely a continuation of these earlier struggles. Nevertheless, the term has been hallowed by custom and will be used here for the sake of convenience.

There is, however, one theme that links the various campaigns of the Hundred Years War and separates them from previous Anglo-French conflicts: the English monarchy's claim to the French throne. When Charles IV, the last of the Capetian kings, died childless in 1328, Edward III became a serious contender for the French royal succession through his mother Isabella, Charles' sister. But the French asserted their ancient custom that royal succession could not pass down through the female line and gave the crown to Philip VI (1328–1350), a first cousin of Charles IV and the founder of the long-lived Valois dynasty. Edward did not at first dispute this decision; but later, when other matters prompted him to take up arms against the French, he revived his claim and used it to justify his invasions. Subsequent kings of England were also to claim the throne of France, and the Valois succession was not finally recognized in England until after the war's end in 1453.

---

[2] Jean le Beau, *Chroniques,* I, 155–56; quoted in McKisack, *Fourteenth Century,* p. 150.

EDWARD III
His tomb effigy at Westminster Abbey. *Copyright A. F. Kersting.*

In the middle and later 1330s Anglo-French relations were severely strained by a number of other disputes. The two lands were at odds over Flanders, which France had long been endeavoring to control but which was extremely important to England as a market for its wool. Moreover, the French had been supporting the Scots in their warfare with England. The old dispute over the remaining English fiefs in southern France remained alive and reached a crisis in 1337 when Philip VI ordered the confiscation of Gascony. And underlying these issues was the fact that the young King Edward and the chivalrous young noblemen he had gathered around him were hungry for adventure and for the pursuit of military glory on the fields of France. In short, a warrior-king and a warrior nobility needed a war.

So it was that in 1338, after elaborate preparations, Edward III led a glittering and hopeful army southward across the English Channel. His plan was to invade France through the Low Countries—to attack on a huge scale not only with his own soldiers but with those of his continental allies as well. For Edward III, like John and Edward I before him, had created a system of alliances with important princes in the Netherlands and Germany. Such a system required staggeringly heavy expenditures for subsidies and bribes, and imposed a considerable strain on English resources. Edward attempted to finance his soldiers and diplomats by means of heavy taxes on wool and by various complex but ineffective schemes to create artificial wool shortages and thereby raise prices and customs revenues. But Edward found that his allies' thirst for bribes was unquenchable and that, when the time for action came, they demanded more money than he was able to give. Accordingly, the campaigning between 1338 and 1340 accomplished very little except to drive the English monarchy far into debt. Edward salvaged one victory from the early phase of the war when in 1340 his fleet annihilated a large French armada at the battle of Sluys, off the Flemish coast. Sluys was an impressive triumph that enabled the English to control the Channel for the next several years. But Edward's initial land campaigns were both frustrating and excessively expensive.

During the 1340s and afterward Edward altered his military strategy. Finding that an alliance system was costly and inefficient, he undertook to send directly into France English armies that were lightly supplied but prepared to forage off the land. The new policy proved its worth in 1342, when a series of English raids against Brittany resulted in the establishment of English control over that strategic province. Again in 1345 Edward sent armies into France—one to Brittany, another to Gascony. In 1346 the king himself crossed the Channel with an army of 10,000 men—immense by the standards of the age. Campaigning in Normandy, he plundered the important town of Caen and from there led his force first southeastward toward Paris, then northward into Ponthieu. At Crécy, a few miles from the Channel, he encountered the French royal army, and the two forces clashed in the first great land battle of the Hundred Years War.

The battle of Crécy, fought on August 26, 1346, resulted in an overwhelming victory for Edward III. It was the most stunning military triumph of his career. Edward's longbowmen decimated the mounted French nobles to such a degree that their military capability was crippled for years to come. In the same month the English occupied the key Channel port of Calais, which was destined to remain in English hands until the midsixteenth century. The campaign of 1346 gave Edward the success and prestige to which he had aspired only in his wilder dreams, and it brought the hegemony of medieval France to a decisive close.

A decade after Crécy the English, again depending heavily on their longbowmen, won another major victory over the French at Poitiers. Edward III was not present at the battle; the English army was led by his eldest son, Edward, known as the Black Prince. Although badly outnumbered, the English put the French to rout, captured the incompetent French king, John the Good, and returned to England with their royal prisoner. English arms had triumphed dramatically once again, and the Black Prince was acclaimed as "the most valiant prince that ever lived in this world, throughout its length and breadth, since the days of Julius Caesar or Arthur."

Crécy and Poitiers were separated by the cataclysmic arrival of the Black Death in Europe. Shattered by two military disasters, the plague, the loss of its king, and the harrying of mercenary companies, France in the later 1350s was prostrate. In 1358 large-scale rebellion of French peasants was put down only after a savage struggle; and in 1359 the Black

TOMB EFFIGY OF EDWARD THE BLACK PRINCE, CANTERBURY CATHEDRAL
This hero of Poitiers and son of Edward III died only one year before his
father, leaving his 11-year-old son, Richard II, to inherit the throne.
Copyright A. F. Kersting.

Prince was able to lead his army across France from the Channel to Burgundy virtually unopposed. At length, in 1360, the two kingdoms concluded a truce on terms exceedingly favorable to Edward III. King Edward temporarily dropped his claim to the French throne but was given vast territories in France, approaching those of the twelfth-century Angevin Empire. And King John of France was ransomed for the staggering sum of half a million pounds—five times the ransom of Richard the Lion-Hearted in the twelfth century!

The impressive gains the English had won in these French campaigns were lost in the course of the next two decades. This reversal in military fortunes resulted from a revival of French royal authority and the dogged, unrelenting pressure of French armies against the overextended English positions. England prospered during the greater part of the 1360s, Edward III basked in the prestige of his earlier victories, and the royal treasury was richly nourished by French ransom payments. But as the 1360s drew to a close, the relative quality of French and English leadership was undergoing a transformation. Edward III's high living had driven him into an early dotage; he became senile in his late fifties and passed his later years as a tool of unscrupulous courtiers and of his even more unscrupulous mistress, Alice Perrers. His eldest son, the Black Prince, fell victim to a lingering illness. On the French side, the inept King John died in 1364 and was succeeded by his intelligent and energetic son, Charles V (1364–1380). King Charles had the good fortune to be served by an able military commander, Bertrand du Guesclin, who was reputed to be the ugliest man in France and the best general in Europe. Charles and Du Guesclin adopted a military policy of remorseless harassment. They avoided major battles but won many skirmishes. From about 1369 on, England's French possessions dissolved steadily until, at Edward III's death in 1377, the English held only Calais, Cherbourg, a little territory around Bordeaux, and a few Breton harbors. A generation was to pass before England, under the vibrant leadership of Henry V, made any serious attempt to recover its losses and resume its quest for the throne of France.

Parliament in the Fourteenth Century

Against the background of foreign military campaigning that characterized much of the fourteenth century, parliament underwent a significant development.[3] Huge military expenditures forced the monarchy to depend increasingly on extraordinary taxation, and the revenues the kings so des-

---

[3] On parliament see the references cited in Chapter 9, note 1. See further the splendid essays of G. T. Lapsley, *Crown, Community and Parliament in the Later Middle Ages* (Oxford, 1951); and H. G. Richardson and G. O. Sayles, *Parliaments and Great Councils in Medieval England* (London, 1961). A comprehensive work on the English administrative structure is T. F. Tout, *Chapters in Mediaeval Administrative History* (6 vols., Manchester, 1920–1937).

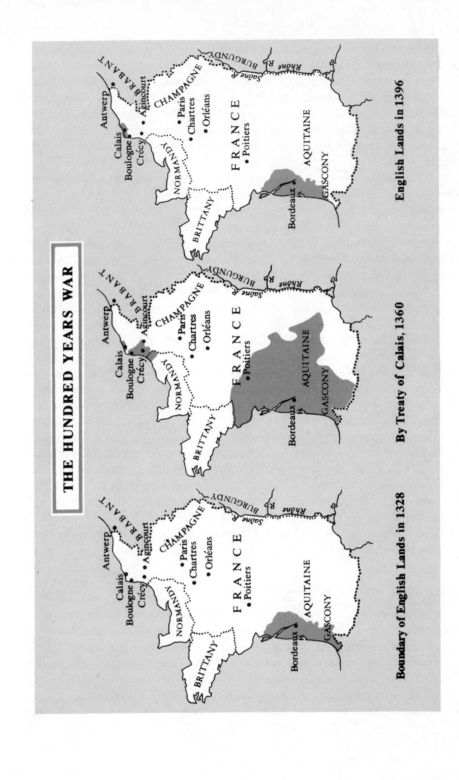

THE HUNDRED YEARS WAR

Boundary of English Lands in 1328

By Treaty of Calais, 1360

English Lands in 1396

perately needed could be obtained only by parliamentary consent. Hence, the parliaments of the fourteenth century were in a good bargaining position. The magnates were generally enthusiastic about the French wars of Edward III and were not inclined to be parsimonious in giving the king their financial support. His policies and his chivalric personality placed him in close rapport with his nobles. Fourteenth-century parliaments included other classes than the nobility, however, and Edward III's aggressive and expensive policies were less captivating to the townsmen and gentry. It was they who objected most strongly to the repeated subsidies necessary to finance his campaigns, and consequently it was they who gained the most politically from his dependence on parliamentary grants.

As the fourteenth century opened, parliament was ill-defined in membership and function. By the end of the century it was coming to assume something of its modern form. It had split into Lords and Commons, and the Commons in parliament had acquired a crucial role in taxation and legislation. By 1399 the parliamentary tradition had become sufficiently etched into the English political system to survive the anarchy of the fifteenth century, the discreet absolutism of the Tudors, and the divine-right monarchy of the Stuarts, to become the fundamental institution of modern English government.

The fourteenth century, therefore, was a crucial epoch in the rise of parliament and, more specifically, in the rise of the Commons. By the time of Edward I's death the summoning of representatives of townsmen and gentry was becoming common practice; and although they were present at only three of the first seven parliaments of Edward II, these representatives attended all but two of the parliaments between 1310 and 1327. They became a normal element in the parliaments of Edward III and were invariably present from the mid-fourteenth century on.

At the very time when representatives of town and shire were becoming an integral part of parliament, the two groups were in the process of coalescing into a single political body. Gradually they came to realize that they had strong common interests. The shire knights remained more powerful and more articulate than the burghers in fourteenth-century parliaments; but the economic resources of the burghers, relative to those of other classes, were expanding throughout this period, and both gentry and townsmen discovered that they could accomplish far more by working in cooperation than by defending their interests alone. Their community of interest was cemented by frequent intermarriages between members of the two classes. Before the fourteenth century was half over they had fused politically into a single parliamentary group: the House of Commons.

This process of fusion began under Edward II and reached its completion under Edward III. Representatives of town and shire may have met together in 1332, and they unquestionably did so in 1339—to deliberate jointly over a royal grant. They were described in the rolls of parliament at that time as "men of the Commons." Thereafter, joint meetings became normal, and the Commons took its place as a vital element in the government of England.

The development of Commons as a separate parliamentary group meant that the members of parliament who were not included in the Commons became, in effect, a separate group themselves. These men—the great magnates and prelates of the realm—became a distinct body known as the House of Lords. The term "house of lords" does not actually appear in documents until the sixteenth century, but the institution itself was in existence from the mid-fourteenth century on.

In the thirteenth century many notables had regarded attendance in parliaments as a burden; but as the fourteenth century progressed they came increasingly to consider it a valuable privilege. Eligibility for attendance in parliaments was now much more rigorously defined than before. Under Edward II there evolved a fixed list of barons who alone and invariably received parliamentary summonses. This select group came to be known as the "peerage." And although the term "peer" literally means "social equal," the peers were in fact, to paraphrase George Orwell, more equal than anyone else in the realm. Fourteenth-century barons who were eligible for a parliamentary summons fell into two groups: (1) the greatest magnates and prelates, who received individual summonses to parliament; and (2) lesser lords, whose tenures were regarded by custom as "baronial" rather than merely "knightly" and who were called by a general parliamentary summons (but often failed to attend). The right of a lord to attend parliament became hereditary and was passed down, like a great baronial estate, from father to eldest son. Thus, the peerage became a permanent and clearly defined group at the apex of the social order.

The process of selecting particular individuals to represent their shires or towns in the House of Commons was far more fluid and complex, and many of the details of the selection process are hidden from us. Normally the shire representative was chosen at a meeting of the shire court, which was usually attended only by the more substantial men of the district. The sheriff was the chief figure at these meetings and was often able to manipulate the elections in his own favor or in behalf of the monarchy. Indeed, the electoral procedures were frequently so ill-defined that the sheriff could simply name his own slate of representatives. Similarly, a powerful local magnate might overawe the court with his private army of retainers and secure the election of his own henchmen. In the later fourteenth century, John of Gaunt exerted virtually absolute control over the selection of shire knights from his vast palatinate of Lancaster; and the great magnates of Yorkshire appear to have dominated the elections of Commons representatives from their county. Such manipulation was still more common in the fifteenth century, when the military power and local autonomy of the great lords was at its height. Prior to 1399, manipulation of county elections by sheriffs or magnates, although widespread, was far from universal. Left to themselves, the county courts were apt to elect knights or squires of unusual wealth and substance; and the same was true of the towns where electoral arrangements were so varied as to defy generalization. Whatever the details, the Commons representatives were generally pillars of their community (unless they were paid royal or baronial agents), and one will look in vain in the fourteenth-century Commons for lower-class protest or revolutionary ferment.

Nevertheless, the emergence of Commons and the progressive extension of its power is a matter of immense significance in the development of English constitutionalism. The fourteenth-century Commons rose primarily by means of its implied power to approve or disapprove extraordinary royal taxes on the classes it represented. And at every opportunity it sought to tighten its control of taxation—to make its power over the royal purse strings increasingly explicit.

In the crisis of 1297 the royal government of Edward I had conceded that all uncustomary taxes must be approved by the community of the realm. It was generally assumed by then, although not specifically stated, that the community was embodied in parliaments. Under Edward III this power to approve taxes, now inherent in parliament, passed gradually into the hands of Commons. It was to be the key to all of that body's future power, and the members of Commons seem to have understood this. When they approved a particular grant, they would often demand and receive greater control over grants in general. Commons was in a strong position, for the increasingly affluent classes it represented were supplying the monarchy with the bulk of its tax revenues. Accordingly, by the end of the fourteenth century the Commons was coming to exercise the exclusive right to originate parliamentary taxation. In 1395 a parliamentary grant was made "by the Commons with the advice and assent of the Lords." This was the first time these exact words were used, but they became the normal formula in years thereafter.

Thus, by 1399 parliament—and more specifically Commons—had a controlling voice in royal taxation. Parliamentary approval was required for all taxes, direct or indirect—even tolls and customs from merchants. Parliament was even supervising and auditing tax revenues and was beginning to specify the uses to which particular taxes could be put. Profiting from the military dangers and general unrest of Richard II's reign (1377–1399), parliament used its fiscal power to establish an ever-greater control over government policies. In 1377 it insisted on overseeing the use to which its grant was put and succeeded in securing the appointment of two London merchants as treasurers of war. And in 1382 the parliamentary representatives imposed their own foreign policy on the royal government by insisting on a military campaign in Flanders. The right to grant or refuse taxes, they were discovering, was an effective avenue to political power.

The relationship between taxation and power is nowhere better illustrated than in the gradual acceptance of Commons' right to legislate. This function, undreamed of at the close of the thirteenth century, was well established a hundred years later. Edward III's first parliament, meeting in 1327, introduced for the first time a Commons petition—a list of grievances that the parliament expected the monarchy to consider seriously in return for the granting of taxes. Parliaments had long been accustomed to receiving and passing on to the king petitions from individuals or groups. The Commons petition differed from these in that it dealt with matters of general interest to the community of the realm. The Commons petition of 1327 was concerned with such matters as the maintenance of Magna Carta, the soundness of English currency, and the size of cloths sold in English markets. Coming at a time of grave political crisis, it received the sympathetic attention of the royal government and gave rise to two statutes and several ordinances and decrees. More important, it set a precedent; similar petitions were introduced in the parliaments of 1333 and 1337, and they appeared regularly from 1343 on. Fourteenth-century parliaments used the Commons petition repeatedly as a device to put pressure on the king to grant their wishes; and as time went on it became increasingly customary for a Commons petition to give rise to royal statutes. Thus the Commons petition was a significant step in the direction of parliamentary legislation. In later years the Commons petition evolved into the Commons bill, and thus the will of the House of Commons became the law of England. Indeed, after the mid-fourteenth century, most statutes resulted directly from Commons petitions or bills rather than from royal initiative, as in the days of Edward I. The mechanism for Commons legislation was thereby established. It remained only to refine it.

Originally, the procedure was for Commons to make a petition and vote a grant. The king would then approve the petition, and it would be translated into statute. But if some item in the petition was offensive to the king, he might ignore it or alter its meaning. In order to prevent this sort of royal tampering and to achieve complete identity between petition and statute, the Commons developed the principle of "redress before supply." Only if and when the king satisfied their petition, both in matter and spirit, would Commons make the requested grant. This principle was an effective weapon indeed against a monarch such as Edward III, who needed money desperately in order to fight his wars and who was not inclined to quibble as long as he received his grant. "Redress before supply," which had become a normal procedure by the early fifteenth century, was a key factor in the transformation of parliament's privilege to petition into parliament's right to make law.

In the course of the fourteenth century, therefore, parliament—and Commons in particular—acquired two vital privileges: consent to taxation and a commanding voice in royal legislation. By the century's end, parliament had established itself firmly and permanently in the English political fabric. A hundred years of war, plague, and social turbulence had seen England move far along the road toward constitutional monarchy.

Law and Administration

The evolution of other branches of the fourteenth-century English government was less spectacular than that of parliament. The functions of the council—now a fixed body of sworn royal counselors—became steadily more elaborate and varied. It remained the organizational core of every parliament. It supervised the entire system of royal justice and functioned, although on a declining scale, as a court of equity to settle cases unadaptable to the common-law courts. It counseled the king (as before), kept watch over the great departments of chancery and exchequer, handled affairs of diplomacy, and enacted royal ordinances—many of which gave rise to royal statutes in parliament. As the fourteenth century progressed, it became increasingly an executive body, authorizing under the Privy Seal, without direct royal mandate, most of the ordinary business of state. These activities and responsibilities had by now become much too complex for direct monarchical supervision; and as time passed the council operated more and more on its own initiative. By the century's close it had achieved sufficient independence to keep separate records of its meetings.

[margin note: Council duties]

Baronial attempts to control council and household had begun, as we have seen, under Henry III and were revived under Edward II—never with lasting success. Edward III, a friend of the barons, normally made it a point to fill his council with nobles or men acceptable to them. This was not invariably the case: in 1341 he submitted very briefly to a degree of parliamentary control over his officers of state. And in his old age, in 1376, Commons undertook an investigation of royal maladministration, secured the appointment of a new royal council, and removed from court—through the novel process of impeachment—the king's chamberlain and the king's mistress. But within months the impeachments were quashed. The crises of 1341 and 1376 proved to be isolated, momentary disturbances in a long and otherwise untroubled period of royal-baronial harmony.

During the second half of his reign, Edward appointed barons and educated laymen to his council at the expense of the ecclesiastical administrators who had traditionally been at the core of royal affairs. Here, as elsewhere, the power of the Church in society was receding. Under Richard II, in the final quarter of the century, monarchy and nobility were again at odds; and the magnates and parliaments succeeded more completely than ever before in establishing their grip on the council and influencing the household. As a result, portions of Richard II's reign were dominated by what may be termed a "conciliar government."

The two departments of chancery and exchequer also drifted farther away from direct royal control. Each had its own seal; both had now gone out of court and were carrying on their functions at Westminster. In the course of the fourteenth century the chancery's administrative independence declined as it came increasingly to share its authority with the household departments of wardrobe and chamber. By the end of the century the chancery's initiative was largely limited to the automatic issuing of judicial writs and the drafting and authenticating of royal documents already authorized elsewhere. The chancellor himself devoted less and less attention to supervising the chancery and its clerks, more and more to great matters of state. Throughout much of the period he was the dominant figure in the council, and as time went on he assumed the further task of presiding over a special tribunal responsible for hearing cases in equity.

Such cases, as we have seen, had traditionally been heard by the full council. But now the council's administrative burdens were growing to such a point that it could no longer serve with much effectiveness as a tribunal. The chancellor, as chief officer in the council, was particularly well equipped to take equity cases under his own jurisdiction. He was likely to be an expert jurist, and his responsibilities included the channeling of pleas into the appropriate common-law courts—King's Bench, Common Pleas, or exchequer. He was therefore in a strategic position to identify cases that were appropriate to none of these courts—cases requiring special, equitable treatment in a court unhampered by the hardening rules and procedures of the common law. Such a court developed in the course of the fourteenth century—a learned group of lawyers and justices selected by the chancellor to aid him in judging cases. Not until later did this tribunal disentangle itself completely from the council to become the official court of chancery; but by the end of Edward III's reign it was already, for all practical purposes, functioning on its own and draining off most of the pleas formerly heard by the council. Its development illustrates once again the growing professionalization and departmentalization of the royal government and the steady drift of its components farther and farther away from direct royal supervision.

This centrifugal drift was caused less by baronial opposition to royal authority than by the increasing scope and bureaucratization of the royal government itself. Under the three Edwards, efforts were made to shift administrative authority from the exchequer and chancery at Westminster to more responsive offices that traveled with the royal household. Edward I depended heavily on the wardrobe, giving it broad fiscal and executive responsibilities and custody of the Privy Seal. The next two reigns witnessed a shift of power from wardrobe to chamber; but by Richard II's time strong baronial objections had reduced the chamber to a small household treasury, which it would remain until Tudor times.

American presidents have complained of the immense difficulty of imposing their will on a vast, inert federal bureaucracy. Fourteenth-century English kings faced the same problem on a smaller scale. It had been convenient enough for William the Conqueror to issue his documents under the Great Seal; but by Edward I's time—with the Great Seal in the chancery's custody at Westminster—the Privy Seal was necessary for the day-by-day exercise of the royal will. In the course of Edward III's reign, the keeper of the Privy Seal himself drifted out of court and settled in Westminster with his large clerical staff so that the king was obliged to depend on various new household seals. Richard II sealed many of his documents with his own signet ring—so many, in fact, that the ring acquired its own office and its own staff of clerks.

Meanwhile the judicial structure was evolving slowly along the general lines established by Edward I. There were no English Justinians in the fourteenth century, and the Common Law remained more or less as it had been at Edward I's death. The lords in parliament continued to function as the highest tribunal. The common-law courts grew increasingly specialized—and increasingly jealous of one another. The court of King's Bench was now responsible primarily for criminal cases; Common Pleas for civil cases; and the exchequer for royal revenue cases. The role of the old itinerant justices was declining through the early decades of the reign as the volume of local judicial business became more than the eyres could handle. They were abolished altogether in 1361—at Commons' insistence—and thereafter the king's justice in the countryside was handled by a new group of officials—usually drawn from the local gentry—known as justices of the peace. The rise of these new officers meant that the gentry had, in effect, won control of the local courts.

The fourteenth-century justice of the peace was to remain a dominant figure in the administrative and judicial organization of the counties for centuries to come. The office evolved out of Edward I's keepers of the peace, who exercised police functions under the authority of the sheriff. A statute of 1330 gave them the responsibility to indict criminals as well as apprehend them; and this new judicial function was greatly broadened by a statute of 1360, empowering the keepers to try felons and trespassers. The statute of 1360, in effect, transformed the keepers of the peace into justices of the peace. Their judicial functions were further elaborated in 1362, when they were directed to hold courts four times a year. These "quarter sessions" gave the justices of the peace pre-eminence in legal affairs over all other county officials, including sheriffs. By the century's close their jurisdictional supremacy had ripened into a general supervision of the county administration, and the quarter sessions had virtually superseded the older shire courts. The justices had also by then assumed the obligation of supervising the recruitment of shire levies. So it was that the justices of the peace became the chief royal officers in the counties and the essential links between crown and shire.

Edward III and the Decline of Royal Authority

The staggering war expenses of Edward III made him even more dependent on parliamentary grants than his predecessors had been, and he won the financial backing of the community by a policy of acceding to most of its demands. He soothed parliament by consulting with it on important matters of policy and appointing no high-handed royal ministers of the sort that parliament found offensive. His pliancy contributed much, as we have seen, to the growth of the power of Commons. And in agreeing to abolish his itinerant justices, he contributed to the decline of royal authority in the countryside. In the absence of justices from the royal court, magnates could often dominate the law and administration of their regions —bribing the local justices of the peace or intimidating them with private armies.

Overall, Edward III was splendidly successful in restoring the prestige of the crown after the disasters of Edward II's reign, and in working harmoniously with his subjects—but at a cost. All was well as long as England remained under the charm of a victorious and venerated king. But Edward's less pliant and less triumphant successors would suffer for his concessions. The Commons, through their control of taxation, could hamstring royal policies with which they disagreed. And the magnates' unprecedented power in the shires would, in the next century, drive England toward political chaos. Not until the coming of the Tudors would the crown regain the supremacy over the nobility it had enjoyed in the twelfth and thirteenth centuries. And never again could it safely ignore the Commons.

The Strange Death of
Medieval England

During the second half of the fourteenth century
England's foreign struggles and constitutional transformation occurred
against a background of plague, cultural change, and growing social upheaval. The Black Death served as the somber backdrop to a deepening
economic crisis, a bitter popular insurrection known as the Peasants' Revolt,
and growing social tensions and religious restlessness. These themes recognize no arbitrary beginning and end such as is so often imposed on them by
historians. They are problems that continued to torment English society
well after 1399, the terminal point of his book, and many of them will be
discussed more fully in the next volume of this series. Together they constitute a turbulent epilogue to England's medieval experience.

The Black Death

As the fourteenth century opened, the general prosperity of the High
Middle Ages was fading. The ever-increasing pressure of population on resources and the shift to a colder, rainier climate was reducing the standard
of living of the peasantry and creating widespread hunger and malnutrition. The towns suffered too, for they were dependent on food from the
countryside; poor harvests and crop failures brought famine to townsmen
and peasants alike. The population may have already begun its downward
trend when a series of terrible floods and famines struck England between
1315 and 1317. The agrarian economy made a partial recovery in the years
that followed, but for the next generation famine remained near at hand.
Then in 1348–1349 the Black Death came, carrying off perhaps a third of
the population of England and Western Europe.

The Black Death appears to have been a combination of two diseases: bubonic plague—which was carried by fleas infesting black rats—and pneumonic plague—which spread by direct contagion. Bubonic plague came first, arriving from the east aboard rat-infested trading ships and spreading swiftly among a population whose resistance was weakened by malnutrition. It was quickly followed by pneumonic plague—which apparently results when a person with a respiratory infection contacts bubonic plague. In these two forms, the Black Death was spread by contacts both between human and flea and between human and human.

Arriving at the Mediterranean ports of southern Europe in 1347, the plague moved northward into France. The French monk Guillaume de Nangis describes it as

> so great a mortality of people of both sexes . . . that it was scarcely possible to bury them. They were only ill for two or three days and died suddenly, their bodies almost sound. And he who was in good health one day was dead and buried the next. They had swellings in the arm-pits and groin, and the appearance of these swellings was an unmistakable sign of death. . . . In many towns, great and small, the priests were terrified and fled, but some monks and friars, being braver, administered the sacraments. Soon, in many places, of every twenty inhabitants only two remained alive. The mortality was so great at the hospital in Paris that for a long time more than 500 bodies were carried off on wagons each day, to be buried at the cemetery of the Holy Innocents. And the holy sisters of the hospital, fearless of death, carried out their task to the end with the most perfect gentleness and humility. These sisters were wiped out by death. . . .

In the summer of 1348 the Black Death came to England. It first broke out at the port of Melcombe Regis in Dorset, then spread through the southwestern shires. By winter it was in London, and by the following summer it was at its peak, ravaging the heavily populated counties of eastern England. "So great a pestilence," writes a Lincolnshire monk, "had never been seen, heard, or written of before this time. . . . Even the flood of Noah's days had not, it was thought, swept away so great a multitude." The fourteenth-century historian Henry Knighton describes it in these words:

> In Leicester, in the little parish of St. Leonard, more than 380 people died; in the parish of the Holy Cross more than 400; and in the parish of St. Margaret in Leicester, more than 700. And so in each parish, they died in great numbers. . . . And the sheep and cattle wandered about through the fields and among the crops, and there was nobody to go after them or to collect them. They perished in countless numbers everywhere, in secluded ditches and hedges, for lack of watching, since there was such a lack of serfs and servants that nobody knew what he should do. . . . Meanwhile there was such a lack of priests everywhere that many widowed churches had no divine services—no masses, matins, vespers, sacraments, or sacramentals. . . . Likewise many small villages and hamlets were completely deserted; not a single house remained in which any inhabitants were still alive. Many such hamlets will probably never again be inhabited.

ſ non eſſent regiſtrantes
et futuris miniſtrantes que
vident et que audiunt .
et illa que eueniunt in diuerſis
temporibus et in ſuis etatibus p
libros et per ſcripturas vbi po
unt magnas curas. pauca ſc
rentur de factis in temporibus

que non viderunt nec ſciunt :
per ſcripturas edocemur.
ſi nos bene recordemur. que ſunt
bona vt amemus. quid ue malii
vt uitemus. Ergo tu ſane cō
clude ama ſcripturas. et ſtude.
et non amabis vicia ſn quib'
ſunt opprobria. Laudandum

BURIAL OF VICTIMS OF THE BLACK DEATH AT TOURNAI, BELGIUM, 1349
There was not always time to construct the numerous coffins shown here.
Often victims were carried off in carts and thrown together into large pits.
Bibliothèque Royale, Brussels.

Contemporary writers, suffering from shock and terror, may have been prone to exaggerate, but modern studies make it clear that the plague's toll was heavy indeed. Some 35 percent of the population of Bristol succumbed; about 44 percent of the beneficed clergy perished in the dioceses of York and Lincoln; and nearly 50 percent in the dioceses of Exeter, Winchester, Norwich, and Ely. It has been estimated that half the English clergy may have died of plague. And yet the surviving population endured this prodigious calamity without general panic or widespread flight. Life went on, agriculture and commerce continued, and the war with France persisted.

By the end of 1349 the Black Death had run its course. There is evidence of unusually numerous marriages and births in the years just following, as the English endeavored to preserve family lines and repopulate the land. But in 1361–1362 the plague returned, striking especially hard at the young people born since 1349. This "children's plague" was followed by further epidemics in 1369, 1379, 1390, 1407, and periodically through the fifteenth century. For a century and a half plague was a normal and recurring hazard, keeping the people in a state of perpetual anxiety for their lives and the lives of their families. The population of England and the continent dropped drastically in the wake of the plague and appears to have continued its decline for the next century or so. It began to rise again after about the mid-fifteenth century, but only very slowly. England's population in the late fifteenth century was probably only about half what it had been in 1300.

The personal grief brought by the plague is immeasurable, but one can comprehend its effects in more tangible ways—in the deserted villages, the temporary decline of the European wool market, and the severe shortage of labor. The Black Death vastly accelerated the already-evident breakdown of high medieval civilization. Among other things, it hastened the demise of the old manorial regime. Because of the rising wages brought about by the labor shortage and the declining grain market resulting from the population drop, land profits and land values plummeted. Demesne farming became increasing profitless and gradually disappeared almost entirely. Landlords tended to abandon direct farming, preferring to divide their old demesne lands into individual peasant plots and live entirely off the rents.

Political and Social Conflict

Social turbulence had been intensifying early in the century during Edward II's reign, and in the later years of Edward III it increased still more. The Black Death had much to do with this, as did Edward III's failing leadership in his old age. But most important was the unhealthy trend toward so-called bastard feudalism that had been gaining momentum ever since Edward I's reign. By the later fourteenth century the custom of assembling permanent private armies of retainers—supported by their lords' wages and clad in their lords' liveries—was reaching its height. This practice of "livery and maintenance" was, in effect, the old feudal household system gone wild. The contract, or indenture, between king and lord and between lord and military retainer had become fully developed in the course of Edward III's French campaigns; and, in the decades following, it contributed much to general social chaos. Private military retinues sometimes terrorized the countryside, bringing about a breakdown of local government and an epidemic of local warfare. The English countryside had been relatively peaceful in the High Middle Ages; in the fourteenth and fifteenth centuries it was afflicted by an accelerating trend toward violence.

The social crisis reached its peak in Edward III's final years and in the reign of his successor. When Edward passed from his long dotage in 1377, he was succeeded by a ten-year-old child, Richard II (1377–1399), son of the Black Prince. For the next decade, England was ruled by a regency government dominated by contending baronial factions. Plague, social disorder, and weak royal government all contributed to the general gloom of the period, as did the series of military humiliations England was suffering at the hands of the French. The years between 1377 and 1380 were darkened by fear of a French invasion of England—a fear that ceased only with the death of the able French monarch Charles V. But France had been suffering, too; and the succession of a child to the French throne in 1380—the fitfully insane Charles VI—brought on a long era of civil strife centering on the rivalry of two royal uncles: the dukes of Burgundy and Orleans. France, which had been tormented so long, was now obliged to endure still more. But England gained no immediate advantage; the duke of Burgundy was sufficiently strong to maintain the military pressure against the English, and Richard II had no taste for large-scale campaigns in France.

Religious Ferment

The turmoil and pessimism of the later fourteenth century were accompanied by a powerful surge of protest against the Church. Outcries against the wealth and spiritual hollowness of the clergy had been heard for centuries, but they were more strident now. Plague and social upheaval had created a mood of violence and radicalism at the very time when the Church was most vulnerable to pious condemnation. Early in the century the papacy had abandoned Rome for Avignon. There it remained for seven decades, under the shadow of the French monarchy, devoting itself more and more to administrative matters and collecting its revenues with ever-greater efficiency. To many, the papacy seemed to have forfeited its international character, and its grasping fiscal policies were therefore all the more resented. For the English, who were at war with France during much of the fourteenth century, the payment of taxes to a French pope aroused growing resentment. One contemporary observed that the pope was supposed to lead Christ's flock, not fleece it. The situation worsened after 1378 when the Church split into two fragments—one led by a pope at Avignon, the other by a pope at Rome. This tragicomic schism persisted to the end of the fourteenth century and beyond.

Opposition to the papacy and the Church proceeded along several lines. The English Franciscan philosopher, William of Ockham, contended not only against the faith-reason synthesis of St. Thomas Aquinas but also against the complacency, greed, and corruption of the contemporary Church. An avowed enemy of papal absolutism, he insisted that the Church should be governed and reformed through ecclesiastical councils, the selection of which was to begin at the parish level. On the continent, similar and even more radical views were finding expression. The clergy, it was suggested, should renounce its wealth or be deprived of it, and the pope should withdraw from politics and restrict his attention to spiritual matters.

As confidence in the established ecclesiastical order waned, piety tended to become more individualized. The later fourteenth century witnessed an upsurge of mysticism, in such works as *The Revelations of Divine Love* by the hermit mystic, Dame Julian of Norwich. The medieval Church had always found room for mystics but had never been entirely comfortable with them. Mysticism involves a direct relationship between the believer and God which—without necessarily questioning the sacraments or the priesthood—has the effect of bypassing them and diminishing their importance. The Church as mediator between God and man was only of secondary importance to the mystic, who needed no intermediary in his quest for the beatific vision.

The alienation of the ecclesiastical hierarchy from the individual believer is illustrated in quite different ways in the writings of two great literary figures of the late fourteenth century, William Langland and Geoffrey Chaucer. The works of these two men mark the assertion of the English language as a dominant literary vehicle after centuries of French linguistic supremacy. And both men disclose—each in his own manner—the growing popular hostility toward the ecclesiastical establishment. Langland, like the contemporary mystics, had no great interest in the sacramental functions of the priesthood. But, unlike the mystics, he was a moralist not a contemplative. He loved the Church as it should be but despised the Church as it was. Perhaps one might more properly say that his love for the essential Church—the Body of Christ—prompted him to condemn the corrupt behavior of contemporary churchmen all the more severely. Langland was neither a revolutionary nor a heretic. He revered the Church as the agent of man's salvation and the vehicle of divine love; but he denounced the friars for their greed, the theologians for their arid complexity, and the papacy for its malign influence on simple Christian believers. More than anything else, Langland condemned the avarice and arrogance of the wealthy and the selfish cruelty of those in power, whether churchmen or laymen. Wealth, to Langland, hardened men and made them uncharitable, and the Church should therefore return to a condition of apostolic poverty. In his masterpiece *Piers Plowman* he writes:

> Ah, well it may be with poverty, for he may pass untroubled,
> And in peace among the pillagers if patience follow him.
> Our prince, Jesus, and his apostles chose poverty together,
> And the longer they lived the less wealth they mastered. . . .
> If possession is poison and makes imperfect orders,
> It would be well to dislodge them for the Church's profit,
> And purge them of that poison before the peril is greater.

Not only the Church, but all society has been corrupted by wealth:

> As weeds run wild on ooze or on the dunghill,
> So riches spread upon riches give rise to all vices.
> The best wheat is bent before it ripens,
> On land overlaid with marl or the dungheap.

And so are surely all such people.
Overplenty feeds the pride which poverty conquers.

Langland was bitterly critical of his society, but like a Hebrew prophet he softened his protests with a strain of hope—hope for a purified humanity moved by love rather than greed.

William Langland's intense moral sensitivity contrasts sharply with the mood of his genial and worldly-wise contemporary, Geoffrey Chaucer (c. 1343–1400). Chaucer's literary genius derived in part from his ability to portray with remarkable insight the personalities and motivations of his characters. He entered into their minds, displayed them for all to see, and yet was able to remain personally aloof. He was not a conscious reformer, not a prophet crying out against the sins of his age, but an acute observer of human character. In this role he was able to illuminate vividly the vices and virtues of contemporary churchmen. The pilgrims depicted in his *Canterbury Tales* include the Parson—a compassionate and well-intentioned village priest—and the Oxford Clerk—absorbed in his disinterested devotion to scholarship. They also include less attractive ecclesiastical types: the superficial, mannered Prioress, the Pardoner who was essentially a salesman of indulgences, the lecherous Summoner, the Monk who was addicted to the pleasures of the hunt, and the corrupt Friar:

> Highly beloved and intimate was he
> With country folk wherever he might be,
> And worthy city women with possessions;
> For he was qualified to hear confessions,
> Or so he said, with more than priestly scope;
> He had a special license from the pope.
> Sweetly he heard his penitents at shrift
> With pleasant absolution, for a gift.[1]

Criticism and resentment of the contemporary Church found expression also at the political level. During the later thirteenth and early fourteenth centuries, the papacy considerably expanded its right of "provision"—of exercising direct control over the appointment of English churchmen at all levels, from parish and canonry to archdiocese. The right of papal provision —which was in keeping with the growing tendency toward ecclesiastical centralization—gave the papacy the power to appoint a large number of churchmen in fourteenth-century England. Resentful of such extensive control of the English Church by the Avignon papacy, parliament gave its support in 1351 to the Statute of Provisors, which succeeded in limiting papal provisions slightly. A second Statute of Provisors in 1390 was more effective, but the popes retained considerable influence on English ecclesiastical ap-

---

[1] *The Canterbury Tales,* Nevill Coghill, tr. (Baltimore, 1952). Langland's *Piers Plowman* is rendered into modern English by, among others, J. F. Goodridge (Baltimore, 1959).

CHAUCER AND THE WIFE OF BATH
(from the Ellesmere Manuscript of
The Canterbury Tales, circa 1390)
The author is wearing a fashionable
longtailed hat known as a "liripipe."
The wife of Bath indicates her unlady-
like assertiveness by riding astride
and carrying a whip. *Henry E.
Huntington Library.*

pointments for some time to come. In doing so, they insured that resentment would continue.

The old issue of appeals to the pope from the church courts of England remained acute throughout the fourteenth century. Papal appeals, like papal provisions, were attacked by statutes. The first Statute of Praemunire (1353) sought to limit such appeals but actually had little effect on them. It was not until the third Statute of Praemunire in 1393 that the practice was seriously curtailed. Finally, Anglo-papal relations during the fourteenth century were clouded by an accelerating conflict over the pope's right to tax the English clergy. There were serious protests against papal taxation in 1375 and 1376, and on two occasions Richard II refused it altogether. These struggles, although inconclusive, had the effect of diminishing the papal hold on the English Church. They constitute a political expression of the rising anticlericalism that affected society at all levels.

Fourteenth-century anticlericalism reached its crescendo in the career of the great Oxford philosopher and ecclesiastical revolutionary, John Wycliffe (d. 1384).[2] Wycliffe's thought was built on the strong tradition of antiecclesiastical protest that had already manifested itself in many ways— in popular opposition to clerical wealth and corruption, in hostility between the English government and the papacy, and in scholarly attacks on medieval theology and the Church hierarchy by men such as Ockham. The mystical doctrine of direct communion with God, short-circuiting the priestly sacramental system, also made a deep impact on Wycliffe. In addition, by the later fourteenth century the Church itself was noticeably weaker than it had been in the High Middle Ages. Its moral authority was declining; it no longer inspired such awe; its monopoly on literacy and learning had long ago been broken, and laymen now occupied high positions in the royal administration and judiciary that had once been the exclusive preserve of clerics. With the decline in land income brought about by the plague, the Church's revenue fell; and it found itself in bitter competition with the equally hard-pressed barons and monarchy for the taxes of the English laity. Many Englishmen were prepared to listen respectfully to Wycliffe's radical reform proposals, and some were ready to follow him.

Wycliffe first attained repute as a highly gifted but fundamentally orthodox Oxford theologian. In the mid-1370s he passed under the protection of the most powerful magnate of the age, John of Gaunt, Duke of Lancaster, fourth son of Edward III. Shielded by John of Gaunt's favor, he became active in politics for a time and began his journey along the road of heresy. After 1378 his radical doctrinal views made it impossible for him to continue his political career, and he devoted his final years to writing. In these years his opposition to the Church and to traditional Catholic doctrine became sharper and more fundamental than ever before. He condemned

---

[2] See K. B. McFarlane, *John Wycliffe and the Beginnings of English Nonconformity* (London, 1952).

ecclesiastical property and suggested that the king had the right to confiscate it. He attacked the traditional medieval doctrine of the eucharist. Inspired by the mystical doctrines that were then in the air, he rejected the entire priestly-sacramental system. To him, the organized Church was not a mediator between God and man, but merely an agency to aid man in his spiritual quest. Indeed, the true Church was not the ecclesiastical hierarchy at all, but the community of believers. Not merely the mystic but every man must confront God directly—without priestly intercession, guided only by his own conscience and Holy Scripture.

Such, in brief, were the religious doctrines of John Wycliffe. Most Englishmen, disenchanted as they were with traditional Catholic Christianity, were not yet ready for them. Langland's longing for a purification of the old order was far more congenial to the contemporary English mood than Wycliffe's call to revolution. Yet Wycliffe's scholarly prestige was great, hostility to the Church was growing, and there were some who adopted his views. These men, known as Lollards, included a handful of Oxford scholars; most of them, however, were from the poor and outcast classes. To them, Wycliffe's religious revolt carried strong overtones of social revolution. Within a few years the heresy had spread to the continent and served as a powerful influence on the career of the Bohemian reformer, John Hus. In 1415 Hus was burned at the stake by the fathers of the Council of Constance; but the doctrines endured to influence the Protestant reformers of the sixteenth century.

England had not produced a major heretic since the days of Pelagius, and Wycliffe appears to have caught English churchmen off guard. In time, however, they reacted to his teachings and had little difficulty in enlisting the support of the lay establishment. Wycliffe himself seems to have enjoyed John of Gaunt's protection to the end and was allowed to die a natural death in 1384. But his doctrines had already been officially condemned before he died; and during the later part of Richard II's reign it became royal policy to hunt down Lollards. This policy of repression was strengthened by a statute of 1401 bearing the ingenuous title, the Statute on the Burning of Heretics. By the early fifteenth century the immediate crisis was over; but the seeds had been planted and continued to germinate.

The Peasants' Revolt

Ecclesiastical wealth evoked a powerful protest in the later fourteenth century, but, as the poetry of Langland demonstrates, popular opposition was directed not only against wealthy churchmen but against wealthy laymen as well:

> The poor may plead and pray in doorways,
> They may quake for cold and thirst and hunger.
> None receives them rightfully and relieves their suffering;
> They are hooted at like hounds and ordered away.

A HARVEST SCENE FROM THE ST. MARY'S PSALTER
The economic system represented by the oppressive overseer in this
illustration was already being strongly challenged by the rural poor of the
14th century. *Bodleian Library.*

These words illustrate a profound sense of grievance that translated itself
into an increasing degree of class antagonism. In 1381 it gave rise to a
bloody uprising known as the Peasants' Revolt.[3] This tragic rebellion fed
on the general gloom and unrest of the age. More specifically, it was a
product of the growing conflict between landlord and tenant that arose from
the Black Death, the falling population, and the shortage of labor. As the
labor supply diminished, wages tended to rise sharply. The landlords, facing
an economic squeeze between rising wages and contracting markets, sought
through legislation to keep wages down. These landlords were not great
magnates for the most part but members of the gentry. Their fears were
manifested in a series of Statutes of Laborers, issued from 1351 onwards in
response to strong pressure from the House of Commons. The Statutes of
Laborers, which aimed at freezing wages by legislative fiat, were successful
in keeping them within bounds but not in halting their rise altogether. Landlords often found themselves in competition with one another for peasants'
services, and a black market on labor seems to have developed. Nevertheless,
the peasant felt wronged by this legislation and tended toward the opinion,
not unfounded, that the ruling orders were conspiring against him.

This conviction was powerfully reinforced by a series of poll taxes
levied between 1377 and 1381. Traditionally, parliamentary grants had been

---

[3] See R. B. Dobson, ed., *The Peasants' Revolt of 1381* (London, 1970). The revolt is
given a Marxist twist in R. H. Hilton and H. Fagan, *The English Rising of 1381*
(1950). Important contemporary documents are collected in G. M. Trevelyan and
E. Powell, eds., *The Peasants' Rising and the Lollards* (London, 1899).

borne chiefly by the wealthier part of the population; but the poll taxes were assessed on rich and poor alike by head. The Commons, hard-pressed by declining land revenues and convinced that the peasants were having things far too much their own way, were captivated by the idea of reducing their own tax burden at peasant expense. The most severe poll tax, that of 1381, was the immediate cause of the Peasants' Revolt.

The revolt lasted scarcely a month—from late May 1381 to the end of June; by then the rebels were suppressed and the old social order was every-where restored. It was a hopeless, wretchedly-led endeavor, but for a brief moment it shook society to its foundations. A violent protest against the miserable conditions resulting from political suppression, war, depression, and plague, it illustrates the deep hostilities that afflicted English society in the later Middle Ages.

The Peasants' Revolt began in Kent and in neighboring Essex. Among its many leaders the most notable were the Kentishman Wat Tyler and the priest John Ball, whose famous couplet symbolizes the radical, Christian-based egalitarianism of the rebels:

When Adam delved and Eve span,
Who was then a gentleman?

Having terrorized the lords and gentry of their respective shires, the two bands merged on London in mid-June and ran wild in the city for two days, burning and murdering. The court took refuge in the Tower, and the arch-bishop of Canterbury was captured and beheaded. Then, writes an anon-ymous observer, the rebel leaders proclaimed

that anyone who could catch any Fleming or other alien of any nation might cut off his head, and so they did forthwith. Then they took the heads of the archbishop and of the others and put them on wooden poles, and carried them before them in procession as far as the shrine of Westminster Abbey. . . . Then they returned to London Bridge and set the head of the archbishop above the gate, with eight other heads of those they had mur-dered, so that all could see them who crossed over the bridge. Thereupon they went to the church of St. Martin's in the Vintry, and found within it thirty-five Flemings, whom they dragged out and beheaded in the street. On that day there were beheaded about 140 or 160 people in all. Then they made their way to the houses of Lombards and other aliens, and broke into their dwellings, and robbed them of all their goods that they could lay hands on. This continued all that day and the night following, amidst hideous cries and horrid tumult.

Although deeply hostile to the nobility and the foreign merchants, the rebels remained respectful of the monarchy, and the frightened court had no recourse but to send out the fourteen-year-old king, Richard II, to nego-tiate. There were two parleys, on two successive days, between the young monarch and the rebel leaders, and from contemporary accounts of these meetings we are able to discern some of the diverse rebel goals. They demanded above all the abolition of villeinage—that is, the freeing of all peasants from the traditional work service on their lords' demesnes. They further demanded a ceiling on rents—not to exceed fourpence per acre. Beyond these specific concessions they sought a series of reforms that would have had no less drastic an effect than the overturning of society: equality of all men before the law, abolition of all lordship except the king's, confiscation and redistribution of all ecclesiastical property not essential to the direct sustenance of churchmen, and the elimination of all English bishoprics but one. Such goals might well have found wide support in later centuries; in 1381 they were wildly unrealistic.

Richard II, having no real choice, submitted for the moment to the peasants' demands. At the second of the two parleys, after the king had made his concessions, the rebel leader Wat Tyler drew his sword (for reasons unclear to us), and the Lord Mayor of London seized him and pulled him from his horse. Wat Tyler was immediately slain, and his followers, surprisingly, refrained from any violent reaction. At the king's request, they simply dispersed. Perhaps they were under the illusion that their cause had triumphed. In fact, however, once the rebels withdrew from London the

THE PEASANTS' REVOLT OF 1381 (from Froissart's Chronicles)
The rebel leader, Wat Tyler, is about to be killed by the Lord Mayor of London in the presence of the 14-year-old Richard II. *British Museum.*

revolt was doomed. Terror continued to afflict the countryside for the next week or two—abbeys were attacked, manors burned, and towns plundered— but the rebellion quickly lost its initial enthusiasm. By the end of June the rebel bands had been hunted down and the old social order restored. The ·concessions were of course forgotten, but the peasantry had gained one thing: the idea of a tax on the entire population was dropped, not to be re- vived until the twentieth century.

> Afterwards the king sent out his messengers into divers parts to capture the evildoers and put them to death. And many were taken and hanged in London, and they set up many gallows around the city of London and in other cities and boroughs of the south country. At length, as it pleased God, the king saw that too many of his faithful subjects would be undone, and too much blood spilled, and he took pity in his heart and granted them full pardon, on condition that they should never rise again, under penalty of death or mutilation, and that each of them should get his charter of pardon, and pay the king, as a fee for sealing the charter, twenty shillings for his enrichment. And so finished this wicked war.

The Peasants' Revolt had no real chance to overturn society; yet some of its leaders' goals were realized in the next few decades through the op- eration of basic economic forces. The old demesne economy was no longer paying its way, and English villeinage was therefore rapidly disappearing of its own accord. A villein was essentially one who was bound to perform work services for his lord; and as demesne lands were divided more and more into tenants' plots, the necessity of work service disappeared. By the early fifteenth century the old manorial regime was all but dead, and villein- age was dying with it.

As the fourteenth century closed, the age of crisis was drawing to an end. The following century, although socially divided and deeply troubled, witnessed no repetition of the Peasants' Revolt and produced no heretic of Wycliffe's stature. Aristocratic warfare reached a new level of intensity, but there were no serious challenges to basic social or ecclesiastical institu- tions. The epoch of transition from medieval to modern England was far from over, but the first great social and cultural upheaval had passed.

The Reign of Richard II (1377–1399)

When the ten-year-old Richard II acceded to the throne in 1377, the political-economic balance between king, magnates, and gentry was sub- stantially different than in the days of Edward I.[4] The ongoing expenses of

---

[4] On Richard II see A. B. Steel, *Richard II* (Cambridge, 1941); and, more recently, R. H. Jones, *The Royal Policy of Richard II: Absolutism in the Later Middle Ages* (Oxford, 1968), a short, perceptive reinterpretation of the reign; also see G. Mathew, *The Court of Richard II* (London, 1968). There are some excellent special studies in F. R. H. DuBolay and C. M. Barron, eds., *The Reign of Richard II: Essays in Honour of May McKisack* (London, 1971).

war had long ago forced the crown to turn to parliament for help; and in the course of Edward III's reign Commons had come to demand an ever-greater voice in royal policy in return for its subsidies. The expansion and consolidation of baronial estates, and the growth of private armies, had raised a handful of magnates to a position of formidable power and wealth. Parliament's efforts to control the royal council had culminated, during the parliament of 1376, in the development of a process by which the Commons could remove unpopular royal ministers by impeachment. And Edward II's fall in 1327 demonstrated that, as a last resort, parliament might even depose the king.

Throughout his reign, Richard II endeavored to reverse the decline of royal power and to restore the monarchy to what he conceived to be its rightful position of authority over the realm. His goal was to establish a regime of royal absolutism; but in pursuing this goal he so alienated a powerful group of magnates that he himself was deposed. It took the English monarchy a century to recover from the catastrophe. Although he has sometimes been viewed as an unsuccessful precursor of the Tudors, his policies can be regarded more accurately as the last hurrah of Norman and Angevin absolutism—as a final effort to recreate the powerful monarchy of the High Middle Ages and bring it to fruition.

Richard himself was a man of courage, as his behavior during the Peasants' Revolt makes clear. He was small in stature and perhaps slightly hunchbacked; his portraits disclose a sensitive, anxious face. He was a thoughtful, moody man, a connoisseur of the arts who lacked distinguished intelligence or unusual political acumen. And he was a devotee of the cult of sacred kingship. Particularly during his last years, he preoccupied himself with the symbols and ceremonies of monarchy: he stressed the sacred qualities of the royal anointment; he displayed the sun on his banners; and he turned ordinary court procedures into elaborate and colorful pageants. In these and other ways he gave visible expression to his lofty notions of royal absolutism. No monarch had ever surrounded himself with so much regal display as Richard; and none had pursued a royalist policy under such unfavorable circumstances.

In 1380 Richard dismissed the regency council that had ruled for him during the opening years of his reign. In the years just following, he surrounded himself with loyal friends, thereby creating a "court party" faithful to the crown. He favored these friends with earldoms, duchies, and high offices at court; and with their advice and support he embarked on his policy of royal absolutism—unheedful of the opinion of magnates and gentry outside his inner circle.

The barons of this period were in no sense a monolithic force; if anything they were even more faction-ridden than in earlier times. They were at odds not only with one another but also with the gentry and townsmen who now exercised considerable power in the House of Commons. But men of all classes were alarmed at the young Richard's independent course; and

RICHARD II
The portrait is by an
unknown artist. *National
Portrait Gallery.*

his position was rendered all the more insecure by a continuing series of English military reverses abroad. Court favorites were suspected of enriching themselves on revenues intended for warfare and of conniving with foreign enemies. In 1381 and 1382 members of parliament unsuccessfully demanded investigations of the king's household expenses; in 1384 two royal favorites were accused of financial irregularities. Richard, showing none of Edward III's pliancy, charged the accusers with defamation and had them punished severely. In 1385 parliament requested an annual review of the household accounts, and although the king permitted the drawing up of an ordinance to that effect, it was never implemented. Richard was determined to isolate his court and household from the meddling of the community.

In 1386 parliament's dissatisfaction became intense. Thus far relations between crown and community had been tempered by the moderating influence of John of Gaunt, Duke of Lancaster and younger son of Edward III. As uncle of the king, Gaunt had a foothold in court; and as England's wealthiest magnate—master of the immense Lancastrian inheritance—he was a political figure of commanding influence. In 1386 he departed for a military adventure in Spain, and in his absence both court and community acted with less restraint. The parliament of autumn 1386 demanded the dismissal of Richard's chancellor, Michael de la Pole. Richard responded that he would not dismiss even one of his kitchen scullions at their request. Thereupon parliament reminded him that if a king refused to govern with the assent of his people, a clear precedent existed "for deposing the king himself from the royal throne and elevating some close relative of the royal line." Abashed, Richard gave in, and Michael de la Pole was impeached by Commons for graft and maladministration. Even more important was parliament's appointment of a new royal council to govern for a year. The council members, hand-picked by parliament, were empowered to control revenues, supervise household expenses, and reform the royal government.

Early in 1387 Richard departed from Westminster—where the council was sitting—taking with him his household and court favorites, including de la Pole. Ruling once again through his inner circle, he ignored the parliament-appointed council and did not return to Westminster until its year of power had almost expired. Meanwhile, he had a series of constitutional questions placed before a group of England's chief justices, and they answered exactly as the king wished: they judged that the parliament-appointed council offended the royal prerogative and was therefore illegal, and that those who had forced it on the king should be punished as traitors (the customary penalty for treason was death). The judges proclaimed further that it was treason to hinder in any way the king's exercise of his royal power; that parliament had no right to make demands on the king prior to granting him requested subsidies; and that the king was empowered to dissolve any parliament at his pleasure. Finally, they stated that parliament could not lawfully impeach any minister of the king without royal consent; and it was treason to view Edward II's deposition as a legal precedent.

These judgments represent a lucid and unqualified assertion of the royal prerogative—a firm statement of the philosophy of absolutism that Richard cherished. According to this view, the king's counsellors were to be chosen by the king alone and were responsible to the king alone. Parliament too was to be a royal tool, summoned and dismissed at the king's will. And anyone who acted contrary to these rules was subject to condemnation for treason.

But the judges' ruling had no effect on the king's enemies; indeed, Richard's defiance united opposition against him. In November 1387, a group of magnates approached the king at Westminster and brought charges of treason against several of his favorites. Richard promised to arrest those accused and hold them until the next parliament, when the "appeal" of treason would be judged. In reality he was merely playing for time, and he permitted his accused favorites to remain at liberty. But in February 1388, a royalist army was routed by the magnates at Radcot Bridge in Oxfordshire, and Richard was left without adequate means to defend himself. Lacking the necessary military power, he was obliged to submit to the magnates and accept their "appeals" against his favorites.

The so-called Merciless Parliament met in 1388 to hear the appeals of five great magnates. These "lords appellant" entered the assembly "arm in arm, clad in cloth of gold," to prosecute their case. Dominated by them and their supporters, the Merciless Parliament convicted the accused counsellors and executed several others as well. Michael de la Pole was sentenced to hang, but he had already fled to France, never to return. Richard's court circle was thus destroyed, and the king was left no choice but to cooperate with his barons and his parliaments. The barons appointed a new royal council, whose members swore to support all acts of parliament. And the five lords appellant were awarded twenty thousand pounds for their efforts and expenses "in procuring the salvation of the realm and the destruction of the traitors."

The Merciless Parliament was the central political event of Richard II's reign. It marks the zenith of parliamentary power and the nadir of the royal prerogative in fourteenth-century England. The lords appellant themselves justified their actions on legal and constitutional grounds, but their acts betray cruelty and vindictiveness. Like so many victorious barons before them, they went too far; and the magnitude of their triumph evoked a reaction of venomous factionalism and widespread dissent. Moreover, England's wars abroad fared no better under the new government than before: the French campaigns remained hopelessly bogged down, and in 1388 an English army was crushingly defeated by the Scots. In 1389 John of Gaunt returned from Spain, and in the years that followed Richard enjoyed his tacit support. With the situation thus turning in his favor, Richard was able in 1389 to dismiss his baronial council and rule once more through counsellors of his own choosing. The baronial council withdrew without protest. Richard was again the master of his court.

For the next eight years the king mended his fences. In the style of Edward III, he cooperated with barons and parliament in the governance of his realm. He did not abandon his dreams of royal absolutism, but he pursued them more wisely and cautiously than before. Gritting his teeth, he showed honor and favor even toward the lords appellant. And slowly he succeeded in building around him a new circle of trustworthy supporters. Meanwhile he sought to free himself from total financial dependence on parliament by bringing the war with France to an end. A definitive peace eluded him, but he did succeed in arranging a twenty-eight-year truce; he sealed it by taking as his royal bride the princess Isabella, eldest daughter of the half-mad king of France, Charles VI. Isabella was a girl of six, but Richard himself was still in his twenties and could seemingly afford to wait a few years for an heir. And Isabella brought with her a dowry of 800,000 francs.

Accordingly, when Richard returned to England with his child-bride late in 1396, his financial position was vastly improved. The dowry helped, and the freedom from war expenses helped still more. No longer was he under such pressure to go begging to parliament, or to permit the need for parliamentary subsidies to hamper the exercise of his royal prerogative. Working through his sheriffs and other local administrators, he packed the spring parliament of 1397 with his own supporters and overawed it with his military retainers. When a member of Commons demanded a reduction in the royal household expenses, he was arraigned for treason and convicted. And the Lords in parliament ratified the king's declaration that anyone who "shall move or excite the Commons of parliament or any other person to make remedy of any matter which touches our person, our government, or our regality shall be considered a traitor."

With the situation so propitious, Richard undertook his long-awaited revenge on the lords appellant. The autumn parliament of 1397, again packed with royalists, moved savagely against all the king's former enemies —depriving them of their lands and liberty, forcing some into exile, executing others. Three of the lords appellant now suffered the irony of being themselves "appealed" in parliament for treason. One of the three was murdered, a second legally executed, and a third banished from the realm. Lands were confiscated on an immense scale and redistributed among a new group of magnates, some of them close friends of the king. A parliament of 1398 formally revoked all the acts of the Merciless Parliament, and everyone involved in anti-royalist activity during 1387 and 1388 was obliged to sue (that is, pay) for the royal pardon. The royalist opinions of the judges in 1387 were now resurrected and, with parliament's assent, declared to be the law of the realm. And Richard, anxious to secure still greater independence from annual parliamentary grants, demanded and received a lifetime privilege of collecting the subsidies on wool. Financially and constitutionally, the English throne had never stood higher.

Intoxicated by these triumphs, Richard lost all restraint. He forced huge loans from the burghers and assessed heavy fines on a number of shires for failing to support him in his struggle against the lords appellant in 1388. In autumn 1398, he banished the two remaining lords appellant, one of whom was Henry Bolingbroke, son and heir of the wealthy and aged John of Gaunt, Duke of Lancaster. When Gaunt died early in 1399, the king refused to consider the claims of the banished heir. Henry Bolingbroke's sentence of exile was extended from ten years to life, and the vast Lancastrian lands reverted to the crown.

Henry Bolingbroke had been a very considerable landholder in his own right; at the time of his exile he held the title duke of Hereford. The addition of the Lancastrian patrimony would have made him a magnate of almost kingly wealth; and it is understandable that Richard would fear the concentration of such prodigious resources in the hands of any single baron —particularly one who had formerly opposed him. Nevertheless, the king's seizure of the Lancastrian inheritance aroused the fear and hostility of the magnates. Ever since the Norman Conquest the inheritance of land had been of vital concern to the nobility. The issue of normal inheritance underlay the civil strife of Stephen's reign in the early twelfth century and now, two hundred fifty years later, England had a king who flaunted the rights of noble heirs. Richard's throne had never seemed so secure as it was in early 1399; yet, in fact, the king could count on little support outside his immediate circle. He had sown hostility among all the articulate classes in the land. Supremely confident, he led an expedition into Ireland in the summer of 1399; while he was away Henry Bolingbroke returned to England to claim his Lancastrian inheritance by force.

As a son of John of Gaunt and a grandson of Edward III, Henry Bolingbroke was a man of royal blood, and when he landed in Yorkshire and moved southward, one great magnate after another rallied to him. The aim of the rebels was not merely to install Bolingbroke in his Lancastrian estates but to make him king of England in Richard's stead. Richard returned from Ireland to find his cause abandoned, and in August 1399 he surrendered to the insurrectionists. Parliament received his abdication in September, declared him deposed, and recognized Henry of Bolingbroke as King Henry IV of England. Richard died in captivity early in 1400—he was probably murdered—and the new Lancastrian dynasty was established on the English throne.

As in 1327, so in 1399 parliament was the instrument of a royal deposition. In neither instance was parliament acting on its own. Rather it was conferring a stamp of legality on an accomplished revolution. Parliament deposed Richard II in the presence of Bolingbroke's army and had little choice in the matter. Nevertheless, the precedent of 1327 was powerfully reinforced in 1399; and Richard II, who had struggled so hard for the full exercise of the royal prerogative, left behind him a crippled monarchy.

Whereas Edward II had been deposed because he was too weak, Richard II was deposed because he was too strong. Richard pitted himself against a long and potent trend toward shared power between crown and community—a trend that by the late fourteenth century had progressed too far to be easily reversed. The magnates were by then very powerful, and townsmen and gentry had become articulate. Neither could be ignored. In his final years Richard tried to control them by fear and failed. A century thereafter, when the Tudors succeeded at last in rebuilding royal authority, they did so on a sturdy foundation of popular support. The idea does not seem to have occurred to Richard II.

Conclusion

The deposition of Richard II marks an appropriate end to a century of violence and turmoil. The act was, in every respect, a fundamental revolution in English politics. A king had been deposed in 1327 but was succeeded by his legitimate and unquestioned heir. With Richard II's deposition in 1399 the very concept of hereditary succession was thrown into question. For Richard was the last of the Plantagenet kings. He had no son. The succession was irregular for the first time in two hundred years. Legitimate succession was basic to the politics of the Middle Ages, and the shattering of that principle in 1399 rocked the political order. For the next century rival families contended for the throne while ordinary Englishmen were ill-ruled and plagued by civil war. Not until the coming of the Tudors in 1485 was the destructive work of 1399 undone and the succession problem settled.

The transition from the medieval to the modern ethos was far from complete in 1399. Englishmen remained troubled by recurring plague, social unrest, and constitutional confusion. In emphasizing a change in dynasty one must not be misled into ignoring more subtle charges that were still in process and would remain so for generations to come. As the period

CANTERBURY CATHEDRAL, CIRCA 1400
An interesting example of the Perpendicular style, Canterbury's late-Gothic columns are molded over the much earlier pillars of a Norman-Romanesque nave. *National Monuments Record.*

closes, England's population was apparently still falling, its struggle with France remained fundamentally unresolved, its economy was spotty, its commitment to the Roman Church was slowly dissolving, and its countryside was turbulent. Yet for all that, England in 1399 was not a society in decline but a society in transition. There was anxiety and suffering, but there was also creativity. Men such as Chaucer, Langland, and Wycliffe display originality of a degree that would ornament any age. More than that, all three demonstrate a heightened sense of national identity. Chaucer and Langland were crucial figures in the development of English as an important literary vehicle, and Wycliffe dreamed of an English translation of the Bible and accorded the king a central position in the governance of the English Church. Richard II's reign was also a great creative age in the development of Perpendicular Gothic architecture—witness the naves of Canterbury and Winchester and the choir of York. The new architectural style was not only impressive in itself but also less cosmopolitan, more distinctly English, than earlier Gothic styles had been. At this same time English merchants, who had once allowed their foreign rivals to dominate English trade, were creating lucrative new markets for themselves across northern Europe.

As the fourteenth century closed, all Europe was slipping gradually from medieval universalism toward modern nationalism. England was still a kingdom, not yet a nation; but it was becoming increasingly English as time went on—moving perceptibly toward the England of the Tudors and Stuarts. In many respects the transition from medieval to modern England involved a rejection of things medieval: feudalism, scholasticism, Christian universalism. But in other respects, modern England was built on medieval foundations: king, council, household, parliament, the university, the tradition of scientific scholarship, the conquest of fields from forest and marsh, the common law. More basic still was the growing awareness among Englishmen that they were a single people—a conviction that began with Bede and Theodore of Tarsus and grew steadily as the Middle Ages progressed. Some of the fundamental ingredients of modern English society and culture are clearly in evidence by 1399. They illustrate the essential medieval contribution to the making of England.

Appendix

The English Kings from Alfred to Henry IV

The Anglo-Saxon Kings

Alfred	871–899
Edward the Elder	899–925
Athelstan	925–939
Edmund	939–946
Edred	946–955
Eadwig	955–959
Edgar the Peaceable	959–975
Edward the Martyr	975–978
Ethelred the Unready	978–1016
Edmund Ironside	1016
Canute	1016–1035
Harold Harefoot	1035–1040
Harthacanute	1040–1042
Edward the Confessor	1042–1066
Harold Godwinson	1066

The Norman Kings

William I	1066–1087
William II (Rufus)	1087–1100
Henry I	1100–1135
Stephen	1135–1154

The Angevin (Plantagenet) Kings

Henry II	1154–1189
Richard I	1189–1199
John	1199–1216
Henry III	1216–1272
Edward I	1272–1307
Edward II	1307–1327
Edward III	1327–1377
Richard II	1377–1399

The Lancastrian Kings

Henry IV	1399–1413

Bibliography

Bibliographies

Altschul, Michael. *Anglo-Norman England: 1066–1154.* Conference on British Studies Bibliographical Handbooks. Cambridge, 1969.

Bonser, Wilfred. *Anglo-Saxon and Celtic Bibliography.* 2 vols. Berkeley, 1957.

Gross, Charles. *The Sources and Literature of English History from the Earliest Times to about 1485.* 2nd ed. London, 1915.

Hall, Hubert. *A Select Bibliography for the Study, Sources and Literature of English Mediaeval Economic History.* London, 1914.

Mullins, E. L. C. *A Guide to the Historical and Archaeological Publications of Societies in England and Wales, 1901–1933.* London, 1968.

————. *Texts and Calendars, An Analytical Guide to Serial Publications.* Royal Historical Society. London, 1958.

Writings on British History, 1901–1933, Vol. II, *The Middle Ages, 450–1485.* Royal Historical Society. London, 1968.

Writings on British History, 1940–1945, Vol. I. Royal Historical Society. London, 1960.

General Works

REFERENCE

Cokayne, George E. *The Complete Peerage of England, Scotland, Ireland, Great Britain and the United Kingdom.* Edited by Vicary Gibbs et al. 13 vols. London, 1910–1949.

Knowles, David, C. N. L. Brooke, and Vera London, eds. *The Heads of Religious Houses, England and Wales, 940–1216.* Cambridge, 1972.

Knowles, David, and R. N. Hadcock, *Medieval Religious Houses, England and Wales.* 2nd ed. London, 1971.

Powicke, F. M., and E. B. Fryde, eds. *Handbook of British Chronology.* 2nd ed. Royal Historical Society. London, 1961.

Sanders, I. J. *English Baronies, A Study of their Origin and Descent, 1086–1327.* Oxford, 1960.

Stephen, Leslie, and Sidney Lee, eds. *Dictionary of National Biography from the Earliest Times to 1900.* 22 vols. Oxford, 1917.

GENERAL MEDIEVAL

Barrow, G. W. S. *Feudal Britain: The Completion of the Medieval Kingdoms, 1066–1314.* London, 1956.

Brooke, C. N. L. *From Alfred to Henry III, 871–1272.* New York, 1961.

———. *The Saxon and Norman Kings.* London, 1963.

Petit-Dutaillis, Charles. *The Feudal Monarchy in France and England from the Tenth to the Thirteenth Century.* London, 1936.

Poole, A. L., ed. *Medieval England.* 2 vols. Oxford, 1958.

Southern, R. W. *Medieval Humanism and Other Studies.* Oxford, 1970.

ROMAN AND ANGLO-SAXON

Alcock, Leslie. *Arthur's Britain: History and Archaeology, A.D. 367–634.* Baltimore, 1973.

Blair, P. Hunter. *An Introduction to Anglo-Saxon England.* Cambridge, 1956.

———. *Roman Britain and Early England, 55 B.C–A.D. 871.* Edinburgh, 1963.

Barlow, Frank. *Edward the Confessor.* Berkeley, Calif., 1970.

Burn, A. R. *Agricola and Roman Britain.* London, 1953.

Chadwick, H. M., et al. *Studies in Early British History.* Cambridge, 1954.

Chadwick, Nora K., et al. *Celt and Saxon: Studies in the Early British Border.* Cambridge, 1963.

Chaney, William A. *The Cult of Kingship in Anglo-Saxon England.* Berkeley, Calif., 1970.

Clemoes, Peter, and Kathleen Hughes, eds. *England Before the Conquest: Studies in Primary Sources Presented to Dorothy Whitelock.* Cambridge, 1971.

Collingwood, R. G. and J. N. L. Myres. *Roman Britain and the English Settlements.* 2nd ed. Oxford, 1937.

Collingwood, R. G. and Ian Richmond. *The Archaeology of Roman Britain.* Rev. ed. London, 1969.

Copley, G. J. *The Conquest of Wessex in the Sixth Century.* London, 1954.

Crawford, S. J. *Anglo-Saxon Influence on Western Christendom, 600–800.* Oxford, 1933.

Duckett, Eleanor S. *Alfred the Great.* Chicago, 1956.

Dudley, D. R., and G. Webster. *The Rebellion of Boudicca.* New York, 1962.

Evison, Vera I. *The Fifth-Century Invasions South of the Thames.* London, 1965.

Fisher, D. J. V. *The Anglo-Saxon Age.* London, 1974.

Frere, Sheppard. *Britannia: A History of Roman Britain.* London, 1967.

Hoskins, W. G. *The Westward Expansion of Wessex.* Leicester, 1960.

John, Eric. *Orbis Britanniae and Other Studies.* Leicester, 1966.

Jolliffe, J. E. A. *Pre-Feudal England: The Jutes.* Oxford, 1933.

Kirby, D. P. *The Making of Early England.* London, 1967.

Körner, Sten. *The Battle of Hastings: England and Europe, 1035–1066.* Lund, 1964.

Larson, L. M. *Canute the Great.* New York, 1912.

Levison, W. *England and the Continent in the Eighth Century.* Oxford, 1946.

Morris, John. *The Age of Arthur: A History of the British Isles from 350 to 650.* New York, 1973.

Nash-Williams, V. E. *The Roman Frontier in Wales.* 2nd ed. Cardiff, 1969.

Plummer, Charles. *The Life and Times of Alfred the Great.* Oxford, 1902.

Porter, H. M. *The Saxon Conquest of Somerset and Devon.* Bath, 1967.

Richmond, I. A., ed. *Roman Britain.* Rev. ed. New York, 1964.

———, ed. *Roman and Native in North Britain.* Edinburgh, 1958.

Ritchie, R. L. G. *The Normans in England Before Edward the Confessor.* Exeter, 1948.

Stention, F. M. *Anglo-Saxon England.* 3rd ed. Oxford, 1971.

———. *Preparatory to Anglo-Saxon England.* Edited by D. M. Stenton. Oxford, 1970.

NORMAN CONQUEST TO MAGNA CARTA

Appleby, John T. *England Without Richard, 1189–1199.* Ithaca, N.Y., 1965.

———. *John, King of England.* New York, 1958.

———. *The Troubled Reign of King Stephen.* New York, 1970.

Barlow, Frank. *The Feudal Kingdom of England, 1042–1216.* 2nd ed. London, 1955.

———. *William I and the Norman Conquest.* London, 1965.

Brown, R. Allen. *The Normans and the Norman Conquest.* London, 1969.

Brundage, James A. *Richard Lion Heart: A Biography.* New York, 1974.

Cronne, H. A. *The Reign of Stephen.* London, 1970.

David, C. W. *Robert Curthose, Duke of Normandy.* Cambridge, Mass., 1920.

Davis, R. H. C. *King Stephen, 1135–1154.* Berkeley, Calif., 1967.

Douglas, David C. *The Norman Achievement, 1050–1100.* Berkeley, Calif., 1969.

———. *William the Conqueror.* Berkeley, Calif., 1964.

Freeman, E. A. *The History of the Norman Conquest of England.* 6 vols. Oxford, 1867–1879.

———. *The Reign of William Rufus and the Accession of Henry I.* 2 vols. Oxford, 1882.

Gibbs-Smith, Charles H. *The Bayeux Tapestry.* New York, 1973.

Haskins, C. H. *Norman Institutions.* Cambridge, Mass., 1918.

Hollister, C. W. *The Impact of the Norman Conquest.* New York, 1969.

Holt, J. C. *The Northerners: A Study in the Reign of King John.* New York, 1961.

Kelly, Amy. *Eleanor of Aquitaine and the Four Kings.* Cambridge, Mass., 1950.

Loyn, H. R. *The Norman Conquest.* London, 1965.

Matthew, D. J. A. *The Norman Conquest.* New York, 1966.

Morton, Catherine and Hope Muntz, eds. *The Carmen de Hastingae Proelio of Guy Bishop of Amiens.* Oxford, 1972.

Nelson, Lynn H. *The Normans in South Wales, 1070–1171.* Austin, Texas, 1966.

Norgate, Kate. *England Under the Angevin Kings.* 2 vols. London, 1887.

Painter, Sidney. *The Reign of King John.* Baltimore, 1949.

Pernoud, Regine. *Eleanor of Aquitaine.* New York, 1968.
Poole, A. L. *From Domesday Book to Magna Carta, 1087–1216.* 2nd ed. Oxford, 1955.
Powicke, F. M. *The Loss of Normandy, 1189–1204.* 2nd ed. Manchester, 1961.
Ritchie, R. L. G. *The Normans in Scotland.* Edinburgh, 1954.
Round, J. H. *The Commune of London and Other Studies.* Westminster, 1899.
_____. *Geoffrey de Mandeville, A Study of the Anarchy.* London, 1892.
Thorpe, Lewis, ed. *The Bayeux Tapestry and the Norman Invasion.* London, 1973.
Warren, W. L. *Henry II.* Berkeley, 1973.
_____. *King John.* London, 1961.
Whitelock, Dorothy, et al. *The Norman Conquest: Its Setting and Impact.* London, 1966.

THIRTEENTH CENTURY

Clifford, E. R. *A Knight of Great Renown: The Life and Times of Othon de Grandson.* Chicago, 1961.
Cuttino, G. P. *English Diplomatic Administration, 1259–1339.* 2nd ed. Oxford, 1971.
Denholm-Young, N. *Richard of Cornwall.* Oxford, 1947.
Galbraith, V. H. *Roger Wendover and Matthew Paris.* Glasgow, 1944.
Jacob, E. F. *Studies in the Period of Baronial Reform and Rebellion, 1258–1267.* Oxford, 1925.
Labarge, Margaret W. *Simon de Montfort.* New York, 1963.
Norgate, Kate. *The Minority of Henry the Third.* London, 1912.
Painter, Sidney. *William Marshal.* Baltimore, 1933.
Powicke, F. M. *King Henry III and the Lord Edward: The Community of the Realm in the Thirteenth Century, 1216–1307.* 2nd ed. Oxford, 1962.
_____. *The Thirteenth Century, 1216–1307.* 2nd ed. Oxford, 1962.
Salzman, L. F. *Edward I.* London, 1968.
Snellgrove, H. S. *The Lusignans in England, 1247–1258.* Albuquerque, N.M., 1950.
Treharne, R. F. *The Lusignans in England, 1247–1263.* Rev. ed. Manchester, 1971.

FOURTEENTH CENTURY

Barrow, G. W. S. *Robert Bruce.* Berkeley, 1965.
Davies, J. C. *The Baronial Opposition to Edward II: A Study in Administrative History.* Cambridge, 1918.
DuBolay, F. R. H. and C. M. Barron, eds. *The Reign of Richard II: Essays in Honour of May McKisack.* London, 1971.
Fowler, Kenneth A. *The Age of Plantagenet and Valois, 1328–1498.* London, 1967.
_____, ed. *The Hundred Years War.* London, 1971.
_____. *The King's Lieutenant: Henry of Grosmont.* London, 1969.
Green, V. H. H. *The Later Plantagenets, 1307–1485.* London, 1955.
Holmes, G. A. *The Later Middle Ages, 1272–1485.* New York, 1962.

Hutchinson, H. F. *Edward II: The Pliant King.* London, 1971.
Jones, R. H. *The Royal Policy of Richard II.* Oxford, 1968.
Keen, M. H. *England in the Later Middle Ages.* London, 1973.
McKisack, May. *The Fourteenth Century, 1307–1399.* Oxford, 1959.
Maddicott, J. R. *Thomas of Lancaster, 1307–1322.* London, 1970.
Mathew, Gervase. *The Court of Richard II.* London, 1968.
Nicholson, Ranald. *Edward III and the Scots.* Oxford, 1965.
Palmer, J. J. N. *England, France, and Christendom, 1377–1399.* London, 1972.
Perroy, Edouard. *The Hundred Years War.* London, 1951.
Phillips, J. R. S. *Aymer de Valence: Earl of Pembroke, 1307–1324.* Oxford, 1972.
Russell, P. E. *The English Intervention in Spain and Portugal in the Time of Edward III and Richard II.* Oxford, 1955.
Steel, A. B. *Richard II.* Cambridge, Mass., 1941.
Tout, T. F. *The Place of the Reign of Edward II in English History.* 2nd ed. Manchester, 1936.
Tuck, Anthony. *Richard II and the English Nobility.* London, 1973.
Wilkinson, Bertie. *The Later Middle Ages in England, 1216–1485.* London, 1969.

SPECIAL SURVEYS

Bloch, Marc. *The Royal Touch: Sacred Monarchy and Scrofula in England and France.* London, 1973.
Colvin, H. M., ed. *The History of the King's Works.* Vols. I and II, *The Middle Ages.* London, 1963.
Dickinson, W. C. *Scotland from the Earliest Times to 1603.* 2nd ed. London, 1965.
Douglas, David C., ed. *English Historical Documents.* Vols. I–IV. London, 1953ff.
Lloyd, J. E. *A History of Wales from the Earliest Times to the Edwardian Conquest.* 3rd ed. 2 vols. London, 1939.
Richardson, H. G. *The English Jewry under the Angevin Kings.* London, 1960.
Roth, Cecil. *A History of the Jews in England.* 3rd ed. Oxford, 1964.

Legal, Constitutional, and Governmental History

GENERAL MEDIEVAL

Bean, J. M. W. *The Decline of English Feudalism, 1215–1540.* Manchester, 1968.
Cam, Helen M. *Law Finders and Law Makers in Medieval England.* London, 1962.
————. *Liberties and Communities in Medieval England.* Cambridge, 1944.
Chrimes, S. B. *An Introduction to the Administrative History of Medieval England.* 3rd ed. New York, 1966.
Denholm-Young, N. *Seignorial Administration in England.* Oxford, 1937.
Edwards, J. G. *Historians and the Medieval English Parliament.* Glasgow, 1960.
Fryde, E. B. and Edward Miller, eds. *Historical Studies of the English Parliament.* Vol. I, *Origins to 1399.* Cambridge, 1970.

Haskins, George L. *The Growth of English Representative Government.* Philadelphia, 1948.

Hearder, H. and H. L. Loyn, eds. *British Government and Administration: Studies Presented to S. B. Chrimes.* Cardiff, 1974.

Howell, Margaret. *Regalian Right in Medieval England.* London, 1962.

Hoyt, Robert S. *The Royal Demesne in English Constitutional History, 1066–1272.* Ithaca, N.Y., 1950.

Hunnisett, R. F. *The Medieval Coroner.* Cambridge, 1961.

Jewell, Helen M. *English Local Administration in the Middle Ages.* New York, 1972.

Jolliffe, J. E. A. *The Constitutional History of Medieval England from the English Settlement to 1485.* 4th ed. New York, 1961.

Keeney, B. C. *Judgment by Peers.* Cambridge, Mass., 1949.

Lyon, Bryce. *A Constitutional and Legal History of Medieval England.* New York, 1960.

_____. *From Fief to Indenture.* Cambridge, Mass., 1957.

Mitchell, Sydney Knox. *Taxation in Medieval England.* New Haven, 1951.

Morris, William A. *The Medieval English Sheriff to 1300.* Manchester, 1927.

Petit-Dutaillis, Charles and Georges Lefebvre. *Studies and Notes Supplementary to Stubbs' Constitutional History.* Manchester, 1930.

Plucknett, T. F. T. *Early English Legal Literature.* Cambridge, 1958.

Pollock, F. and F. W. Maitland. *The History of English Law Before the Time of Edward I.* Rev. reissue of 2nd ed. 2 vols. Cambridge, 1968.

Poole, A. L. *Obligations of Society in the XII and XIII Centuries.* Oxford, 1946.

Ramsay, J. H. *A History of the Revenues of the Kings of England, 1066–1485.* 2 vols. Oxford, 1925.

Richardson, H. G. and G. O. Sayles. *Parliaments and Great Councils in Medieval England.* London, 1961.

Schramm, Percy E. *A History of the English Coronation.* Oxford, 1937.

Stubbs, William A. *The Constitutional History of England.* 5th ed. 3 vols. Oxford, 1891–1896.

Tout, T. F. *Chapters in the Administrative History of Medieval England.* 6 vols. Manchester, 1920–1937.

Wilkinson, Bertie. *The Constitutional History of Medieval England, 1216–1399.* 3 vols. New York, 1948–1958.

_____. *The Creation of Medieval Parliaments.* New York, 1972.

_____. *Studies in the Constitutional History of the Thirteenth and Fourteenth Centuries.* Manchester, 1937.

Wolffe, B. P. *The Royal Demesne in English History: The Crown Estate in the Governance of the Realm from the Conquest in 1509.* London, 1971.

Young, Charles R. *The English Borough and Royal Administration, 1130–1307.* Durham, N.C., 1961.

ROMAN AND ANGLO-SAXON

Chadwick, H. M. *Studies on Anglo-Saxon Institutions.* Cambridge, 1905.

Harmer, F. E. *Anglo-Saxon Writs.* Manchester, 1952.

Hollister, C. W. *Anglo-Saxon Military Institutions on the Eve of the Norman Conquest.* Oxford, 1962.

John, Eric. *Land Tenure in Early England.* Leicester, 1960.

Oleson, T. J. *The Witenagemot in the Reign of Edward the Confessor.* Toronto, 1955.

NORMAN CONQUEST TO MAGNA CARTA

Brown, R. Allen. *Origins of English Feudalism.* London, 1973.

Cheney, C. R. *Hubert Walter.* London, 1967.

Hollister, C. W. *The Military Organization of Norman England.* Oxford, 1965.

Holt, J. C. *Magna Carta.* Cambridge, 1965.

————, ed. *Magna Carta and the Idea of Liberty.* New York, 1972.

Howell, Margaret. *Regalian Right in Medieval England.* London, 1962.

Jolliffe, J. E. A. *Angevin Kingship.* 2nd ed. London, 1963.

Kealey, Edward. *Roger of Salisbury, Viceroy of England.* Berkeley, 1972.

Keeton, G. W. *The Norman Conquest and the Common Law.* London, 1966.

Poole, R. L. *The Exchequer in the Twelfth Century.* Oxford, 1912.

Richardson, H. G., and G. O. Sayles. *The Governance of Mediaeval England from the Conquest to Magna Carta.* Edinburgh, 1963.

————. *Law and Legislation from Aethelberht to Magna Carta.* Edinburgh, 1966.

Round, J. H. *Feudal England.* London, 1895.

Sutherland, Donald W. *The Assize of Novel Disseisin.* Oxford, 1973.

Stenton, Doris M. *English Justice Between the Norman Conquest and the Great Charter, 1066–1215.* Philadelphia, 1964.

Stenton, F. M. *The First Century of English Feudalism, 1066–1166.* 2nd ed. Oxford, 1961.

Turner, Ralph V. *The King and His Courts, 1199–1240.* Ithaca, N.Y., 1968.

Van Caenegem, R. C. *The Birth of the English Common Law.* Cambridge, 1973.

————. *Royal Writs in England from the Conquest to Glanvill.* Seldon Society. London, 1959.

West, Francis J. *The Justiciarship in England, 1066–1232.* Cambridge, 1966.

Young, Charles R. *Hubert Walter, Lord of Canterbury and Lord of England.* Durham, N.C., 1968.

THIRTEENTH CENTURY

Cam, Helen M. *Studies in the Hundred Rolls.* Oxford, 1921.

Clarke, M. V. *Representation and Consent.* London, 1936.

Ellis, Clarence. *Hubert de Burgh.* London, 1952.

Kantorowicz, Hermann. *Bractonian Problems.* Glasgow, 1941.

Plucknett, T. F. T. *Edward I and Criminal Law.* Cambridge, 1960.

————. *The Legislation of Edward I.* Oxford, 1949.

Powicke, Michael. *Military Obligation in Medieval England: A Study in Liberty and Duty.* Oxford, 1962.

Prestwich, M. C. *War, Politics and Finance Under Edward I.* London, 1972.

FOURTEENTH CENTURY

Bellamy, J. G. *The Law of Treason in the Later Middle Ages.* Cambridge, 1970.

Cuttino, G. P. *English Diplomatic Administration, 1259–1339.* Oxford, 1940.

Edwards, J. G. *The Commons in Medieval English Parliaments.* London, 1958.
Hewitt, H. J. *The Organization of War under Edward III, 1338–1362.* Manchester, 1966.
Lapsley, G. T. *Crown, Community and Parliament in the Later Middle Ages.* Edited by Helen M. Cam and Geoffrey Barraclough. Oxford, 1951.
Mackenzie, Kenneth R. *The English Parliament.* Rev. ed. Baltimore, 1959.
McKisack, May. *The Parliamentary Representation of the English Boroughs During the Middle Ages.* Oxford, 1932.
Powell, J. E. and K. Wallis. *The House of Lords in the Middle Ages.* London, 1968.
Willard, J. F., et al., eds. *The English Government at Work, 1326–1337.* 3 vols. Cambridge, Mass., 1940–1950.

Economic and Social History

GENERAL MEDIEVAL

Arnold, Ralph C. M. *A Social History of England, 55 B.C. to A.D. 1215.* New York, 1967.
Ault, Warren O. *Open-Field Farming in Medieval England: A Study of English By-Laws.* London, 1972.
Baker, A. R. H. and R. A. Butlin, eds. *Studies of Field Systems in the British Isles.* Cambridge, 1973.
Baker, Timothy. *Medieval London.* London, 1970.
Barraclough, Geoffrey, ed. *Social Life in Early England.* New York, 1960.
Beresford, Maurice. *The Lost Villages of England.* London, 1954.
——. *New Towns of the Middle Ages: Town Plantation in England, Wales and Glascony.* New York, 1967.
——, and J. K. W. St. Joseph. *Medieval England: An Aerial Survey.* Cambridge, 1958.
Brooke, G. C. *English Coins.* 3rd ed. London, 1950.
Douglas, David C. *The Social Structure of Medieval East Anglia.* Oxford, 1927.
DuBoulay, F. R. H. *The Lordship of Canterbury: An Essay on Medieval Society.* New York, 1966.
Finberg, H. P. R. *Tavistock Abbey: A Study in the Social and Economic History of Devon.* 2nd ed. Newton Abbot, 1969.
Harding, Alan. *A Social History of English Law.* Baltimore, 1966.
Hill, J. W. F. *Medieval Lincoln.* Cambridge, 1948.
Keen, M. H. *The Outlaws of Medieval Legend.* Toronto, 1961.
King, Edmund. *Peterborough Abbey, 1086–1310: A Study in the Land Market.* Cambridge, 1973.
Lunt, William. *Financial Relations of the Papacy with England to 1327.* Cambridge, Mass., 1939.
Miller, Edward. *The Abbey and Bishopric of Ely.* Cambridge, 1951.
Orwin, Charles S., and Christabel S. Orwin. *The Open Fields.* 3rd ed. Oxford, 1967.
Pollard, S., and D. W. Crossley. *The Wealth of Britain, 1085–1966.* London, 1968.

Postan, M. M. *Essays on Medieval Agriculture and General Problems of the Medieval Economy.* Cambridge, 1973.

———. *The Medieval Economy and Society: An Economic History of Britain, 1100–1500.* Berkeley, Calif., 1972.

———. *Medieval Trade and Finance.* Cambridge, 1973.

Power, Eileen. *The Wool Trade in English Medieval History.* Oxford, 1941.

Pugh, Ralph B. *Imprisonment in Medieval England.* New York, 1968.

Raftis, J. A. *The Estates of Ramsey Abbey.* Toronto, 1957.

———. *Tenure and Mobility: Studies in the Social History of the Medieval English Village.* Toronto, 1964.

Russell, J. C. *British Medieval Population.* Albuquerque, N.M., 1948.

Searle, Eleanor. *Lordship and Community: Battle Abbey and Its Banlieu, 1066–1538.* Toronto, 1974.

Seebohm, F. *The English Village Community.* 4th ed. London, 1890.

Stenton, Doris M. *English Society in the Early Middle Ages (1066–1307).* 2nd ed. Baltimore, 1952.

———. *The English Woman in History.* London, 1957.

Tait, James. *The Medieval English Borough.* Manchester, 1936.

Vinogradoff, Paul. *The Growth of the Manor.* 2nd ed. London, 1911.

———. *Villainage in England.* Oxford, 1892.

Williams, Gwyn A. *Medieval London: From Commune to Capital.* London, 1963.

ROMAN AND ANGLO-SAXON

Boon, G. C. *Roman Silchester, The Archaelogy of a Romano-British Town.* London, 1957.

Dolley, R. H. M., ed. *Anglo-Saxon Coins: Studies Presented to Sir Frank Stenton.* London, 1961.

———. *Anglo-Saxon Pennies.* London, 1964.

Finberg, H. P. R., ed. *The Agrarian History of England and Wales, A.D. 43–1042.* Cambridge, 1972.

Home, G. C. *Roman London, A.D. 43–457.* 2nd ed. London, 1948.

Jackson, K. H. *Language and History in Early Britain.* Edinburgh, 1953.

Liversidge, Joan E. A. *Britain in the Roman Empire.* London, 1968.

Maitland, F. W. *Domesday Book and Beyond.* Cambridge, 1897.

Margary, I. D. *Roman Roads in Britain.* 2 vols. London, 1955–1957.

Merrifield, Ralph. *The Roman City of London.* London, 1965.

Quennell, M., and C. H. B. Quennell. *Everyday Life in Anglo-Saxon, Viking and Norman Times.* Rev. ed. London, 1959.

Whitelock, Dorothy. *The Beginnings of English Society.* Baltimore, 1952.

NORMAN CONQUEST TO MAGNA CARTA

Dolley, R. H. M. *The Norman Conquest and the English Coinage.* London, 1966.

Finn, R. Welldon. *The Domesday Inquest and the Making of Domesday Book.* London, 1961.

———. *An Introduction to Domesday Book.* New York, 1963.

———. *The Norman Conquest and Its Effects on the Economy, 1066–1086.* London, 1971.

Galbraith, V. H. *The Making of Domesday Book.* Oxford, 1961.
Lennard, Reginald V. *Rural England, 1086–1135.* Oxford, 1959.
Painter, Sidney. *Studies in the History of the English Feudal Barony.* Baltimore, 1943.
Tomkieff, Olive G. *Life in Norman England.* London, 1966.
Urry, William. *Canterbury Under the Angevin Kings.* 2 vols. London, 1967.
Vinogradoff, Paul. *English Society in the Eleventh Century.* Oxford, 1908.
Wightman, W. E. *The Lacy Family in England and Normandy, 1066–1194.* Oxford, 1966.

THIRTEENTH CENTURY

Altschul, Michael. *A Baronial Family in Medieval England: The Clares, 1217–1314.* Baltimore, 1965.
Hilton, R. H. *A Medieval Society: The Western Midlands at the End of the Thirteenth Century.* New York, 1966.
Homans, George C. *English Villagers of the Thirteenth Century.* Cambridge, Mass., 1941.
Kosminsky, E. A. *Studies in the Agrarian History of England in the Thirteenth Century.* Oxford, 1956.
Titow, J. Z. *English Rural Society, 1200–1350.* London, 1969.
Treharne, R. F. *Essays on Thirteenth-Century England.* London, 1971.

FOURTEENTH CENTURY

Barnie, John. *War in Medieval English Society: Social Values and the Hundred Years War.* Ithaca, N.Y., 1974.
Bird, Ruth. *The Turbulent London of Richard II.* London, 1949.
Bridbury, A. R. *Economic Growth: England in the Later Middle Ages.* London, 1962.
Dobson, R. B., ed. *The Peasants' Revolt of 1381.* London, 1970.
DuBoulay, F. R. H. *An Age of Ambition: English Society in the Late Middle Ages.* London, 1970.
Hilton, R. H. *The Decline of Serfdom in Medieval England.* London, 1969.
——, and H. Fagan. *The English Rising in 1381.* London, 1950.
Holmes, G. A. *The Estates of the Higher Nobility in Fourteenth-Century England.* Cambridge, 1957.
Lunt, W. E. *Financial Relations of the Papacy with England, 1327–1534.* Cambridge, Mass., 1962.
McFarlane, K. B. *The Nobility of Later Medieval England.* Oxford, 1973.
Myers, A. R. *England in the Late Middle Ages.* [1307–1536]. Baltimore, 1952.
Shrewsbury, J. F. D. *A History of the Bubonic Plague in the British Isles.* Cambridge, 1970.
Thrupp, Sylvia. *The Merchant Class of Medieval London, 1300–1500.* Chicago, 1948.
Ziegler, Philip. *The Black Death.* London, 1969.

Religious History

GENERAL MEDIEVAL

Colvin, H. M. *The White Canons in England.* Oxford, 1951.
Dickinson, John C. *Monastic Life in Medieval England.* New York, 1961.
Hall, Donald J. *English Medieval Pilgrimage.* London, 1965.
Kemp, E. W. *An Introduction to Canon Law in the Church of England.* London, 1957.
Knowles, David. *The English Mystical Tradition.* New York, 1961.
———. *The Monastic Order in England, 940–1216.* 2nd ed. Cambridge, 1963.
———. *The Religious Orders in England.* 3 vols. Cambridge, 1950–1959.
Lawrence, C. H., ed. *The English Church and the Papacy in the Middle Ages.* New York, 1965.
Moorman, J. R. H. *The Grey Friars in Cambridge, 1225–1538.* Cambridge, 1952.
Roth, Francis. *The English Austin Friars, 1249–1538.* Vol. I, *History.* New York, 1966.
Southern, R. W. *Western Society and the Church in the Middle Ages.* Baltimore, 1970.

ROMAN AND ANGLO-SAXON

Barley, M. W., and R. P. C. Hanson, eds. *Christianity in Britain, 300–700.* Leicester, 1968.
Barlow, Frank. *The English Church, 1000–1066: A Constitutional History.* London, 1963.
Chadwick, Nora K. *The Age of the Saints in the Early Celtic Church.* London, 1961.
Deanesly, Margaret. *The Pre-Conquest Church in England.* 2nd ed. London, 1963.
———. *Sidelights on the Anglo-Saxon Church.* London, 1962.
Duckett, Eleanor S. *Saint Dunstan of Canterbury: A Study of Monastic Reform in the Tenth Century.* London, 1955.
Godfrey, John. *The Church in Anglo-Saxon England.* Cambridge, 1962.
Mayr-Harting, Henry. *The Coming of Christianity to Anglo-Saxon England.* London, 1972.

NORMAN CONQUEST TO MAGNA CARTA

Brooke, Z. N. *The English Church and the Papacy from the Conquest to the Reign of John.* Cambridge, 1931.
Cantor, Norman F. *Church, Kingship and Lay Investiture in England, 1089–1135.* Princeton, N.J., 1958.
Cheney, C. R. *English Bishops' Chanceries, 1100–1250.* Manchester, 1950.
———. *From Becket to Langton: English Church Government, 1170–1213.* Manchester, 1956.

Dickinson, J. C. *The Origins of the Austin Canons and Their Introduction into England.* London, 1950.

Hill, Bennett D. *English Cistercian Monasteries and Their Patrons in the Twelfth Century.* Urbana, Ill., 1968.

Jones, Thomas M. *The Becket Controversy.* New York, 1970.

Knowles, David. *Episcopal Colleagues of Archbishop Thomas Becket.* Cambridge, 1951.

———. *Thomas Becket.* Stanford, 1970.

Macdonald, A. J. *Lanfranc.* 2nd ed. London, 1944.

Morey, Adrian, and C. N. L. Brooke. *Gilbert Foliot and His Letters.* 2 vols. Cambridge, 1965.

Matthew, D. J. A. *The Norman Monasteries and Their English Possessions.* London, 1962.

Nicholl, Donald. *Thurstan, Archbishop of York (1114–1140).* York, 1964.

Powicke, F. M. *Stephen Langton.* Oxford, 1928.

Saltman, Avrom. *Theobald, Archbishop of Canterbury.* London, 1956.

Scammell, G. V. *Hugh du Puiset, Bishop of Durham.* Cambridge, 1956.

Smalley, Beryl. *The Becket Conflict and the Schools: A Study of Intellectuals in Politics in the Twelfth Century.* Totowa, N.J., 1973.

Southern, R. W. *Saint Anselm and His Biographer: A Study in Monastic Life and Thought, 1059–c. 1130.* Cambridge, 1963.

Squire, Aelred. *Aelred of Rievaulx: A Study.* London, 1969.

THIRTEENTH CENTURY

Brentano, Robert J. *Two Churches: England and Italy in the Thirteenth Century.* Princeton, N.J., 1968.

———. *York Metropolitan Jurisdiction and Papal Judges Delegate, 1279–1296.* Berkeley, Calif., 1959.

Douie, D. L. *Archbishop Pecham.* Oxford, 1952.

Hinnebusch, W. A. *The Early English Friars Preachers.* Rome, 1951.

Moorman, J. R. H. *Church Life in England in the Thirteenth Century.* Cambridge, 1945.

Parker, Thomas W. *The Knights Templars in England.* Tucson, 1963.

Wood, Susan. *English Monasteries and Their Patrons in the Thirteenth Century.* London, 1955.

FOURTEENTH CENTURY

Aston, Margaret. *Thomas Arundel: A Study of Church Life in the Reign of Richard II.* Oxford, 1967.

Dahmus, Joseph H. *William Courtenay, Archbishop of Canterbury, 1381–1396.* London, 1966.

McFarlane, K. B. *John Wycliffe and the Beginnings of English Nonconformity.* London, 1953.

Pantin, W. A. *The English Church in the Fourteenth Century.* Cambridge, 1955.

Robson, J. A. *Wyclif and the Oxford Schools.* Cambridge, 1961.
Thompson, A. Hamilton. *The English Clergy and Their Organization in the Later Middle Ages.* Oxford, 1947.
Workman, H. B. *John Wyclif.* 2 vols. Oxford, 1926.

Intellectual and Cultural History

GENERAL MEDIEVAL

Chambers, R. W. *On the Continuity of English Prose from Alfred to More and His School.* London, 1932.
Craig, H. *English Religious Drama in the Middle Ages.* Oxford, 1955.
Gardner, Arthur. *English Medieval Sculpture.* Rev. ed. Cambridge, 1951.
Harrison, F. L. *Music in Medieval Britain.* New York, 1958.
James, M. R. *Two Ancient English Scholars: St. Aldhelm and William of Malmesbury.* Glasgow, 1931.
Knowles, David. *Saints and Scholars.* Cambridge, 1962.
Mallet, Charles E. *A History of the University of Oxford.* Vol. I. London, 1924.
Oakschott, W. *The Sequence of English Medieval Art, Illustrated Chiefly from Illuminated MSS., 640–1450.* London, 1950.
Orme, Nicholas. *English Schools in the Middle Ages.* London, 1973.
Rickert, M. J. *Painting in Britain: The Middle Ages.* 2nd ed. Baltimore, 1965.
Simson, Otto von. *The Gothic Cathedral.* 2nd ed. New York, 1962.
Stone, L. *Sculpture in Britain: The Middle Ages.* London, 1955.
Talbot, Charles H. *Medicine in Medieval England.* London, 1967.
Webb, G. *Architecture in Britain: The Middle Ages.* London, 1956.
Woodforde, Christopher. *English Stained and Painted Glass.* Oxford, 1954.

ROMAN AND ANGLO-SAXON

Clapham, A. W. *English Romanesque Architecture Before the Conquest.* Oxford, 1930.
Duckett, Eleanor S. *Alcuin, Friend of Charlemagne.* New York, 1951.
____. *Anglo-Saxon Saints and Scholars.* New York, 1947.
Greenfield, S. B. *A Critical History of Old English Literature.* New York, 1965.
Hanning, Robert W. *The Vision of History in Early Britain from Gildas to Geoffrey of Monmouth.* New York, 1966.
Jones, C. W. *Saints' Lives and Chronicles in Early England.* Ithaca, N.Y., 1947.
Kendrick, T. D. *Anglo-Saxon Art to A.D. 900.* London, 1938.
Kennedy, C. W. *The Earliest English Poetry.* Oxford, 1943.
Rice, D. Talbot. *English Art, 871–1100.* Oxford, 1949.
Stanley, E. G., ed. *Continuations and Beginnings: Studies in Old English Literature.* London, 1966.
Stoll, Robert. *Architecture and Sculpture in Early Britain: Celtic, Saxon, Norman.* New York, 1967.
Thompson, A. Hamilton, ed. *Bede, His Life, Times and Writings.* Oxford, 1935.
Toynbee, J. M. C. *Art in Britain Under the Romans.* Oxford, 1964.

NORMAN CONQUEST TO MAGNA CARTA

Boase, T. S. R. *English Art, 1100–1216.* Oxford, 1953.
Clapham, A. W. *English Romanesque Architecture after the Conquest.* Oxford, 1934.
Darlington, R. R. *Anglo-Norman Historians.* London, 1947.
Henry, Desmond P. *The Logic of St. Anselm.* Oxford, 1967.
Legge, M. Dominica. *Anglo-Norman in the Cloisters: The Influence of the Orders upon Anglo-Norman Literature.* Edinburgh, 1950.
_____. *Anglo-Norman Literature and Its Background.* Oxford, 1963.
Liebeschütz, Hans. *Mediaeval Humanism in the Life and Writings of John of Salisbury.* London, 1950.
Tatlock, J. S. P. *The Legendary History of Britain.* Berkeley, Calif., 1950.
Williams, G. H. *The Norman Anonymous of 1100 A.D.* Cambridge, Mass., 1951.
Zarnecki, G. *Later English Romanesque Sculpture, 1140–1210.* London, 1953.

THIRTEENTH CENTURY

Brieger, P. H. *English Art, 1216–1307.* Oxford, 1957.
Callus, D. A. P., ed. *Robert Grosseteste, Scholar and Bishop.* Oxford, 1955.
Crombie, A. C. *Robert Grosseteste and the Origins of Experimental Science, 1100–1700.* Oxford, 1953.
Leff, Gordon A. *Paris and Oxford Universities in the Thirteenth and Fourteenth Centuries: An Institutional and Intellectual History.* New York, 1968.
Vaughan, Richard. *Matthew Paris.* Cambridge, 1958.

FOURTEENTH CENTURY

Brewer, D. S. *Chaucer.* 3rd ed. London, 1973.
Evans, Joan. *English Art, 1307–1461.* Oxford, 1949.
Hussey, S. S. *Chaucer: An Introduction.* London, 1971.
Leff, Gordon A. *Bradwardine and the Pelagians.* Cambridge, 1957.
Norton-Smith, John. *Geoffrey Chaucer.* London, 1974.
Robbins, R. H. *Historical Poems of the Fourteenth and Fifteenth Centuries.* New York, 1959.

Military History

Beeler, John. *Warfare in England, 1066–1189.* Ithaca, N.Y., 1966.
Birley, Eric B. *Research on Hadrian's Wall.* Kendal, Eng., 1961.
_____. *Roman Britain and the Roman Army.* Kendal, Eng., 1953.
Brooks, F. W. *The English Naval Forces, 1199–1272.* London, 1933.
Brown, R. Allen. *English Castles.* London, 1962.
Burne, A. H. *The Agincourt War: A Military History of the Latter Part of the Hundred Years War from 1369 to 1453.* London, 1956.
_____. *The Crécy War: A Military History of the Hundred Years War from 1337 to the Peace of Brétigny, 1360.* London, 1955.
Davidson, H. R. E. *The Sword in Anglo-Saxon England: Its Archaeology and Literature.* New York, 1962.

Hewitt, H. J. *The Black Prince's Expedition of 1355–1357.* Manchester, 1958.

Marcus, Geoffrey J. *A Naval History of England.* Vol. I, *The Formative Centuries.* Boston, 1961.

Renn, D. F. *Norman Castles in Britain.* London, 1968.

Simpson, W. Douglas. *Castles in England and Wales.* London, 1969.

Index

1 2 3 4 5 6 7 8 9 10